21 世纪高等学校专业英语系列规划教材

人力资源管理专业英语

English for Human Resources Management

主编　董晓波

清华大学出版社
北京交通大学出版社
·北京·

内 容 简 介

本书所选的国外原版阅读文章涵盖了人力资源管理专业核心课程的重要领域，反映了当前许多国内外人力资源管理学科最前沿的知识信息。全书共 15 个单元，以人力资源管理实务环节来规划内容，内容涉及工作分析与职位评析、人力资源计划与招聘、人员使用与调配，以及绩效管理、薪酬管理、人员培训、组织文化、职业计划与发展、劳动关系、跨文化管理等方面。

本书可作为高校人力资源管理相关专业的高年级本科生、研究生及 MBA 学生的教材，也可以作为经贸英语专业高年级阅读课程教材，还可用作其他各类专业本科生及研究生的选修课或课外泛读教材，也适用于企业管理人员的在职培训。

图书在版编目（CIP）数据

人力资源管理专业英语 / 董晓波主编. —北京：北京交通大学出版社：清华大学出版社，2019.10（2025.1 重印）

　ISBN 978-7-5121-4083-7

　Ⅰ. ① 人⋯　Ⅱ. ① 董⋯　Ⅲ. ① 人力资源管理–英语–高等学校–教材　Ⅳ. ① F243

中国版本图书馆 CIP 数据核字（2019）第 227136 号

人力资源管理专业英语
RENLI ZIYUAN GUANLI ZHUANYE YINGYU

责任编辑：孙晓萌
出版发行：清 华 大 学 出 版 社　　邮编：100084　　电话：010-62776969　　http://www.tup.com.cn
　　　　　北京交通大学出版社　　邮编：100044　　电话：010-51686414　　http://www.bjtup.com.cn
印 刷 者：北京虎彩文化传播有限公司
经　　销：全国新华书店
开　　本：185 mm×260 mm　　印张：13.25　　字数：331 千字
版　　次：2019 年 10 月第 1 版　　2025 年 1 月第 3 次印刷
书　　号：ISBN 978-7-5121-4083-7/F·1918
定　　价：48.00 元

本书如有质量问题，请向北京交通大学出版社质监组反映。对您的意见和批评，我们表示欢迎和感谢。
投诉电话：010-51686043，51686008；传真：010-62225406；E-mail：press@bjtu.edu.cn。

前　言

伴随着习近平总书记"一带一路"伟大倡议的提出，中国正以更快的步伐融入全球化的浪潮中，在构建人类命运共同体的伟大实践中，越来越多的中国企业向国际化管理模式转变，中国企业"走出去"战略的实施，对工商管理人才、商务英语专业人才培养模式提出了更高的要求。我国日益频繁的对外商务交往也急需培养大量外语基础好且精通国际商贸规则的高素质的复合型商务英语人才和管理人才。为了满足各大专院校培养复合型工商管理人才、商务英语人才及社会各阶层商务管理工作者的需要，我们特编写了《人力资源管理专业英语》一书。

阅读是语言学习者最重要的信息获取形式之一，本书的编写设计以学习者的需求为出发点，重在培养学习者的语言应用能力。文章的选取力求做到广泛、专业、精要，宏观与微观领域并重，能够全面涵盖人力资源管理领域各个环节的知识。内容具有先进性、科学性、时代性和实用性。全书共 15 个单元，以人力资源管理实务环节来规划章节，内容涉及工作分析与职位评析、人力资源计划与招聘、人员使用与调配，以及绩效管理、薪酬管理、人员培训、组织文化、职业计划与发展、劳动关系、跨文化管理等方面。全书用文均选自英美人力资源管理最前沿的著作和论文，语言纯正、地道，读者可以通过英语了解人力资源管理学科最前沿的知识信息，也可以通过学习学科专业知识，掌握专业英语。每单元包含 2 篇精读文章，紧扣单元主题且配有中文导读、注释和练习，并附有 Tips 版块，对人力资源管理相关知识做专题介绍，内容丰富、专业性强，以便于教学之用。为了方便自学，所有练习也都在文后附有参考答案。

在整个编写过程中，我们力求完美，但由于水平所限，难免有疏漏和欠妥之处，恳请广大读者不吝指正，以便充实与完善本书。

董晓波

2018 年 11 月于南京河西

E-mail: dongxiaobo@163.com

目　　录

PART Ⅰ　Recruitment & Deployment

PART Ⅱ　Training & Development

PART Ⅲ　Performance Management

PART Ⅳ   Benefits Management

PART Ⅴ   Career Design & Development

PART Ⅵ   Organizational Management & Development

PART Ⅰ
Recruitment & Deployment

Managing the Corporations

Text A

Staff Recruitment — a Qualitative Aspect of the Human Resources Management

导读： 招聘是根据工作需要，运用相关方法和技术，吸引并选择最适当人选的过程。其任务是确保企业能够获得充足的职位候选人，并能以合理的成本从职位申请人中选拔出最符合企业需要的员工。在构成一个企业的员工、品牌、效益、利润四大元素中，员工占有首要地位。在一个真正以人为本的企业中，员工的素质直接影响企业的效益和利润，挑战企业的生存和发展空间，所以，招聘一个企业所需要的合格员工是人力资源部门的重要职责。

The staff recruitment has an immediate impact both on the lives of the people and on the organizations. Therefore, one can say that the act of recruitment is one of the key acts of management. The success or the failure of the recruitment process has a significant impact on the enterprises and the organizations. Its quality relies mostly on the adopted strategy but also on the preparation of the manager.

When Churchill wanted to recruit the commandant of the British army in Northern Africa in the Second World War, he would have chosen the least agreeable one of his superior officers, and he declared to the state that "If the commandant was so disagreeable to us, then he should be odious to his enemies." So, the question is how we can recruit the most competitive person.

The goal of the recruitment activity is to identify a large number of applicants, so that the ones who fulfil the requirements are selected. Recruitment ensures the selections according to the principle of performance.

John Kador thinks that there are just a few organizations who are satisfied with hiring employees who are able to reach only a reasonable performance level. The organizations only want to hire superstars for each level of the organization. These organizations are looking for applicants who can offer remarkable results and who are able to overcome the traditional thresholds of performance.

The process of ensuring staff from within or outside an organization can be regarded as a series of activities which are necessary to fulfil the individual and organizational objectives. The process of ensuring staff from outside of an organization consists of recruitment, selection and orientation or integration of the staff, while ensuring staff from the interior of an organization involves promotions, qualification, developments as well as prospective retirements, reassignments, dismissals or deaths.

According to George T. Milkovich and John W. Boudreau, recruitment is the first step in the process of ensuring staff, as well as the first step in the process of selecting human resources[1]. At the same time, in spite of the fact that more attention was given to the selection of the staff, staff recruitment has to have another priority, because an efficient selection of the personnel can be accomplished only if the recruitment process provides a large number of competitive candidates. In other words, the most efficient methods or selection procedures of the personnel are limited by the efficiency of the recruitment process.

The recruitment of the human resources also takes into account the analysis of the vacancies and the projection of labour, because the basic results of these activities, the descriptions and the specifications for the jobs, are essential in the recruitment process of the personnel. This means that the person who recruits or hires has to have not only the necessary information regarding the features of the job, but also the qualities of the future employee.

The recruitment effort of an organization and the methods which have to be used depend on the planning process of the human resources and of the specific requirements of the jobs which are going to be taken. Knowing the need for staff or anticipating this, as a consequence of the human resources planning process, allows for a good and successful completion of the staff recruitment process. Recruitment can be carried out directly, contacting the recruitment source or indirectly through mass media. The process should take place according to a correct methodology, facilitating in this way the identification and attracting the most adequate persons.

The process of recruitment begins when new jobs appear in the organization or when the existing ones become vacant due to transfers or retirement. It starts with the detailed inventory of the needs that is the job description, qualifications and necessary experience. The recruitment process takes place according to the nature of the activities and it may be a permanent process or a process which takes place when a certain need appears.

Staff recruitment is the process of attracting the suitable qualified candidates for a certain job who will stay in the enterprise for a reasonable period of time after accepting the employment. The recruitment relies on internal and external sources. The recruitment from within an enterprise has not only a series of advantages but also some disadvantages as compared to the external recruitment[2].

In what the internal recruitment[3] is concerned, each enterprise may have its own training program in order to train the staff for certain jobs. For example, IBM[4], a worldwide well known company, relies on an important practice — internal recruitment and promotion. In the context of globalization, staff recruitment related to the evolution of the mentalities is more and more favourable for the mobility. Victor Ernoult wrote that "On a European level labour legislation allows more fluidity. This aspect involves not only more possibilities and opportunities both for the one who recruits and for the applicant, but also more competitiveness". Therefore, it is necessary for a sustained professionalization of recruitment.

In the case of the external recruitment, the sources are different according to the type of the jobs and the size of the organization.

The external recruitment process can be: recruitment offices, newspapers, placement agencies, references, training programs.

Although there are various sources, one of the traditional practices is the recruitment of a number of individuals, larger than necessary, so that after selection the best should be chosen. Another way is to identify the place where the best candidates come and to recruit from those sources.

There are also negative recruitment techniques which use insults and sarcasm, interview under stress and which test the ability of the employees to face certain difficulties. These practices should be avoided; if they are used, the prospective employees should be warned so they do not have an unfavourable image about the organization.

The development potential of the candidate is identified by the psychologist in the selection process and is transmitted to the decisive persons in the organization. The development potential of the candidate can be identified by testing four large plans: skills, intellect, motivation and character-values. According to these plans one can make a prognosis for each candidate.

The recruitment of human resources also takes into account the analysis of the jobs and designing the labour because the basic results of these activities, the descriptions and the specifications of the jobs are essential in the staff recruitment process. This means that the person who recruits or hires has to have the necessary information regarding the characteristics of the job and the qualities of the future employee.

In the recruitment process, the job has to be presented as real as possible, so that the employees would not quit even if their expectations have not been fulfilled. Staff recruitment requires not only identifying and attracting candidates but also their first screening. The most frequently used criteria in the process of recruitment are: competencies, professional experience, development potential of the candidate.

The competencies-based recruitment systems are "focused on filtering methods which allow the fast and efficient selection of a small number of valuable candidates from an important group".

These recruitment systems are focusing on the identification of some major competencies which can satisfy the following criteria: (1) competencies already possessed by the candidates and which have been proved in their professional life (for example initiative); (2) competencies which may estimate on a long term success of the candidates. These competencies are difficult to develop through professional training or experience (competencies regarding the necessary motivation for the activity); (3) competencies which can be evaluated through reliability, by using the maintenance of the behavioral events. For example when "the participant management of the team" is a required competence, the interviewed are required to integrate in a group and to carry out a certain activity. The given answers are codified before getting an assessment of the discussed competencies which have been proven or not; (4) competencies represent a set of observable behaviors, knowledge, skills, interests and personality. All organizations are interested in candidates which are able to give quick results; (5) competence is "... a fundamental feature of a person, which may include a trait, an ability, an intention, a set of knowledge, an aspect of the self-image or of the social role..."; (6) competencies are defined in terms of traits, reasons, motives, knowledge and behavioral skills; (7) competencies are distinct dimension of behaviors which are relevant for the performances in the job. The level of performance is affected by the way in which an individual behaves.

There are two tendencies in the practices of the organizations: (1) organizations which recruit only young people because they start from the premises that they can be easier trained and modeled, and their requirements are more modest; (2) organizations which recruit only personnel with a certain experience, starting either from the principle of quality and avoiding the training costs, or from principles which are imposed by normative acts which govern certain sectors of activity.

In practice these two exacerbated tendencies do not give good results, because the recruitment has to focus on the competence and quality of the employee and not on the economic costs. The best recruitment has to take into account the accomplishment of an age pyramid from the young to the elderly. Therefore, if we maintain the pyramid, we can send the future generation the professional information and secrets.

The seniority-based recruitment system[5] can be found in the public organizations. The system appreciates the degree and the seniority, and this aspect is characteristic both for the person and for the job. One starts from the idea that all these aspects are correlated with the proven ability.

In conclusion, the human resources recruitment process is related to other staff activities as for example: the evaluation of the performances, the rewards given to employees, training and developing the personnel and the relations with the employees. Therefore, the candidates with corresponding preparation have better performances, and the constant preoccupations for performance also involve the identification and attraction of competitive candidates. The recruitment effort of an organization and the methods which should be used rely on the human resources planning process and the specific requirement for the jobs which are to be taken. Knowing the necessary staff need or anticipating it, as a consequence of the human resources planning process, facilitates a better and successful staff recruitment process.

Words & Expressions

1. commandant	*n.*	司令官，指挥官	
2. fulfil	*v.*	满足，完成	
3. threshold	*n.*	门槛，极限	
4. dismissal	*n.*	解雇，免职	
5. vacancy	*n.*	空缺，空位	
6. anticipate	*v.*	预期，期望	
7. inventory	*n.*	存货清单，详细目录	
8. psychologist	*n.*	心理学家，心理学者	
9. placement	*n.*	人员配置	
10. criteria	*n.*	标准，条件（criterion 的复数）	
11. filter	*v.*	过滤，滤除	
12. modest	*a.*	谦虚的，谦逊的，适度的	
13. exacerbate	*v.*	使加剧，使恶化	
14. external	*a.*	外部的	
15. seniority	*n.*	老资格，前任者的特权，长辈	

Notes

1. **Human resources**：人力资源，简称 HR，指在一个国家或地区中，处于劳动年龄、未到劳动年龄和超过劳动年龄但具有劳动能力的人口之和。人力资源也指一定时期内组织中的人员所拥有的能够被企业所用且对价值创造起贡献作用的教育、能力、技能、经验、体力等的总称。从狭义上讲，人力资源是指企事业单位独立的经营团体所需人员具备的能力（资源）。

2. **External recruitment**：外部招聘，指企业通过外部渠道吸收和接纳员工的形式，常见的外部招聘方式包括：广告招聘、职工引荐、校园招聘、委托可信赖的就业第三方中介机构（如猎头公司）招聘。

3. **Internal recruitment**：内部招聘，指在单位出现职务空缺后，从单位内部选择合适的人选来填补这个位置。内部招聘可以分为广义和狭义两种：广义上的内部招聘是指公司内部员工自荐或推荐亲朋好友及子女到公司工作；狭义上的内部招聘是指招聘范围仅限于公司内部的在岗员工，相当于人员内部调动，具体又分为提拔晋升、工作调换、工作重换和人员重聘几种方法。

4. **IBM**：国际商业机器公司或万国商业机器公司，全称为 International Business Machines Corporation。总公司在美国纽约州阿蒙克市，由托马斯·沃森于 1911 年创立于美国，是全球最大的信息技术和业务解决方案公司，拥有全球雇员 30 多万人，业务遍及 160

多个国家和地区。

5. Seniority-based recruitment system：论资排辈招聘制度，指通过对应聘者的个人背景、工作与生活经历进行分析，来判断其对未来岗位适应性的一种招聘体制。近年来，这一方式越来越受到人力资源管理部门的重视，被广泛地用于人员选拔等人力资源管理活动中。这一方式既可以用于初审个人简历，迅速排除明显不合格的人员，也可以根据与工作要求相关性的高低，事先确定履历中各项内容的权重，把应聘者各项得分相加后，根据总分确定选择决策。

I. Match the words on the left with the meanings on the right.

1. threshold   a. when someone is removed from his job
2. anticipate   b. the act of finding a place for someone to live or work
3. placement   c. you have worked there for a long time and have some official advantages
4. seniority   d. to expect that something will happen and be ready for it
5. dismissal   e. the level at which something starts to happen or have an effect

II. Fill in the blanks with the following words and change the forms if necessary.

internal	recruitment	priority	seniority	evaluate

1. The goal of the _____ activity is to identify a large number of applicants, so that the ones who fulfil the requirements are selected.

2. The human resources recruitment process is related to other staff activities as for example: the _____ of the performances, the rewards given to employees, training and developing the personnel and the relations with the employees.

3. At the same time, in spite of the fact that more attention was given to the selection of the staff, staff recruitment has to have another _____, because an efficient selection of the personnel can be accomplished only if the recruitment process provides a large number of competitive candidates.

4. In what the_____ recruitment is concerned, each enterprise may have its own training program in order to train the staff for certain jobs.

5. The seniority-based recruitment system can be found in the public organizations. The system appreciates the degree and the_____, and this aspect is characteristic both for the person and for the job.

III. Decide whether the following statements are true (T) or false (F).

(   ) 1. The goal of the recruitment activity is to identify a small group of elites from all applicants, so that the ones who fulfil the requirements are selected.

(   ) 2. The process of ensuring staff from outside of an organization consists of recruitment, selection and orientation or integration of the staff, while ensuring staff from the interior of an organization involves promotions, qualification, developments as well as prospective retirements, reassignments, dismissals or deaths.

(   ) 3. The external recruitment process can be: recruitment offices, newspapers, placement agencies, references, training programs.

(   ) 4. The development potential of the candidate is identified by the deputy manager in the selection process and is transmitted to the decisive persons in the organization.

(   ) 5. The best recruitment has to take into account the accomplishment of an age pyramid from the young to the elderly. Therefore, if we maintain the pyramid, we can send the future generation the professional information and secrets.

Text B

How to Use Social Media as a Recruiting Tool?

导读: "不花钱找不到人，花钱找到的却是不好用的人。"现在，越来越多企业的人力资源管理人员正面临这样的尴尬处境。在网络时代到来之前，信息传播的局限性使得企业不知从何处找人才。如今最让企业招聘人员头疼的是，如何才能从互联网上征集来的一大批简历中找到自己想要的人。

There are millions of people on social media sites like LinkedIn[1], Facebook[2] or Twitter[3]. More companies are using social media to target candidates. Here's how to use social media as a way to find your next hire.

As a recruiter, you want to be where the most qualified, talented, and largest pool of applicants are. Human resources can leverage social media to tap into potential recruits. This type of head hunting is called social recruiting. It's about engaging with users and using social media tools to source and recruit talent. LinkedIn, Facebook, and Twitter have over 535 million combined users. That equals a lot of potential talent for your company. But how do you find the right person for the job you have available using social media? Here's how to get started.

Understanding Each Social Network

By now you should be familiar with LinkedIn, Facebook, and Twitter. But just in case you're not, here is a quick overview.

"LinkedIn is an interconnected network of experienced professionals from around the world, representing 170 industries and 200 countries. You can find, be introduced to, and collaborate with qualified professionals that you need to work with to accomplish your goals," states the company's website. That is the corporate way of saying they are a giant jobs board and you can connect to other professionals. There are over 65 million professionals on LinkedIn.

Facebook is the largest of the social networking sites with over 400 million users. Facebook is a social utility that connects people with friends and others who work, study, and live around them. It is intended to connect friends, family, and business associates. The model has expanded to include connections to organizations, businesses, and interests — not just individual people.

Twitter is a microblogging social networking service. Messages, better known as tweets, are no more than 140 characters. According to their website, "Twitter is a simple tool that helps connect businesses more meaningfully with the right audience at the right time."

So, now that you know what the major social media sites are, which one should you use and how do you use it?

Using LinkedIn

The most obvious ways to use LinkedIn are to post jobs you have available and search for candidates. It costs $195 to post a job for 30 days. Or you can buy job credits and pay less per job posting if you buy more credits. You can also sign up for LinkedIn Talent Advantage. It is an exclusive suite of tools for recruiters. But if you don't have the budget to pay for job postings or join the Talent Advantage, you can still tap into the free resources LinkedIn offers.

You should start by building connections to people you already know. This could include former co-workers, current clients, local entrepreneurs and even friends and family. Because you never know who someone else may be connected to that could make for a top-notch candidate. You should also join groups where you might connect with potential candidates. For example, if you are always looking for IT consultants, you can find an affiliated group on LinkedIn. Once you join relevant groups, find ways to begin discussions with people in the group. If you notice people who are active in the group, always ask questions and answer others' questions, those might be the people you hone in on for job opportunities.

There is also a free way to advertise that you are hiring on LinkedIn without posting a job. Use your network activity box (also known as a status box) to broadcast that you are hiring. "Looking for an IT consultant. If you know someone, maybe even you. Contact me."

When you find someone who may be a good fit for your company, you have to evaluate their LinkedIn profile. Do they have a complete profile including a picture? Do they have recommendations from peers, managers and colleagues? Are they a member of groups relevant to their field? Do you have any 2nd or 3rd degree connections to the person to get a more personal referral? You can find out a lot about a person from their profile before contacting them for an interview.

As small business owners, you can easily leverage LinkedIn to find talent.

Using Facebook

How many candidates do you have in your database? Whatever the number is it doesn't come close to how many potential candidates are on Facebook. Facebook provides easy and affordable ways to increase your applicant pool. First utilize the Facebook Directory to search for users, pages, groups and applications.

You can post a job for free in the Facebook Marketplace. The ad requires basic information such as location, job category, subcategory, title, why you need to fill this position, description and if you want to post your photo with the job posting or another image. The limitation of a free job posting is that you can't target it to a specific group of people like you can with a Facebook Ad.

Facebook Pages are another free resource within Facebook. A Facebook page is a public profile that enables you to share your business and products with Facebook users. If you don't have a Facebook page you can search other Facebook pages to find people both active and interested in your field or that would be interested in your available position. If your company has a Facebook page you may want to use it as a recruiting tool. Make sure the information about your company is relevant and up-to-date. You can also post job openings for your fans to see. These people are passionate about your company and can be just as passionate about working for your company.

Another option is to post a Facebook Ad if you aren't getting the results you want from searching. The advantage of the ad platform on Facebook over its rivals Google AdWords and Yahoo! Advertising is that Facebook has laser targeting ability. With a Facebook Ad you can choose the exact audience that you are looking to target. The system will ask a series of questions about the characteristics of the people you want to see your job posting ad. You will be asked about the group's age, sex and specific keywords related to the position. Facebook will then calculate how many users fit that criteria. You have the choice to pay per click (how many people clicked on your job ad), pay per impression (how many people potentially saw your ad) and set how much you are willing to pay. You can decide whether to run the job ad continuously or only during a certain time.

For example, if your company is in Minneapolis and you are not including relocation in the budget for this position, you can target the job posting to only be shown to people that live in Minnesota or bordering states. If the position is an entry-level position, you can target the job posting to a younger age demographic. It is normally a violation of EEOC[4] to target for or against a specific gender but a Facebook Ad is a loophole to bypass that. Because if you know a woman would be better suited for your position, you can target your job posting to only be seen by women. The options are endless to how narrow a field you can define. Be careful to not make the criteria too specific or you may not get the applicants you want.

Using Twitter

Twitter can be powerful for small companies or a recruiter who wants to get an edge over the competition. The easiest way to recruit is to tweet jobs you have available. "Looking for a Sales

Rep[5] in NYC. Very competitive salary. Apply at..."

If your company has a Twitter account but not a lot of followers you can expand your network and build relationships with clients and job candidates on Twitter. Run a quick search on Twitter (search.twitter.com) for anybody discussing a specific keyword and you can get hundreds of contacts. You can search for people you know, by location, by industry or interest, by hashtag, by popularity, by time and more.

To make your job posting tweets standout, you can also use hashtags. Tags are used as a way to filter and find information on Twitter. All you have to do is to include the hashtag with a keyword in your tweet and it becomes instantly searchable. You can use more than one hashtag in your tweet but remember you are limited to 140 characters, so be strategic in which hashtag or tags you use.

You can engage with candidates and see what topics they tweet about. There is also the opportunity to market events you will be attending. "Stop by our career booth at the Sales Tech Expo."

There are companies like AdLogic that help businesses target to a particular Twitter audience. AdLogic lets clients create custom job feeds and corresponding specialized Twitter profiles for each area that they recruit for.

Your company Twitter account is also an opportunity to inform potential hires about your company. Your tweets say a lot about the company and what topics are important to your company.

When you find a potential candidate on Twitter, evaluate their activity to see how often they tweet, if they have a healthy balance between followers and following, how big is their network and the quality of their tweets. Do they keep a balance between personal and professional tweets? Do they only post updates or do they respond to others and retweet others fully utilizing what Twitter is about?

Return on Investment

Social media recruiting helps an employer get to know a potential job candidate. Is this a highly skilled, well-rounded individual that fits with your team? As with any job opening, using social media recruiting requires time and effort but it's an investment which will benefit for your company in longer-term. Using LinkedIn, Facebook and Twitter takes recruiting back to its grass roots of networking but for a digital age.

Words & Expressions

1. leverage	v.	用……手段，利用
2. tap into		挖掘，接近
3. exclusive	a.	独有的，专一的
4. top-notch	a.	一流的，拔尖的

5. affiliated group		附属团体
6. evaluate	*v.*	评价
7. database	*n.*	数据库，资料库
8. affordable	*a.*	负担得起的
9. subcategory	*n.*	子范畴，亚类
10. relocation	*n.*	重新安置
11. entry-level	*a.*	入门的，初级的
12. loophole	*n.*	漏洞
13. tag	*n.*	标签
14. engage with		交战，与……接洽
15. well-rounded	*a.*	多才多艺的

1. LinkedIn：全球最大的职业社交网站，是一家面向商业客户的社交网络（SNS），2002 年创立于美国加利福尼亚州山景城。网站的目的是让注册用户维护他们在商业交往中认识并信任的联系人，俗称"人脉"。用户可以邀请他认识的人成为"关系"（connections）圈的人。2014 年，LinkedIn 简体中文版网站正式上线，并宣布中文名为"领英"。

2. Facebook：美国的一个社交网络服务网站，创立于 2004 年，总部位于美国加利福尼亚州的帕罗奥图，2012 年发布 Windows 版桌面聊天软件 Facebook Messenger，主要创始人为马克·扎克伯格。

3. Twitter：全球广受欢迎的社交网络及微博服务网站，允许用户将自己的最新动态和想法以移动电话中的短信形式（推文）发布（发推），可绑定 IM 即时通信软件。所有的 Twitter 消息都被限制在 140 个字符之内。截至 2018 年 3 月，Twitter 共有 3.36 亿活跃用户，Twitter 被形容为"互联网的短信服务"。

4. EEOC：公平就业机会委员会，是依照相关法律反对就业歧视的美国独立联邦执法机构。该机构主要基于种族、肤色、国籍、宗教、性别、年龄等因素受理就业歧视诉讼，其可代表上诉的受害者对雇佣者提起歧视诉讼。

5. Sale Rep：销售代表（sale representative）的简称，销售代表是指代表公司与客户进行直接沟通并负责最终销售产品的人。从销售代表自身来看，在知识方面，优秀的销售代表要有丰富的产品知识、行业知识、营销知识。在技能方面，优秀的销售代表要有良好的沟通技巧、团队精神。在态度方面，优秀的销售代表第一要充满激情和上进心；第二要对自己、对产品、对公司充满自信；第三要从心底里面有对成功的渴望；第四要养成勤劳的习惯；第五要喜欢来自市场的挑战；第六要有善于沟通、善于合作等基本素质。

I. Match the words on the left with the meanings on the right.

1. well-rounded   a. to link an organization very closely with another larger one
2. affordable   b. to make a judgment
3. criterion   c. able to pay for something
4. evaluate   d. a standard or principle by which sth is judged, or with the help of which a decision is made
5. affiliate   e. providing or showing a variety of experience, ability, etc.

II. Fill in the blanks with the following words and change the forms if necessary.

expand   business   collaborate   utility   interconnect

1. Facebook is a social _____ that connects people with friends and others who work, study, and live around them.
2. Twitter is a simple tool that helps connect _____ more meaningfully with the right audience at the right time.
3. LinkedIn is an _____ network of experienced professionals from around the world, representing 170 industries and 200 countries.
4. Now the model has _____ to include connections to organizations, businesses, and interests — not just individual people.
5. You can find, be introduced to, and _____ with qualified professionals that you need to work with to accomplish your goals.

III. Decide whether the following statements are true (T) or false (F).

(   ) 1. Facebook is an interconnected network of experienced professionals from around the world, representing 170 industries and 200 countries.

(   ) 2. The most obvious ways to use LinkedIn are to post jobs you have available and search for candidates.

(   ) 3. There are over 65 million professionals on Twitter.

(   ) 4. Linkedin is a social utility that connects people with friends and others who work, study, and live around them.

(   ) 5. If you notice people who are active in the group, they always ask questions and answer others questions, those might be the people you hone in on for job opportunities.

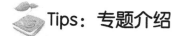Tips：专题介绍

外 部 招 聘

外部招聘的渠道大致有人才交流中心和招聘洽谈会、传统媒体广告、网上招聘、校园招聘、人才猎取和员工推荐等。

1. 人才交流中心和招聘洽谈会

我国很多城市都设有专门的人才交流服务机构，这些机构常年为企事业用人单位提供服务。他们一般建有人才资料库，用人单位可以很方便地在资料库中查询条件基本相符的人才的资料。通过人才交流中心选择人员，有针对性强、费用低廉等优点。

人才交流中心或其他人才交流服务机构每年都要举办多场人才招聘洽谈会，用人单位的招聘者和应聘者可以直接进行接洽和交流。招聘会的最大特点是应聘者集中，用人单位的选择余地较大，费用也比较合理，而且还可以起到很好的企业宣传作用。

2. 传统媒体广告

通过报纸杂志、广播电视等媒体进行广告宣传，向公众传达招聘信息，具有覆盖面广、速度快的优点。在报纸、电视中刊登招聘广告费用较大，但容易醒目地体现组织形象；很多广播电台也都设有人才交流节目，播出招聘广告的费用较少，但效果比报纸、电视广告差一些。

招聘广告应该包含以下内容：

（1）组织的基本情况；

（2）招聘的职位、数量和基本条件；

（3）招聘的范围；

（4）薪资与待遇；

（5）报名的时间、地点、方式及所需的材料等。

媒体广告招聘的优点是：信息传播范围广、速度快，应聘人员数量大、层次丰富，组织的选择余地大，组织可以招聘到素质较高的员工。

媒体广告招聘的缺点是：招聘时间较长、广告费用较高、要花费较多的时间进行筛选。

3. 网上招聘

网上招聘是一种新兴的招聘方式。它具有费用低、覆盖面广、时间周期长、联系快捷方便等优点。用人单位可以将招聘广告张贴在自己的网站上，或者张贴在某些网站上，也可以在一些专门的招聘网站上发布信息。

网络招聘由于信息传播范围广、速度快、成本低，供需双方选择余地大，且不受时间、空间的限制，因而被广泛采用。当然这种方式也存在一定的缺点，比如应聘者鱼目混珠，筛选手续繁杂，以及对高级人才的招聘较为困难等。

4. 校园招聘

学校是人才高度集中的地方，是公司获取人力资源的重要源泉。对于大专院校应届毕业生，可以选择在校园直接进行。校园招聘主要包括学校举办的毕业生招聘会、招聘讲座、毕

业生就业办公室推荐等。

校园招聘的优势有：

（1）公司可以在校园中招聘到大量的高素质人才；

（2）大学毕业生虽然经验较为欠缺，但是具备巨大的发展潜力；

（3）由于大学生思想较为活跃，可以给公司带来一些新的管理理念和新的技术，有利于公司的长远发展。

但是，校园招聘也存在明显的不足之处：

（1）高校毕业生普遍缺少实践经验，公司需要用较长的时间对其进行培训；

（2）新招聘的大学毕业生无法满足公司即时的用人需要，要经过一段较长的相互适应期；

（3）招聘所费时间较多，成本也相对较高；

（4）在大学中招聘的员工到岗率较低，而且经过一段时间后，离职率较高。

5. 人才猎取

一般认为，"猎头"公司是一种专门为雇主"猎取"高级人才和尖端人才的职业中介机构。

6. 员工推荐

通过企业员工推荐人选，是公司招聘的重要形式。

Interviewing

Text A

10 Tips for Crafting S.M.A.R.T. Interviewing Stories

导读：面试是一种经过组织者精心设计，在特定场景下，以考官对考生的面对面交谈与观察为主要手段，由表及里测评考生的知识、能力、经验等有关素质的一种考试活动。面试是公司挑选职工的一种重要方法。面试给公司和应聘者提供了进行双向交流的机会，能促使公司和应聘者之间相互了解，从而双方都可以更准确地做出聘用与否、受聘与否的决定。那么面试有哪些技巧呢？

With small businesses following Fortune 500 companies in the hot trend toward behavioral interviewing[1], it's critical that job seekers be prepared to deliver fact-filled stories when responding to the query, "Tell me about a time when you...". Many interviewers prefer that job seekers deliver interview responses, or stories, using the CAR[2] or STAR[3] method (acronyms for Challenge, Action, Result or Situation, Task, Action, and Result).

For our purposes, we'll use the S.M.A.R.T. format, which stands for Situation with Metrics, Actions, Results, and Tie-in. The last item, Tie-in, is key. It neatly links the response back to the employer's competency question, allows the individual to inquire further into the employer's needs, and helps focus the conversation on how the candidate can DO the job instead of simply AUDITION for the job.

These 10 tips can serve as a guide for crafting S.M.A.R.T. stories.

Tip 1

Use the "it's about them, not me" perspective when describing your stories. This means that, ultimately, your S.M.A.R.T. stories must be related to "them"— the employer and their needs. Think in terms of what will motivate the employer to buy, the return-on-investment you offer, and your benefits vs features.

Tip 2

Craft S.M.A.R.T. stories about your work at each of your past employers. The heaviest concentration of stories should be about your current or most recent experiences. Pen a S.M.A.R.T. story for each recent accomplishment on your resume.

Tip 3

Assign themes to your S.M.A.R.T. stories that underscore competencies for the target position. For instance, competencies for a customer service representative might include customer-focused orientation, interpersonal judgment[4], communication skills, teamwork, problem solving, listening skills, empathy, and initiative.

Tip 4

Craft S.M.A.R.T. stories for non-work experiences if you are just entering the work force. It is fair game to draw on volunteer work, school experiences, and general life incidents. (If you sense you need additional experience, identify and quickly act on how you can best prepare yourself through reading, attending a course, job-shadowing[5], volunteering, or taking a relevant part-time job.)

Tip 5

Regardless of what point your career life is at, everyone should recollect influential or life-altering events throughout youth and adulthood. Craft S.M.A.R.T. stories about these times.

Tip 6

Numbers speak louder than words! Load the stories with numbers, dollar amounts, productivity measurements, comparisons, and the like. Be cautious about conveying proprietary or confidential company information. Be specific and offer proof. Instead of saying, "I learned the program quickly," make it crystal clear with language like, "I studied the manual at night and, in three days, I knew all the basic functions; in two weeks I had mastered several of the advanced features; and by the end of the month, I had experienced operators coming to me to ask how to embed tables into another program."

Tip 7

Include emotions and feelings. When describing the situation, don't be afraid to include details such as these: "the tension among the team was so serious that people were resigning"; "the morale was at an all-time low"; or "the customer was irate about receiving a mis-shipment that occurred because of our transportation vendor." When writing about emotions or feelings, be mindful NOT to whine or disparage anyone, even if through a veiled reference.

Tip 8

Avoid personal opinions. You can, however, include the opinion of a supervisor or another objective party. Instead of saying, "I believe my positive outlook really helped keep the customer happy," rely on someone's opinion: "My supervisor commented in a memo how my outlook helped us save a key account that was in jeopardy of being lost. I have a copy of that memo if you'd like to see it."

Tip 9

Pace the stories so that each is approximately 2-3 minutes in length. Set up the story briefly with facts, place the greatest weight on the action portion of the story, wrap it up with numbers-driven results, and tie it back to the interviewer's needs. Occasionally, vary the delivery by dropping in a result at the front end of the story.

Tip 10

Make the stories relevant. You have a myriad of experiences in your background. Sift through them and select the stories that best substantiate your competencies, knowledge, skills, and motivation to excel in the target job.

Words & Expressions

1. craft	v.	精巧地制作
2. critical	a.	关键的，决定性的
3. query	n.	疑问，质问
4. acronym	n.	首字母缩略词
5. metrics	n.	度量，作诗法，韵律学
6. tie-in	n.	关联，关系，搭卖的广告
7. audition	v.	试听，对……进行面试，让……试唱
8. underscore	v.	强调
9. empathy	n.	感同身受，同感，共鸣
10. convey	v.	传达，运输，让与
11. proprietary	a.	专有的，私人拥有的，专利的
12. confidential	a.	机密的，表示信任的，获信任的
13. crystal	a.	水晶的，透明的，清澈的

14. embed	v.	使嵌入，使插入，使深留脑中
15. morale	n.	士气，斗志
16. irate	a.	生气的，发怒的
17. whine	v.	抱怨，发牢骚，哭诉
18. veiled	a.	隐藏的，含蓄的，蒙上面纱的，不清楚的
19. pace	v.	放稳步调，踱步，缓慢而行
20. myriad	n.	无数，极大数量，无数的人或物
21. substantiate	v.	证实，使实体化
22. vendor	n.	卖主，小贩
23. excel	v.	优于，胜过，擅长

1. Behavioral interviewing：行为面试，是一种能有效排除个人的主观因素，以行为依据和目标为导向的有效选才工具。行为面试通过面试者的行为描述来判断其背后的品行、思想，其准确概率较一般的面试方法要高。通过行为面试，能了解到应聘者的品行是否与岗位要求吻合，深入探索应聘者的动机和兴趣点。行为面试中常用的一种技巧是 STAR。

2. CAR：一种面试方式，包括 challenge（挑战）、action（行动）、result（结果）。挑战指应聘者所处的困境，以助解释其为何有这样的表现；行动指应聘者应对上述挑战所做出的行为或言语反应，透过这些行为或言语反应，可了解应聘者之前的工作表现；结果指应聘者采取行动而产生的效果，从而判断其行动是否积极有效。

3. STAR：面试中经常用来考察应聘者的一种方法，包括 situation（情境）、task（任务）、action（行动）、result（结果）。情境指所参与或负责的项目背景；任务指项目的具体内容、性质、规模及与需求岗位技能要求的匹配度；行动指应聘者在项目实施过程中表现出的反应；结果指应聘者对项目的影响度及总结。

4. Interpersonal judgment：人际关系判断，在面试中，面试官通过询问应聘者一系列与人际交往方面相关的问题，根据应聘者的回答判断其人际关系的处理能力，从而分析其与所应聘岗位的匹配度。

5. Job-shadowing：影子计划，指为了帮助新员工进一步了解感兴趣的工作，企业安排其跟随某位业内人士接受相关培训，从而更快适应工作环境、进入工作状态的一种培训方式。

I. Match the words on the left with the meanings on the right.

1. query   a. to do something very well or much better than most people
2. embed   b. spoken or written in secret and intended to be kept secret
3. excel   c. a question that you ask to get information or to check the truth
4. whine   d. to put something firmly and deeply into something else
5. confidential   e. to complain in a sad annoying voice about something

II. Fill in the blanks with the following words and change the forms if necessary.

measure	portion	deliver	adulthood	veil

1. Regardless of what point your career life is at, everyone should recollect influential or life-altering events throughout youth and _____ .
2. Numbers speak louder than words! Load the stories with numbers, dollar amounts, productivity _____ , comparisons, and the like.
3. When writing about emotions or feelings, be mindful NOT to whine or disparage anyone, even if through a _____ reference.
4. Set up the story briefly with facts, place the greatest weight on the action _____ of the story, wrap it up with numbers-driven results, and tie it back to the interviewer's needs.
5. Many interviewers prefer that job seekers _____ interview responses, or stories, using the CAR or STAR method.

III. Decide whether the following statements are true (T) or false (F).

(   ) 1. Craft S.M.A.R.T. stories about your work at each of your past employers. The heaviest concentration of stories should be about your remotest experiences.
(   ) 2. Regardless of what point your career life is at, everyone should recollect influential or life-altering events throughout youth and adulthood.
(   ) 3. Be specific and offer proof. Words speak louder than numbers.
(   ) 4. S.M.A.R.T. stories can include personal opinions. Also you can include the opinion of a supervisor or another objective party.
(   ) 5. Sift through your experiences and select the stories that best substantiate your competencies, knowledge, skills, and motivation to excel in the target job.

Text B

Interview Preparation Wins Candidate Competitions

导读： 古代智者提出"不打没有把握的仗"，今天流行的面试语是"不做准备的人，就是准备失败的人"。求职者在求职道路上应该尽力去做有把握的事情，所以他们从接到面试通知的那一刻开始，就应该抖擞精神去进行面试前的准备工作。从着装、文具清单到交通线路、心理状态、面试问题等各个环节都要做最精妙而全面的准备。

The "will to win" is overrated. If you think about it, who doesn't have the will to win? What makes people successful — whether in sports competitions or job interviews — is what basketball coach Bob Knight called "the will to prepare to win."

"That's what sets people apart," said Lisa Panarello, founder and CEO of Careers Advance, a professional training and coaching agency in New York.

She said applicants should put in at least 15 minutes of research just to compose an effective cover letter.

"That basic homework, it makes you look interested and really engaged in the process, but it also makes you more confident in the interview," said Kay Piatt, employment manager[1] of the Houstonian Hotel, Club & Spa in Houston. "It's good for both parties."

Piatt has conducted many interviews as the head of employment and recruiting for the luxury hotel, and she knows when a candidate is prepared and when they're not.

But just doing the obvious research isn't enough at the $100k-plus level.

Piatt said job seekers should be well versed in how a company is structured, industry trends that are relevant to the position they're seeking and any current events involving the company. You might even want to study up on the person who will be interviewing you, she added.

According to Piatt, a lot of the basic information you'll need for preparation can be found online or — better yet — from someone you know who may work there.

Mark Grimm, a public speaking trainer and author of *Everyone Can Be a Dynamic Speaker*, stresses offering your interviewer value — and that entails doing the homework necessary to know what she's looking for.

"Go to their Web site," Grimm said, "There's no excuse for not doing research now."

He suggested calling the office, chatting up the secretary and fishing out as much information as you can.

"What do you have to lose?" he said, "Find out as much as you can about what they really want."

When it comes to online research, sometimes cyberspace can become overwhelming. There's just too much information to process.

Not a problem, Panarello said: "Narrow it down to what is most relevant for the position at hand and the growth of the company. Peg it to the future."

Be methodical and efficient, she said. "Google one or two key people from the company, and print out the articles," she said. "Read an article. Try to come up with three questions. Then try to answer it."

This strategy, she said, will help focus you for the interview. And once you've done the research, bring physical evidence of your work to the interview.

"Treat an interview as if it's a business meeting. Bring the printouts in a folder," Panarello advised. "Pull out the article and reference it. They're going to think, 'This person is going to come to a meeting like this.'"

"Next, take your homework to the next level," Panarello said, "and do the same research about the company's competitors."

"When somebody is sitting across my desk, it is really interesting to talk about competitors rather than my list of 10 questions," Piatt said.

"When a candidate can demonstrate a full understanding of the company's competitive needs," Grimm said, "that person is in the best position to make a convincing case."

"The more you talk about how you help the company — rather than help yourself — the better their hearing gets," Grimm said.

As you prepare for your interview, go through the following list and think of how you might answer some of these questions. However, don't recite "rehearsed" answers at the interview!

Tell me about yourself.

(1) What are your strengths? Weaknesses?

(2) What do you think you can offer this company/position?

(3) How do you think your previous employment relates to this position?

(4) What did you like most about your last job? Least?

(5) Why did you leave your last job?

(6) What kind of supervision do you prefer?

(7) Why do you want to work for this company?

(8) Why do you think you would be successful in this job?

(9) How would you describe yourself?

(10) Can you explain the gaps in your work history?

(11) Are you willing to travel?

(12) What are your long term goals?

(13) How do you keep current in your career area?

(14) What accomplishments are you most proud of?

(15) What will your references say about you?

(16) Would your last employer rehire you? Why or why not?

(17) Why do you want this job?

(18) Give an example of a problem in your life and how you handled/resolved it.

(19) Let's say your supervisor harshly criticizes your work. Describe how you handle that

criticism.

 (20) What are your salary expectations?

 (21) Explain how you handle stress.

 (22) What two or three things are the most important things you need in a job?

 (23) Your resume suggests you may be over-qualified for this position. What are your thoughts?

 (24) What is your management style?

 (25) What important trends do you see in this industry and how have you kept up with them?

 (26) What do you want to be doing in 5 years?

 (27) When are you available to start working?

 (28) What questions do you have for me?

Words & Expressions

1. overrate	v.	过高估计，估价过高
2. engage	v.	参与，从事，吸引，占用，使参加
3. recruit	v.	补充，招聘，聘用，征募
4. luxury	a.	奢侈的，豪华的
5. versed	a.	精通的，熟练的
6. dynamic	a.	动态的，动力的，有活力的
7. entail	v.	使必要，使必需，使承担
8. fish out		掏出，摸索出
9. cyberspace	n.	网络空间
10. overwhelming	a.	压倒性的
11. peg	v.	限制，钉木钉，孜孜不倦地做某事
12. methodical	a.	有系统的，有方法的
13. printout	n.	打印出的资料
14. folder	n.	文件夹，折叠式印刷品
15. convincing	a.	令人信服的，有说服力的

Notes

1. employment manager：人事经理，负责计划、指导和协调机构的人事活动，确保人力资源合理利用，负责处理纠纷、人事策略和招聘活动等。

I. Match the words on the left with the meanings on the right.

1. engage
2. overwhelming
3. entail
4. hypothetical
5. convince

a. to make you believe that something is true or right
b. to be doing or to become involved in an activity
c. as strong as to be irresistible
d. to involve something as a necessary part or result
e. based on a situation that is not real but might happen

II. Fill in the blanks with the following words and change the forms if necessary.

involve	recite	across	engage	position

1. It makes you look interested and really _____ in the process, but it also makes you more confident in the interview.
2. Job seekers should be well versed in how a company is structured, industry trends that are relevant to the position they're seeking and any current events _____ the company.
3. When somebody is sitting _____ my desk, it is really interesting to talk about competitors rather than my list of 10 questions.
4. When a candidate can demonstrate a full understanding of the company's competitive needs, that person is in the best _____ to make a convincing case.
5. As you prepare for your interview, go through the following list and think of how you might answer some of these questions. However, don't _____ "rehearsed" answers at the interview!

III. Decide whether the following statements are true (T) or false (F).

(   ) 1. Applicants should put in at most 15 minutes of research just to compose an effective cover letter.

(   ) 2. Narrow it down to what is most relevant for the position at hand and the growth of the company.

(   ) 3. Panarello has conducted many interviews as the head of employment and recruiting for the luxury hotel.

(   ) 4. Job seekers should be well versed in how a company is structured, industry trends that are relevant to the position they're seeking and any current events involving the company.

(   ) 5. When a candidate can demonstrate a full understanding of the company's competitive needs, that person is in the best position to make a convincing case.

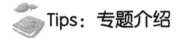 Tips：专题介绍

HR 筛选简历的五大步骤

简历筛选是招聘工作中的一个关键环节，也是招聘人员的一项基本功。怎样才能快速、高效地筛选简历，准确地从众多简历中发现最合适的候选人呢？

1. 简历的粗筛

粗筛简历时，每份简历平均用时大约一秒钟。在粗筛简历之前，应当花一些时间认真思考以下几个问题，以提高粗筛效率。

（1）是否已经充分理解了岗位的职责和资格要求；

（2）应聘者应具备的充分和必要条件，这些条件在简历中可能体现为哪些内容，有哪些表现形式；

（3）用人部门是否有特殊的未在岗位描述中体现的隐形要求；

粗筛简历的关键词，包括岗位、职责、学历、工作年限、地点等。关键词可以帮助招聘者迅速判断应聘者是否符合岗位描述的资格要求。一般而言，粗筛简历的方法基本上是使用关键词从在线简历列表、简历收件箱标题中迅速发现和排除不符合岗位描述的应聘者简历。粗筛简历的诀窍是"只看否定项，不看符合项"，即只要在某一关键词上，不符合岗位描述的条件和要求，就直接予以排除。

经过"一秒钟粗筛"，大约只有 10%的简历能够进入"简历的细选"。

2. 简历的细选

在细选简历阶段，每份简历的平均用时大约六秒钟。"六秒钟细选简历"主要审视的内容包括以下几个方面。

（1）应聘者的主要数据。应聘者的名字、教育背景、目前的公司和岗位、目前岗位的起始时间、上一公司和岗位、上一岗位的起始时间；

（2）应聘者最近的工作经历中与岗位描述相匹配的内容。这里包括三个关键词：最近、大致、匹配。也就是说，细选简历时，只看重最近的工作经历中与岗位描述中相吻合的经验；只求"大致"匹配，不要求严格吻合；

细选简历的关键要点包括以下几个方面。

（1）只看简历，不读简历。不求精确，只要合适。过度解读简历，很容易将一些优秀的应聘者排除在外。另外，简历写得好的人不一定就是最合适的应聘者；

（2）只看"有没有"，不看"配不配"。在细选简历阶段，不必纠结应聘者在关键要素上是否匹配，只需关注应聘者是否具有招聘岗位所需要的核心元素；

（3）不因简历的格式不对而淘汰应聘者。简历细选阶段的重点是看应聘者有没有岗位描述中所要求的关键要素，而不是纠结于简历格式是否正确。如果在格式不对的简历中发现了需要的信息，那就应当留下它，转入下一阶段。

3. 简历的精读

精读简历重点在于解读以下四个方面的内容。

（1）应聘者既往经历的主要职责和工作内容；

（2）应聘者既往取得的成就和成功经验；

（3）应聘者既往的管理幅度和管理经验；

（4）应聘者简历中存在的疑问和瑕疵。

对上述四个方面的解读，有助于招聘者辨别和确认应聘者解决问题的能力和经验、领导风格、文化适应性、书面沟通能力、团队建设能力、效率改善能力等。

那么，如何通过精读应聘者的简历，获得对应聘者上述诸方面的初步印象呢？

1）既往公司的规模和性质

关注应聘者既往公司的规模、性质、知名度、行业排名等，有助于判断该应聘者的工作经验、专业能力和文化适应性等。例如，一个在外企工作多年的应聘者转到民营企业，可能存在"水土不服"的问题；在日韩企业工作多年的应聘者工作风格多偏于严格、服从、执行；从民营企业出来的应聘者抗压能力和实操能力明显强于其他人，但可能缺乏高度和深度；在外企工作多年的候选人专业度和职业精神更出色。

2）既往的角色和职责

招聘者不仅要关注应聘者做了哪些事，还要特别关注其在其中担任的角色是什么，承担的责任有哪些。主持项目和参与项目的责任不同，获得的经验也不同。

对角色和职责的判断有两个关键词："相关性"和"最近"。相关性是指应聘者在既往的工作经历中与所应聘岗位的角色、职责的吻合度；"最近"是指最近 3~5 年，最多不超过 10 年的工作经历和成就。

3）专业管理幅度

专业管理幅度包含管理范围、团队大小、职务功能范围。例如，负责集团统筹的应聘者和仅负责部分公司的应聘者获得的经验不同；管理过较大团队的应聘者要比只管理过人数较少团队的应聘者经验要丰富一些；具有单一功能职务经验的应聘者往往经验丰富、具有较强的专业性和专业高度，对迅速提升公司的业务和管理水平有很大帮助；具有多种职务经历的应聘者一专多能，可塑性和潜力较大。

4）经验和成就

主要考察应聘者既往的工作经验和成就是否与所应聘的岗位有重叠，是否符合岗位需要。重叠较多时，意味着该应聘者能够迅速进入角色，得心应手地投入工作，较快地满足岗位描述的要求。

对于经验而言，参加一个行业领先的研究项目获得的经验通常比一般性项目获得的经验要多；有综合管理经验可能比只有单一功能管理经验的应聘者更受欢迎；著名的、具有举足轻重地位的奖项比一般性奖项更有"江湖"地位。

对于成就的考量，重点是看是否有量化的数据，有量化数据的成就和贡献才是值得相信的。

5）教育背景和资质

对于技术性较强的岗位，是否是科班出身、是否具备必要的专业资质和法定的资格证书非常重要。但是，如果招聘者硬性规定管理岗位的应聘者必须要有 MBA 学历，就会体现出人才招聘部门对人才识别的不自信。

6）工作风格和个性

在简历筛选过程中，应聘者领导能力的判断相对比较容易，但领导风格的辨别相对较难。

一个简单判断应聘者领导风格的方法就是，看应聘者如何介绍他的项目成就。如果应聘者在介绍时，采用比较多的形容词且用词华丽，那么其领导风格可能偏重表面，比较务虚；如果展现比较多的数据和细节，那么该应聘者可能比较严谨、细致。当然这只是初步判断，具体还需要在面试时加以深究和确认。

7）工作期限和职业发展

应聘者的每一段工作经历如果少于三年，通常意味着应聘者的稳定性较弱。如果应聘者在两段工作经历之间存在"工作间隔"，需要引起重视。另外，关注应聘者的职业发展线路是上行、下行或波浪式，对判断应聘者的能力和整体素质有积极的意义。当然，如果应聘者在小公司处于高职位，而后来在大公司处于低职位，这是符合职业发展逻辑的。

8）自相矛盾和明显错误

对于应聘者简历中的语法错误、标点符号错误、错别字等，需要给予一定的关注。这些问题除了说明应聘者书面交流能力较差以外，还暗示着该应聘者对工作的认真程度。

4. 简历的匹配和善后

简历的匹配是整个简历筛选过程的核心。简历筛选的目的只有一个：发现和所招聘岗位要求相匹配的合格简历，进入下一阶段——面试。因此，简历如何匹配显得尤为重要。

1）直接匹配法

直接匹配法又称简单匹配法，是一种最常用也是最简单的简历匹配方法。它对岗位需求中的关键要素与应聘者工作经历和经验进行简单对比和匹配，能够完全对应匹配的，被认为是合适的应聘者。

直接匹配法的一个核心是确定所招聘岗位的关键要素。关键要素的确定取决于该岗位的岗位需求和公司对应聘者在该岗位发挥作用和取得成就的期望。不同的企业、不同岗位的关键要素并不完全相同。

即使在同一企业，不同岗位的关键要素也不相同。关键要素通常包括行业经验、岗位经验、工作年限要求、学历和资质要求等。

2）模糊匹配法

在招聘实践中，通常能够直接匹配的简历并不多见，更多遇到的是应聘者的简历中有些关键要素符合岗位描述的要求，而岗位描述中的另外一些需求则不能满足。

模糊匹配法是通过分析关键要素的匹配量、匹配程度，以及对应聘者具备的"可转移技能"的判断，进行相关性的模糊匹配。大部分关键要素相匹配，而且匹配度较高，而一些次要要素不匹配，或者部分不匹配的关键要素可以通过应聘者的"可转移技能"进行弥补，则模糊匹配成功。

Staff Deployment

Text A

Smart Staff Deployment

导读： 人员调配是指经主管部门决定而改变人员的工作岗位职务、工作单位或隶属关系的人事变动，包括企业之间和企业内部的变动。人员调配的目的和作用，从根本上讲是促进人与事的配合及人与人的协调，充分开发人力资源，实现组织目标。为了适应组织不断变化的外部环境、内部条件及组织目标和任务的变化，需要不断地进行人员调配，以便维持组织的正常运转和推动组织的发展壮大。

Danish retailer reduces queuing and frees up staff to deliver superior customer experience.

Dansk Supermarked Group[1] is the number one retail group in Denmark, operating brands including the Netto discount chain, large format Fotex supermarkets and Bilka hypermarkets.

In 2008, Dansk Supermarked Group became the first retailer in Denmark to roll out self-checkouts, which enable shoppers to scan, pack and pay for goods themselves. The retailer opted for NCR[2] SelfServ Checkout technology from global market leader NCR, which today can be found nationwide in twenty Fotex stores, seven Netto stores and a Bilka store.

"Self-checkouts are far more compact than regular checkouts," notes Greg Mann, NCR SelfServ solution specialist for EMEA[3]. "This means retailers can make far more tills available for customers and free up some staff for other important in-store roles that help to drive up sales and service levels."

Research shows that significant numbers of shoppers fail to spend all they intended to because of "out-of-stocks", difficulties in finding products and the prospect of queues at the checkout.

NCR's technology can help on all three counts. Self-checkouts enable retailers to make smarter use of their staff by making more tills available to speed up checkout times and ensuring shoppers to get the help they need in the aisles.

According to Steffen Skov Larsen, Dansk Supermarked's programme manager: "Between 30 and 50 per cent of customers are opting to use our self-checkouts, depending on the store. We have indications that customer throughput has increased over the last year."

Larsen sees significant potential for the technology in the future: "We anticipate that 60 to 80 per cent of our stores will be suitable for self service. In 2010 alone we are looking at rolling out the technology to 25 more stores nationwide and anticipate further expansion in the future."

Prior to the early deployments, NCR's customer experience consulting team looked at traffic patterns through each of the existing checkouts and the space they occupy. The consultants model the optimum mix of assisted- and self-service lanes and their ideal location to minimise queuing at peak times.

NCR also provides training to help the retailers' self-checkout attendants actively manage the area. Staff are coached on how to observe customer behaviour and the overhead tri-lights to identify if someone needs help.

The NCR SelfServ Checkouts are proven to be intuitive to use — even for first-time users. The latest version enables shoppers to insert loose change in bulk, rather than feeding coins individually as payment. In addition, coin and note recycling means the units need to be replenished less often.

Dansk Supermarked Group is known for being innovative in its format and service offerings. It introduced the concept of supermarkets offering non-food and food goods in Denmark in 1960, launched the discount chain Netto in the early eighties and was the first to market with self-checkouts. The company's ongoing commitment to customer service innovation has enabled it to become Denmark's number one retailer and is designed to keep it in pole position in the future.

Words & Expressions

1. queue	*n.*	队列，长队
2. brand	*n.*	商标，牌子
3. format	*n.*	格式，版式，开本
4. hypermarket	*n.*	超大型自助商场，大规模超级市场
5. scan	*v.*	扫描，浏览，细看，详细调查
6. till	*n.*	放钱的抽屉，备用现金
7. aisle	*n.*	通道，走道，走廊
8. throughput	*n.*	生产量，生产能力
9. anticipate	*v.*	预期，期望，占先，提前使用

10. optimum	*a.*	最适宜的
11. peak	*n.*	山峰，最高点，顶点
12. intuitive	*a.*	直觉的，凭直觉获知的
13. bulk	*n.*	体积，容量，大多数，大部分，大块
14. replenish	*v.*	补充，再装满，把……装满，给……添加燃料
15. ongoing	*a.*	不间断的，进行的，前进的
16. pole position	*n.*	领先位置

1. Dansk Supermarked Group：丹麦超级市场公司，拥有数家连锁店，其旗下的连锁店大部分只在丹麦经营，但 Netto 除外，目前 Netto 已经在几个欧洲国家开设连锁店。该公司是由 Herman Salling 创立的。

2. NCR：美国计算机服务公司，是一家美国技术公司，专门从事零售、金融、旅游、医疗、食品服务、娱乐、游戏和公共部门等行业的服务。其主要产品有自助服务站、销售点终端、自动柜员机、检查处理系统、条码扫描器和商用消耗品。他们还提供 IT 维护支持服务。从 1988 年到 1997 年，他们赞助了非小说类的 NCR 图书奖。

3. EMEA：欧洲、中东和非洲地区，全称为 Europe, Middle East and Africa。

I. Match the words on the left with the meanings on the right.

1. replenish   a. most favorable condition or greatest degree or amount possible under given circumstances

2. throughput   b. obtained through intuition rather than from reasoning or observation

3. intuitive   c. fill something that had previously been emptied

4. optimum   d. make a prediction about; tell in advance

5. anticipate   e. the amount passing through a system from input to output

II. Fill in the blanks with the following words and change the forms if necessary.

expand	prospect	coach	compact	offer

1. Self-checkouts are far more _____ than regular checkouts.
2. Dansk Supermarked Gruppen is known for being innovative in its format and service _____ .
3. In 2010 alone we are looking at rolling out the technology to 25 more stores nationwide and anticipate further _____ in the future.
4. Staff are _____ on how to observe customer behaviour and the overhead tri-lights to identify if someone needs help.
5. Research shows that significant numbers of shoppers fail to spend all they intended to because of "out-of-stocks", difficulties in finding products and the _____ of queues at the checkout.

III. Decide whether the following statements are true (T) or false (F).

(   ) 1. Dansk Supermarked Gruppen became the first retailer in Denmark to roll out self-checkouts, which enable shoppers to scan, pack and pay for goods themselves.

(   ) 2. The latest version enables shoppers to feed coins individually as payment.

(   ) 3. Retailers can make far more tills available for customers and free up some staff for other important in-store roles that help to drive up sales and service levels.

(   ) 4. In 2010 alone we are looking at rolling out the technology to 25 stores nationwide and anticipate further expansion in the future.

(   ) 5. The company's ongoing commitment to customer service innovation has enabled it to become Denmark's number one retailer and is designed to keep it in pole position in the future.

Text B

Staff Deployment Planning

导读： 人员调配需秉承以下原则：① 因事择人原则。因事择人是企业员工配备的首要原则。② 人职匹配原则。员工所具备的能力、知识必须与其履行职务的工作任务所需的能力、知识相适应。③ 用人之长原则。对多数员工来讲，最大的愿望是能充分发挥自己的业务专长。④ 人事动态平衡原则。

Efficient Staff Deployment

Forget about staff bottlenecks, underutilized staff, poor service and low productivity! Deploy your valuable human resources more efficiently. TIMENSION Staff Deployment Planning[1] supports the decision-making task by enhancing your ability to efficiently deploy personnel. Planning with TIMENSION Staff Deployment Planning (including on-duty and standby duty planning) is such a pleasure, because it helps you deploy your staff exactly.

This high quality tabular overview shows you immediately who is at the workplace, who is on duty or on standby duty, and when. The result: the right staff at the right job at the right time. You concentrate on your planning goals and leave the routine work to TIMENSION Staff Deployment Planning.

The Right Worker — in the Right Place — at the Right Time

To ensure that your human resources efficiently match your labour needs, TIMENSION Staff Deployment Planning works with information such as staff competencies, job specifications, working time models, vacation periods, training.

You can plan for any period you wish — from a 5-minute-grid, an hour, a single day, several weeks or even longer-term capacity planning over user-defined periods.

In next to no time, you can obtain a staff deployment plan (standby duty schedule or on-duty plan). All contextual relationships are clearly displayed, enabling you to see at a glance who is working over what time period and also the target staffing levels for each job.

Staff Deployment Planning and Standby Duty Scheduler

TIMENSION Staff Deployment Planning is a user-optimized solution and can be deployed in any company department and in any industry.

Typical uses might be manpower planning for assembly operations, manpower planning for project groups, or the staffing of service phones or departments. In manufacturing companies, in call centres, in department stores, hotels or security companies, TIMENSION Staff Deployment Planning is an ideal solution both in terms of performance and technological excellence.

On-duty Planner

The on-duty planner is arranged in two rows to make it easy for you to directly compare core and flexible times with the actual time worked. The planner also shows the difference between the possible target times and the actual target time.

Good to Know

You need no special knowledge to use TIMENSION Staff Deployment Planning. Because it is tailored to your needs, staff deployment becomes so easy. Planners have much less administration work; human resources staffs get more accurate information.

Fast Response to Change

Perfect planning gives you more freedom. TIMENSION Staff Deployment Planning opens up a wealth of new possibilities for scheduling, simulation and rescheduling.

You remain independent of changed circumstances. Restructuring, strategies designed to improve customer orientation, unexpected rush orders, the sudden loss of an employee or deadline rescheduling can all quickly be incorporated into your planning. With TIMENSION Staff Deployment Planning, you can produce a new staff deployment plan in no time, avoiding under-utilization of manpower and making sure your quality standards are maintained.

Enjoy more independence.

HR as a Business Partner

To provide you with an active structure analysis, TIMENSION Staff Deployment Planning creates a target/actual comparison from existing planning and time data in TIMENSION Staff Time Management, taking into account details such as absences or changes in working hours.

The comparison highlights any deviations from the norm and provides a powerful platform for your future planning. The result is an organization that focuses on the requirements of your company, which in turn means increased customer focus and customer loyalty, and smoother-running organizational processes that help your business to grow and be more successful. There is no more convincing way to establish HR as an effective business partner.

Words & Expressions

1. bottleneck	n.	瓶颈，障碍物
2. underutilize	v.	未充分使用
3. standby	a.	备用的，待命的
4. contextual	a.	上下文的，前后关系的
5. manpower	n.	人力，人力资源，劳动力
6. core	n.	核心，要点，果心
7. tailored	a.	定做的，合适的
8. a wealth of		很多的，大量的
9. simulation	n.	仿真，模拟，模仿
10. orientation	n.	方向，定向，定位
11. incorporate	v.	包含，吸收，体现，把……合并
12. highlight	v.	突出，强调，使显著，加亮
13. deviation	n.	偏差，误差，背离
14. convincing	a.	令人信服的，有说服力的
15. tabular	a.	扁平的，列成表格

Notes

1. staff deployment planning：人员调配计划，人员调配计划的任务是对企业已有员工进行数量、质量、结构的调整，使企业工作任务与工作人员得到更好的组合。在实际工作中，人员调配计划包括工作人员与工作职位的横向流动、纵向升迁，以及员工辞退等方面的内容。

I. Match the words on the left with the meanings on the right.

1. contextual   a. arranged in rows across and down a page; in the form of a table
2. core   b. the angle or position of an object, or the direction in which it is facing
3. orientation   c. the most important or central part of something
4. incorporate   d. relating to a particular context
5. tabular   e. to include something as part of a group, system, plan, etc.

II. Fill in the blanks with the following words and change the forms if necessary.

wealth	tailor	match	loyal	standby

1. This high quality tabular overview shows you immediately who is at the workplace, who is on duty or on _____ duty, and when.
2. To ensure that your human resources efficiently _____ your labour needs, TIMENSION Staff Deployment Planning works with information such as staff competencies, job specifications, working time models, vacation periods, training.
3. Because it is _____ to your needs, staff deployment becomes so easy. Planners have much less administration work; human resources staffs get more accurate information.
4. Perfect planning gives you more freedom. TIMENSION Staff Deployment Planning opens up a _____ of new possibilities for scheduling, simulation and rescheduling.
5. The result is an organization that focuses on the requirements of your company, which in turn means increased customer focus and customer _____, and smoother-running organizational processes that help your business to grow and be more successful.

III. Decide whether the following statements are true (T) or false (F).

(   ) 1. According to TIMENSION Staff Deployment Planning, you can only plan for a certain period.

(   ) 2. Typical uses might be manpower planning for assembly operations, manpower planning for project groups, or the staffing of service phones or departments.

(   ) 3. The on-duty planner is arranged in two rows to make it easy for you to directly compare core and flexible times with the actual time worked.

(   ) 4. You need no special knowledge to use TIMENSION Staff Deployment Planning.

(   ) 5. You remain dependent on changed circumstances. Restructuring, strategies designed to improve customer orientation, unexpected rush orders, the sudden loss of an employee or deadline rescheduling can all quickly be incorporated into your planning.

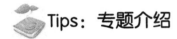Tips：专题介绍

人员调配的类型和程序

1. 人员调配的类型
从类型上看，人员调配大体上有以下四种。

1）工作需要

这种类型是指因地区、部门或单位事业上的发展，如建立新的部门、公司等，形成新的生产和经营能力，需要调动一部分技术和管理骨干组建新单位；或者对于正在发展中的组织充实工作骨干，加强技术力量和管理队伍；或者因退休、调离等，须补充缺额而引发的人员调动。

2）调整优化

这种类型是指对一些使用不当、用非所长或专业不对口的人员进行的工作调整；或者因优化组合，对富余人员、超编人员进行的工作调动。

3）照顾困难

这种类型是指针对职工的一些具体困难，如夫妻两地分居、父母身边无子女、子女入学困难、上班离家太远、长期支边等情况实施的照顾性调动。

4）落实政策

这种类型是指根据国家有关政策，对相应人员的隶属关系、工作关系所做的工作调整。

从涉及的范围上看，调配可分为全国调配、地区或部门间协商调配、单位间协商调配、单位内部调配。

2. 人员调配的程序
一般而言，凡因工作需要进行的人员调动，应按照管理权限直接由调出、调入的批准机关审核决定，进行直接调配。在调配前，单位领导应找本人说明情况，做好工作。

凡因个人原因要求组织调动的，一般按下列程序进行。

（1）本人提出申请，填写调动审批表；

（2）组织审核；

（3）调出、调入单位双方协商；

（4）调入单位发出调动通知；

（5）办理调动手续。

PART Ⅱ
Training & Development

Staff Training

Text A

Assessment: A Must for Developing an Effective Training Program

导读： 培训是一种有组织的知识传递、技能传递、标准传递、信息传递、信念传递和管理训诫行为。培训的目的是通过目标规划设定、知识和信息传递、技能熟练演练、作业达成评测、结果交流公告等现代信息化的流程，让员工通过一定的教育训练技术手段，最终提高自身技能和水平。影响培训效果的至关重要的环节是前期的培训评估，它统领整个培训项目的框架，决定培训的目标、方法、实施步骤等各方面。

Training needs assessment is an ongoing process of gathering data to determine what training needs exist so that training can be developed to help the organization accomplish its objectives. Conducting needs assessment is fundamental to the success of a training program. Often, organizations will develop and implement training without first conducting a needs analysis. These organizations run the risk of overdoing training, doing too little training, or missing the point completely.

There are four main reasons why needs analysis must be done before training programs are developed.

(1) To identify specific problem areas in the organization. HR and management must know what the problems are so that the most appropriate training (if training is the answer) will be directed to those organizational problems. For example, if a manager approached the HR department with a request for a communications program, too often the trainer's response (eager to serve management) will be to proceed to look around for a good communications program and conduct training without

conducting a needs assessment first. This approach will inevitably fail. Nodding their heads appreciatively, everyone says "That was a good program," but when they go back to their departments, work proceeds as usual because the training was not directed to the real needs of the participants. The proper response should have been, "Yes, but let us start by taking a look at the situation. We will talk to a few people to find out what the problems are. Then when we develop the program, we can zero in on a specific situation rather than just use a random approach."

(2) To obtain management support. Management usually thinks training is a "nice thing to do". This stance can be laid directly at the doorstep of a poor (or nonexistent) needs assessment. The way to obtain management support is to make certain that the training directly affects what happens in that manager's department. Trainers should view themselves the same way that management does, making a direct contribution to the bottom line. Management will be committed to training when HR can show that it clearly improves performance on the job. As a result, training programs and budgets will not be the first things cut or trimmed.

(3) To develop data for evaluation. Unless informational needs are developed prior to conducting training, the evaluations that take place after the program may not be valid. In conducting a needs analysis first, trainers can measure the effectiveness of a program.

(4) To determine the costs and benefits of training. Training is usually looked upon as a nuisance rather than a contribution to the bottom line of the organization. This happens when trainers fail to develop a cost-benefit analysis for the training they conduct. Few managers would balk at spending $20,000 to correct a problem costing them $200,000 a year. Yet, most of the time trainers complain that management will not spend money on training. However, a thorough needs assessment that identifies the problems and performance deficiencies, allows management to put a cost factor on the training needs.

The major question trainers need to address in cost-benefit analysis is, "What is the difference between the cost of no training versus the cost of training?" This entails finding out what the costs (out-of-pocket, salary, lost productivity, etc.) would be if the need continues without being met. Next, an analysis must be made of the cost of conducting the training program that can change the situation. The difference between these two factors will usually tell both the trainer and manager whether or not the training should be conducted.

Human resources professionals and line managers also need to be aware that training is not the "cure all" for organizational problems. Neither should it be used as a tool to reward excellent performance, or as motivation to correct poor performance. The purpose of training is to support the achievement of organizational goals by increasing the necessary skills of its employees.

Training is appropriate when your organization can expect to gain more benefit from the training than it invested in its cost. The value of any training investment to the organization must rely on the vision and judgment of line supervisors and managers. You may authorize training to build skills and knowledge levels that help employees better contribute to your organizational mission(s). In some cases, the need is immediate and the training remedial; in other cases, the aim is to update and maintain professional knowledge; and in still others, the goal is to prepare for requirements anticipated by higher level officials.

The following factors might indicate training or development needs of your employees:

(1) Development of employee/management skills to fill a current need

- Trainee or intern training plans
- Reduction in force [1](RIF) placements
- New employees
- New supervisors
- Managerial competency assessments
- Reassignments
- Promotions

(2) Employee relations/organizational problems

- Performance problems
- Production problems
- Safety problems
- Inspection deficiencies

(3) Meet changing needs

- New technology
- New equipment or programs
- Modernization of equipment
- Mission changes
- Laws and regulations

(4) Career development

- Employees' requests
- Career enhancement plans

The Purpose and Objective for Conducting Needs Assessment

Identifying training needs for your employees requires careful scrutiny of mission objectives, personnel, production, raw materials, costs, and other factors. The training requirements you identify factor into the total training budget forecasted for your organization and your installation, and impact the amount of funds that are allocated by senior management.

Conducting a needs assessment is useful in identifying:

(1) Organizational goals and its effectiveness in achieving these goals;

(2) Gaps or discrepancies between employee skills and the skills required for effective job performance;

(3) Problems that may not be solved by training. If policies, practices, and procedures need to be corrected or adjusted, this is a concern for top management, not a training concern;

(4) Conditions under which the training and development activity will occur.

In addition to providing a clear direction for identifying training needs, a needs analysis also serves as a basis for evaluating the effectiveness of the training program. Upon completion of the analysis, you have a basis for comparison. In the absence of a needs analysis, training results are usually subjective and might not be attributable to the training.

Implementing and developing training programs can be expensive, so it makes sense to analyze training needs at the outset so that training can be tailored to focus on specific needs and withstand evaluation after training.

Conducting a Needs Analysis

In selecting which training needs analysis techniques to use, one requires answers to questions such as the following:

(1) What is the nature of the problem being addressed by instruction?

(2) How have training needs been identified in the past and with what results?

(3) What is the budget for the analysis?

(4) How is training needs analysis perceived in the organization?

(5) Who is available to help conduct the training needs analysis?

(6) What are the time-frames for completing the exercise?

(7) What will be the measure of a successful training needs analysis report?

The time spent and the degree of formality will differ according to particular needs and the organization involved. There are, however, four basic steps:

(1) Gather data to identify needs.

This can be accomplished through:

- surveys or questionnaires
- interviews
- performance appraisals
- observations
- tests
- assessment centers
- focus groups
- document reviews
- advisory commitments

Each method has special characteristics that can affect both the kind and quality of the information obtained. For instance, an interview can reflect the interviewer's biases, while a questionnaire can have sampling biases if only a few participants return the survey. It is best to use more than one method to help validate the data, as you can get different types of information from the different methods. For example, you can use questionnaires to gather facts and utilize follow-up interviews to delve more into why people answered questions the way they did.

It is also important to include persons from a cross-section of the target employees for training. Sample people with varying experience levels or you will not have a valid sample, and training will only be effective for a certain part of the total population you targeted.

(2) Determine what needs can be met by training and development.

If there is indication of performance deficiency, the next step is to determine what needs can be met by training and development. If the problems relate to employee relations such as poor morale, lack of motivation, or inability to learn, training is not a solution. Human resources professionals who use training as a motivator misunderstand the purpose of training, which is simply to pass on missing skills and knowledge to employees who are willing and able to learn. Problems arising from non-training issues such as insufficient rewards or obsolete equipment can be identified and referred to management.

(3) Propose solutions.

After determining that training is a potential solution, human resources professionals will need to closely examine if formal training is the best way to meet the need. You might find that practice or feedback is all that is needed.

Practice is useful if a particular skill was taught but not used. For example, an employee might be trained in all aspects of a word processing program but use only a small portion of those skills. If the job requires expansion of those skills, the employee may need time to review additional word processing material and practice using them.

Feedback to employees concerning their work is critical in maintaining quality. Managers and supervisors need to periodically evaluate job performance and tell employees what they are doing correctly or incorrectly to avoid work skills diminishing. If an employee was not able to perform a certain skill, using an existing program to retrain or designing a new program may be the appropriate solution.

(4) Identify the next step.

Once needs have been analyzed and identified, the next step is to develop the training proposal itself. It should spell out the need for training, the expected results, the people to be trained, and the expected consequences if training is not conducted. A key decision is whether to use an existing program or design a new training program.

We have seen that the rationale for developing a training program relies heavily on identifying training needs, and justifying the costs and benefits to the organization. Without a clear understanding of needs, training efforts are at best randomly useful and at worst, useless. The trainer will only be successful and perceived as such to the extent that needs are carefully assessed, and programs are developed and carried out that meet those needs. The end result is a more precise picture of training needs, which can lead to a performance improvement oriented training program and better results from training.

Words & Expressions

1. zero in on		注意力集中于，对准
2. stance	*n.*	立场，姿态，位置
3. trim	*v.*	削减，修剪，整理
4. valid	*a.*	有效的，有根据的，正当的

5. nuisance	n.	讨厌的人，麻烦事，讨厌的东西
6. balk at		回避，畏缩
7. deficiency	n.	缺陷，缺点，缺乏
8. entail	v.	使必要，使必需，使承担
9. remedial	a.	治疗的，补救的，矫正的
10. intern	n.	实习生
11. inspection	n.	视察，检查
12. scrutiny	n.	详细审查，细看
13. forecast	v.	预报，预测，预示
14. installation	n.	安装，装置，就职
15. allocate	v.	分配，拨出，使坐落于，指定
16. discrepancy	n.	不符，矛盾，相差
17. attributable	a.	可归于……的，可归属的
18. outset	n.	开始，开端
19. formality	n.	正式，礼节，正式手续
20. appraisal	n.	评价，估价，估计
21. validate	v.	证实，验证，确认
22. obsolete	a.	废弃的，老式的

1. Reduction in force：强制裁员，这是雇员因商业原因（例如某些职位不再必要或业务放缓的时候）而遭到暂时停职或永久离职的方式。它最初指的是工作的临时中断，就像工厂的周期性工作中断一样。该词现在通常指的是永久性地消除某一职位。

I. Match the words on the left with the meanings on the right.

1. stance   a. a difference between two details, reports, etc. that should be the same

2. nuisance   b. something that you must do as an official part of an activity

3. remedial   c. an opinion that is stated publicly

4. discrepancy   d. to correct something that has been done wrong

5. formality   e. a person, thing, or situation that annoys you or causes problems

II. Fill in the blanks with the following words and change the forms if necessary.

commit	outset	practice	zero	appropriate

1. We will talk to a few people to find out what the problems are. Then when we develop the program, we can _____ in on a specific situation rather than just use a random approach.
2. HR and management must know what the problems are so that the most _____ training will be directed to those organizational problems.
3. Management will be _____ to training when HR can show that it clearly improves performance on the job.
4. Implementing and developing training programs can be expensive, so it makes sense to analyze training needs at the _____ so that training can be tailored to focus on specific needs and withstand evaluation after training.
5. If the job requires expansion of those skills, the employee may need time to review additional word processing material and _____ using them.

III. Decide whether the following statements are true (T) or false (F).

(　　) 1. When everyone says "That was a good program", it means that this is a fruitful training program.

(　　) 2. Only when HR can demonstrate that training may improve performance on employees' jobs, the management will support training and not cut the budget of training program.

(　　) 3. The purpose of training is to reward excellent performance and to cure all for organizational problems.

(　　) 4. Different organizations and particular needs lead to different time spent and the degree of formality of training program.

(　　) 5. Trainers will have a valid sample when people come from a fixed section of the target employees for training.

Text B

How to Make Training Work?

导读：企业为了提高劳动生产率和个人对职业的满足度，使其更直接有效地为企业生产经营服务，须不断采取各种方法，对企业的各类人员进行教育培训。企业必须对员工进行深入的、专门的技能培训，才能使员工逐步达到企业不断发展的要求。专业化的培训有其技巧及注意点，这是影响培训效果至关重要的因素，它对于整个培训项目的结构安排，培训的目标、方法、实施步骤等各方面都起着重要的作用。

This article is about making employee training transfer to the workplace and produce the results you need for your organization.

How much money did your organization invest last year in training and development that failed to provide the results you sought? You are not alone if employee training classes rarely resulted in the transfer of immediately useful information to your workplace.

Real employee behavioral change, based on the training content, is even harder to demonstrate in most organizations. Discouraging? You bet. So what's an organization to do is to ensure employee training transfer to the workplace?

You can create a training and development support process that will ensure that the employee training you do works. You can make training and development more effective within your organization. These ten suggestions and approaches will make your employee training more effective and transferable; their application will result in measurable differences to your bottom line performance.

Creating Training Stickiness Before the Employee Training Session

You can do the following in advance of the employee training session to increase the likelihood that the training you do will actually transfer to the workplace.

(1) Make sure the need is a training and development opportunity.

Do thorough needs and skills analysis to determine the real need for employee training and development. Make sure the opportunity you are pursuing or the problem you are solving is a training issue.

If the employee is failing in some aspect of his job, determine whether you have provided the employee with the time and tools needed to perform the job. Does the employee clearly understand what is expected from her on the job? Ask yourself whether the employee has the temperament and talent necessary for her current position; consider whether the job is a good skill, ability, and interest fit.

(2) Create a context for the employee training and development.

Provide information for the employee about why the new skills, skill enhancement, or information is necessary. Make certain the employee understands the link between the training and his job.

You can enhance the impact of the training even further if the employee sees the link between the training and his ability to contribute to the accomplishment of the organization's business plan and goals.

It's also important to provide rewards and recognition as a result of successful completion and application of the training. (People like completion certificates, for instance. One company I know lists employee names and completed training sessions in the company newsletter.)

This contextual information will help create an attitude of motivation as the employee attends the training. It will assist the employee to want to look for relevant information to apply after the session.

(3) Provide training and development that is really relevant to the skill you want the employee to attain or the information he needs to expand his work horizons.

You may need to design an employee training session internally if nothing from training providers exactly meets your needs. Or, seek out providers who are willing to customize their offerings to match your specific needs.

It is ineffective to ask an employee to attend a training session on general communication when his immediate need is to learn how to provide feedback in a way that minimizes defensive behavior. The employee will regard the training session as mostly a waste of time or too basic; his complaints will invalidate potential learning.

Whenever possible, connect the employee training to the employee's job and work objectives. If you work in an organization that invests in a self-development component in the appraisal process, make sure the connection to the plan is clear.

(4) Favor employee training and development that has measurable objectives and specified outcomes that will transfer back to the job.

Design or obtain employee training that has clearly stated objectives with measurable outcomes. Ascertain that the content leads the employee to attaining the skill or information promised in the objectives.

With this information in hand, the employee knows exactly what he can expect from the training session and is less likely to be disappointed. He will also have ways to apply the training to the accomplishment of real workplace objectives.

(5) Provide information for the employee about exactly what the training session will involve, prior to the training.

Explain what is expected of the employee at the training session. This will help reduce the person's normal anxiety about trying something new. If she knows what to expect, she can focus on the learning and training transfer rather than her potential discomfort with the unknown. (When I offer a team building session, as an example, people invariably ask me if they will have to touch each other or "do group hugs". They don't, but this really drives home the point for me about letting people know what to expect prior to attending the session.)

(6) Make clear to the employee that the training is his responsibility and he needs to take the employee training seriously.

He is expected to apply himself to the employee training and development process before, during, and after the session. This includes completing pre-training assignments, actively participating in the session, and applying new ideas and skills upon returning to work.

(7) Make sure that internal or external training providers supply pre-training assignments.

Reading or thought-provoking exercises in advance of the session promote thoughtful consideration of the training content. Exercises or self-assessments, provided and scored in advance of the session, save precious training time for interaction and new information. These ideas will engage the employee in thinking about the subject of the session prior to the training day. This supplies important paybacks in terms of his interest, commitment, and involvement.

(8) Train supervisors and managers either first or simultaneously so they know and understand the skills and information provided in the training session.

This will allow the supervisor to model the appropriate behavior and learning, provide an environment in which the employee can apply the training, and create the clear expectation that she expects to see different behavior or thinking as a result of the training. An executive, who has participated in the same training as the rest of the organization, is a powerful role model when he is observed applying the training.

(9) Train managers and supervisors in their role in the training process.

The average supervisor has rarely experienced effective training during his career. Even rarer is the supervisor who has worked in an environment that maximized transfer of training to the actual workplace. Thus it is a mistake to believe that supervisors automatically know what must happen for effective training to take place.

You can coach supervisors about their role. Provide a handy tip sheet that explains in detail the organization's expectations of the supervisor in support of effective training. At one General Motors[1] location, the education and training staff provided a three-hour class called The Organization and the Training Process. The session was most effective in communicating roles and responsibilities to supervisory staff.

(10) Ask supervisors to meet with employees prior to the training session to accomplish all that have recommended in this article.

Discuss with the individual what he hopes to learn in the session. Discuss any concerns he may have about applying the training in the work environment. Determine if key learning points are important for the organization in return for the investment of his time in the training. Identify any obstacles the employee may expect to experience as he transfers the training to the workplace.

The following case study will illustrate the power of paying attention to employee training transfer before, during and after the training and development sessions or activities.

Before the Employee Training

In a mid-western university, the Director of Human Resources Development (HRD)[2] created a new employee training series for supervisory staff members. She began the needs assessment process with focus groups that included both prospective participants and supervisors to identify the key skills and ideas needed from the training.

She consulted with outside experts to determine employee training content. She observed employee training programs and met with other university HRD Directors to compare notes before developing the employee training. She formed a university-wide advisory committee to review and assist with the employee training design and delivery.

Then, working with internal and external training and development vendors, she developed the objective-based employee training sessions. Managers of trainees are required to attend an initial meeting which introduces the employee training session content. These meetings also teach participants the role of the manager in supporting the training efforts. Gradually, more and more managers are attending the complete training as well.

During the Employee Training

She piloted sessions with the first couple of employee training groups. Sessions were redesigned based on feedback. Trainers present relevant examples and activities during the sessions.

The participants fill out multi-page evaluations that provide feedback about content, learning, and the effectiveness of the sessions. These are due within a week and not required at the end of the session so participants have time for thoughtful review.

After the Employee Training

Training redesign is an ongoing process based on feedback.

A couple of months after the sessions, the HRD Director meets with employees who participated to assess their satisfaction and learning transfer over time. She also meets with their supervisors to assess whether the employees are applying the skills in the workplace. She is working to provide actual testing and 360 degree feedback to strengthen the training transfer component of the employee training program.

Is the employee training program a success? You bet. She spent the time implementing the ten steps recommended in this article and the university is reaping great results from the resources invested in the employee training. You can experience these results, too, by paying attention to the transfer of employee training to your workplace.

Well, these ten points are the result of the evolution of my thinking over the past thirty years. I know they were influenced by many of you in the training and development field. So, I thank you all for your contribution. No one develops thoughts such as these on an island.

Words & Expressions

1. demonstrate	v.	证明，展示，论证，示威
2. stickiness	n.	黏性
3. likelihood	n.	可能性，可能
4. pursue	v.	追求，继续，从事，追赶
5. temperament	n.	气质，性情，性格
6. enhancement	n.	增加，放大
7. certificate	n.	证书，执照，文凭
8. newsletter	n.	时事通信
9. contextual	a.	上下文的，前后关系的
10. relevant	a.	有关的，中肯的，有重大作用的
11. horizon	n.	地平线，视野，眼界，范围
12. customize	v.	定做，按客户具体要求制造
13. defensive	a.	自卫的，防御用的
14. invalidate	v.	使无效，使无价值

15. component	*n.*	成分，组件，元件
16. appraisal	*n.*	评价，估价，估计
17. specify	*v.*	指定，详细说明，列举，把……列入说明书
18. ascertain	*v.*	确定，查明，探知
19. invariably	*ad.*	总是，不变地
20. simultaneously	*ad.*	同时地
21. supervisory	*a.*	监督的
22. vendor	*n.*	卖主，小贩
23. pilot	*v.*	驾驶，领航，试用
24. reap	*v.*	收获，获得，收割

1. General Motors：通用汽车公司，成立于 1908 年，自创立以来，通用汽车在全球生产和销售包括雪佛兰、别克、GMC、凯迪拉克、霍顿、欧宝、沃克斯豪尔及五菱等一系列品牌车型并提供服务。通用汽车旗下多个品牌全系列车型畅销于全球 120 多个国家和地区，包括电动车、微车、重型全尺寸卡车、紧凑型车及敞篷车。

2. Human resources development：人力资源开发，该概念由美国学者 Nadler 提出，是指一个企业或组织在现有的人力资源基础上，依据企业战略目标、组织结构变化，对人力资源进行调查、分析、规划、调整，提高企业现有的人力资源管理水平，使人力资源管理效率更高，为企业创造更大的价值。

I. Match the words on the left with the meanings on the right.

1. pursue   a. something determined in relation to something that includes it

2. ascertain   b. having a bearing on or connection with the subject at issue

3. temperament   c. carry out or participate in an activity

4. relevant   d. your usual mood

5. component   e. establish after a calculation, investigation, experiment, survey or study

II. Fill in the blanks with the following words and change the forms if necessary.

thought	link	ensure	disappoint	temperament

1. You can create a training and development support process that will _____ that the employee training you do works.
2. Ask yourself whether the employee has the _____ and talent necessary for her current position; consider whether the job is a good skill, ability, and interest fit?
3. You can enhance the impact of the training even further if the employee sees the _____ between the training and his ability to contribute to the accomplishment of the organization's business plan and goals.
4. With this information in hand, the employee knows exactly what he can expect from the training session and is less likely to be _____.
5. The participants fill out multi-page evaluations that provide feedback about content, learning, and the effectiveness of the sessions. These are due within a week and not required at the end of the session so participants have time for _____ review.

III. Decide whether the following statements are true (T) or false (F).

(   ) 1. It is right to believe that supervisors automatically know what must happen for effective training to take place.

(   ) 2. The average supervisor has often experienced effective training during his career.

(   ) 3. It's also important to provide rewards and recognition as a result of successful completion and application of the training.

(   ) 4. It is effective to ask an employee to attend a training session on general communication when his immediate need is to learn how to provide feedback in a way that minimizes defensive behavior.

(   ) 5. With this information in hand, the employee knows exactly what he can expect from the training session and is less likely to be disappointed.

Tips：专题介绍

员工培训的八种形式

1. 讲授法

讲授法属于传统的培训方式，优点是运用起来较为方便，便于培训者控制整个过程；缺点是单向传递信息，反馈效果差。讲授法常用于一些理念性知识的培训。

2. 视听技术法

通过现代视听技术（如投影仪、DVD、录像机等工具），对员工进行培训。优点是运用视觉与听觉的感知方式，直观鲜明。缺点是学员的反馈与实践效果较差，且制作和购买的成本高，内容易过时。它多用于企业概况介绍、技能传授等培训内容，也可用于概念性知识的培训。

3. 讨论法

讨论法按照费用与操作的复杂程序又可分成研讨会与小组讨论两种方式。研讨会多以专题演讲为主，中途或会后允许学员与演讲者进行交流。优点是信息可以多向传递，与讲授法相比反馈效果较好，但费用较高。小组讨论的特点是信息交流为多向传递，学员的参与性高，费用较低。讨论法多用于巩固知识，训练学员分析、解决问题的能力和人际交往的能力，但运用时对培训教师的要求较高。

4. 案例研讨法

案例研讨法通过向培训对象提供相关的背景资料，让其寻找合适的解决方法。这一方式费用低，反馈效果好，可以有效训练学员分析解决问题的能力。另外，近年来的培训研究表明，案例研讨的方法也可用于知识类的培训，且效果更佳。

5. 角色扮演法

受训者在培训教师设计的工作情境下扮演角色，其他学员与培训教师在学员表演后做适当的点评。该方法具有信息传递多向化、反馈效果好、实践性强、费用低的优点，因而多用于人际关系能力的训练。

6. 自学法

这一方法适合于一般理念性知识的学习。成人学习具有偏重经验与理解的特性，让具有一定学习能力与自觉的学员自学是既经济又实用的方法，但此方法也存在监督性差的缺陷。

7. 互动小组法

该方法也称敏感训练法。此方法主要适用于管理人员的人际关系与沟通训练。让学员在培训活动中通过亲身体验来提高其处理人际关系的能力。其优点是可明显提高处理人际关系的能力，但其效果在很大程度上依赖于培训教师的水平。

8. 网络培训法

这是一种新型的计算机网络信息培训方式，投入较大，但由于使用灵活，符合分散式学习的新趋势，可节省学员集中培训的时间与费用。这种方式信息量大，新知识、新观念传递优势明显，更适合成人学习，因此特别被实力雄厚的企业所青睐，也是培训发展的一个必然趋势。

Leadership

Text A

Thoughts on Corporate Leadership

导读： 领导力包括领导者的个体素质、思维方式、实践经验及领导方法等，是影响具体领导活动效果的个性心理特征和行为的总和。领导力是领导者素质的核心。企业经理人有三个必备核心：专业知识、管理技巧及领导力。其中影响力最大、最为重要的便是领导力。本文阐述了一名真正的领导者在领导力方面应具备的各项素质。

In a recent panel session at the Foreign Policy Association[1]'s World Leadership Forum 2000 conference, I said that I don't think that the corporate leaders of tomorrow will differ greatly from today's company chief executives. Leaders serve. They can only do so well if they have the right attitude.

Let me tell you a story about attitude. Two summers ago we brought in an intern from a prominent Ivy League university to help do administrative and research work.

On the first day she appeared promptly, dressed appropriately for the office, met and was briefed by everyone on our then small staff, and behaved altogether positively. She seemed interested in what our firm does, was inquisitive, congenial and helpful. On day two she arrived in somewhat less formal attire, was not quite so positive in outlook, and by mid-afternoon departed the premises never to be seen again.

We had her and about three other staffers stuff envelopes for a mailing. That did it. In a long e-mail sent to me the next day she complained that she could learn nothing by stuffing envelopes and performing other menial tasks. She had, in the current parlance, "copped an attitude". I thought the university dean should know about this behavior in case they were considering her for other internships — or sending future interns like her our way — and received a polite response to the effect that the university could not control its students' attitudes.

I recount this little tale because I think leadership is primarily about attitude. And that won't change in this new millennium. In the case of corporate leadership the attitude must be one of concern for customers, employees and shareholders. Respect for the authority of the CEO position is key.

There will be some differences in the skills of future corporate leaders. For sure, tomorrow's CEOs will be even more computer-literate than today's leaders. They will be altogether more comfortable with new technologies. Many if not most future CEOs will have served their companies overseas and will be at ease dealing with foreign cultures and international markets. Finally, tomorrow's great leaders will be used to unceasing change at an even more rapid pace, change in their marketplace, how they meet their customers' needs, change among their employees and shareholders. And with the flattening of corporate hierarchies typified by emerging companies in this country, CEOs will have to adapt even more to managing teams, even being members of teams. But, overall, great leadership skills are ageless.

Corporate leaders, like political leaders, are leaders of leaders. That means being able to manage people as smart as you are, even smarter maybe. That takes amazing tact or guile or even bullying from a very strong power base. Leading leaders obviously means delegating. It also means you have to encourage those leadership traits of the people under you, many of whom are after your job. And as a recent *Harvard Business Review* article pointed out, intuition is critical. Great leaders have management intuition. They read people well.

The competition is crucial. It's what our enterprise system is all about, competition among companies, industrial and technological competition among nations, and competition among managers within companies. To get a continuous flow of brilliant ideas — for new products, marketing, training people, for keeping your best people in a tight labor market — a real leader must set up constructive competition within his management team. People naturally want to outshine others. I don't care if they're academics, legislators, judges, rabbis and priests, professional athletes or salesmen. A real leader must nurture this competition from within the organization if the company is going to compete effectively with other companies.

But the leader may have to keep a lid on the ambitions of some of his underlings. Too tight a lid, and they'll leave, and that's bad for the company and its shareholders. Too loose, and they'll talk the board of directors into suggesting to you that you'd be more comfortable "upstairs", as chairman, perhaps, but no longer CEO. It's an amazing balance to achieve, and that's why I have such admiration for really effective CEOs, people like Jack Welch of GE[2], John Louden of Royal Dutch Shell[3], Carly Fiorina of Hewlett-Packard[4], Marvin Bower of McKinsey[5], David Ogilvy of Ogilvy & Mather, Lou is Gerstner of IBM, Ken neth Chenault of American Express, Bridget Macaskill of Oppenheimer Funds, Bob Crandall of American Airlines, John Chambers of Cisco Systems, and the list goes on.

We hear a lot lately about "transformational leaders", people who can effect major change in a company. Behind every change in a company, for better or worse, is a leader. Usually it is the CEO. Often it is one or two people on the board, supporting and challenging the CEO, or, occasionally, at odds with the CEO. But transformational leaders are not only chief executives. Often they're outside directors, and they may be CEOs in their own companies. Such transformational leaders on boards led the charge to replace a number of very prominent CEOs earlier this decade. And recently there have been a number of high-profile CEOs who have been eased out of power by impatient boards.

A marvelous characteristic of great CEO leaders in this country is their ability to work within our corporate governance system, which accords strong, but often misunderstood, power to boards of directors. Boards represent the owners of our public companies, the share-owners. Share-owners are institutional investors (many of them managing the retirement savings of tens of millions of people) and individual investors. The prime responsibility of a board is to enhance shareholder returns or shareholder value. To achieve this goal, it hires the best managers it can find. That's the board's most important responsibility. In our system, CEO leaders report to boards made up of other leaders, most of them also from the corporate world. There really is no equivalent arrangement in government that I can think of.

So, here we have these overachieving corporate CEO leaders having to report to boards. They're not the ultimate bosses, after all. The great CEOs handle this reporting relationship very well. Great boards know how to get the most out of their CEOs. And great CEOs know how to get the most out of their boards, to learn from directors who have specialized knowledge, in technology, for example, or in managing overseas investments, or in developing corporate strategies. My point here is that great CEOs never stop learning. Like the rest of us they have two ears and one mouth, but they probably maintain the intake-outgo balance better than most people do. They know that they don't know it all. They milk their boards for information and expertise. So a great corporate leader is a learning leader. That, and our board governance system, is not going to change dramatically.

The great CEO is also a teaching leader. The ability to communicate one's ideas and experience to others in a compelling way is another trait of great leaders in the business and financial world. It's not just the corporate vision or mission, it's determining how to reach the mission's goal, and then working with people to achieve that goal, getting it done.

A good corporate leader knows how to sell his ideas. Before making the big decisions he monitors the thinking of his best people, not just his managers, but his customers and suppliers, and in ferreting out what these people have to contribute he has the opportunity to do a little pre-selling of what he or she thinks. So when the decision is made, many people feel a part of it, even if they don't agree totally with the outcome. They've participated. They've "voted", as it were.

Great leaders are highly motivated, driven to one or more goals. One might be productivity, another might be profitability, another might be quality and customer service. Or all of the above.

Motivation is never a problem for a leader. I doubt that future CEOs, with all of the competitive challenges and opportunities they will face, will lack for motivation.

Words & Expressions

1. panel	*n.*	座谈小组，全体陪审员
2. intern	*n.*	实习生，实习医师
3. inquisitive	*a.*	好奇的，好问的，爱打听的
4. congenial	*a.*	意气相投的，性格相似的，适意的，一致的
5. attire	*n.*	服装，盛装
6. premise	*n.*	前提，上述各项
7. menial	*a.*	卑微的，仆人的，适合仆人做的
8. parlance	*n.*	说法，用语，语调，发言
9. cop	*v.*	抓住
10. unceasing	*a.*	不断的
11. flatten	*v.*	击败，摧毁，使……平坦
12. hierarchy	*n.*	层级，等级制度
13. tact	*n.*	机智，老练，圆滑，鉴赏力
14. guile	*n.*	狡猾，诡计，欺诈
15. bullying	*n.*	恃强欺弱的行为
16. intuition	*n.*	直觉，直觉力，直觉的知识
17. outshine	*v.*	使相形见绌，胜过，比……更亮
18. rabbi	*n.*	拉比（犹太人的学者），法师，犹太教律法专家，先生
19. lid	*n.*	盖子，眼睑，限制
20. underling	*n.*	下属，部下，走卒
21. odds	*n.*	概率，胜算，不平等，差别
22. high-profile	*a.*	高调的，备受瞩目的，知名度高的
23. compelling	*a.*	引人注目的，强制的，激发兴趣的
24. ferret	*v.*	搜出，查获，搜索，侦破

Notes

1. Foreign Policy Association：（美国）外交政策协会，成立于 1918 年，是一个非营利组织，致力于激发美国民众更多地了解世界，加深美国民众对全球问题的认识和理解，并提供关于这些问题的意见。该协会还鼓励美国民众参与外交政策事务。
2. GE：通用电气公司，创立于 1892 年，是世界上最大的提供技术和服务业务的跨国公司。

目前，公司业务遍及世界上 100 多个国家和地区，拥有员工超过 30 万人。2016 年，通用电气公司位于全球 100 大最有价值品牌第十名。2017 年，通用电气公司宣布在天津空港经济区启用其首个美国以外、服务于多个业务部门的智能制造技术中心。在 2017 年《财富》美国 500 强排行榜中，通用电气公司排第十三名。

3. Royal Dutch Shell：荷兰皇家壳牌集团，是目前世界上第一大石油公司，总部位于荷兰海牙和英国伦敦，由荷兰皇家石油与英国的壳牌两家公司合并组成。它是国际上主要的石油、天然气和石油化工的生产商，也是全球最大的汽车燃油和润滑油零售商。它也是液化天然气行业的先驱，并在融资、管理和经营方面拥有相当丰富的经验，业务遍及全球 140 多个国家和地区。

4. Hewlett-Packard：惠普公司，世界上最大的信息科技公司之一，成立于 1939 年，总部位于美国加利福尼亚州。惠普下设三大业务集团：信息产品集团、打印及成像系统集团和企业计算机专业服务集团。

5. McKinsey：麦肯锡，由美国芝加哥大学商学院教授 James O'McKinsey 于 1926 年在美国创建，现在麦肯锡公司已经成为全球最著名的管理咨询公司，在全球 44 个国家和地区开设了 80 多间分公司或办事处。

I. Match the words on the left with the meanings on the right.

1. inquisitive   a. expressed in the words that most people use

2. attire   b. the use of clever but dishonest methods to deceive someone

3. congenial   c. clothing of a distinctive style or for a particular occasion

4. parlance   d. pleasant in a way that makes you feel relaxed

5. guile   e. to ask too much questions and try to find out details about sth. or sb.

II. Fill in the blanks with the following words and change the forms if necessary.

outshine	intern	underling	ferret	premise

1. Two summers ago we brought in an _____ from a prominent Ivy League university to help do administrative and research work.

2. On day two she arrived in somewhat less formal attire, was not quite so positive in outlook, and by mid-afternoon departed the _____ never to be seen again.

3. A real leader must set up constructive competition within his management team. People naturally want to _____ others.

4. But the leader may have to keep a lid on the ambitions of some of his _____. Too tight a lid, and

they'll leave. Too loose, and they'll talk the board of directors into suggesting to you that you'd be more comfortable "upstairs", as chairman, perhaps, but no longer CEO.

5. A good corporate leader knows how to sell his ideas. Before making the big decisions he monitors the thinking of his best people, not just his managers, but his customers and suppliers, and in _____ out what these people have to contribute he has the opportunity to do a little pre-selling of what he or she thinks.

III. Decide whether the following statements are true (T) or false (F).

(　　) 1. The prime responsibility of a board is to enhance shareholder returns or shareholder value.

(　　) 2. It is believed that the corporate leaders of tomorrow will differ greatly from today's company chief executives.

(　　) 3. To get a continuous flow of brilliant ideas, a real leader must set up constructive competition within his management team.

(　　) 4. The author thinks that future CEOs, with all of the competitive challenges and opportunities they will face, will lack for motivation.

(　　) 5. The ability to communicate one's ideas and experience to others in a compelling way is another trait of great leaders in the business and financial world.

Text B

Leadership Is Prime: How to Measure Leadership Excellence?

导读： 领导力是一系列行为的组合，领导是引导团队成员实现目标的过程。作为优秀的领导者，需要具备引导、授权、关系管理、战略制定和执行管理、领导创新和组织变革的能力。

Leading, planning, controlling and organizing are the four interrelated areas of activity that collectively constitute the systematic process which is known as management. Leadership is the behaviour associated with the activity of leading and, in some ways, represents one of the great problem areas both for the student of management and for the practising manager. A voluminous literature has emerged concerned with those who led the organizations of yesterday, who lead them today and what is required of the leaders of the future. When it comes to such a group of leaders, what characteristics are possessed and what is inevitably seen in them to be uniquely elite that enables its members to distinguish themselves from the largely undifferentiated many and to be recognized by others as distinctive and holding authority over them? Much of management literature has been concerned with finding an answer to such questions and, given the complexity of the earliest studies of leadership were those which sought to provide an answer by discerning the traits that all leaders held in common.

Leadership Traits

This approach was primarily the realm in which psychologists sought to identify the personal traits of leaders based upon the assumption that leaders were not born but made. The task then became one of discovering measurable leadership traits which, once discovered, could be compared with the traits that characterized those who never advanced beyond the role of follower and, moreover, of comparing the traits exhibited by effective and ineffective leaders. It was the failure of this approach to make any meaningful statements about leadership that prompted researchers to try to isolate the behaviour that made leaders effective. So instead of trying to ascertain what makes effective leaders, the task became one of trying to discover what effective leaders did to achieve success.

Leadership Behaviour

Here the focus was upon two aspects of leadership behaviour, namely leadership function and leadership styles. As far as the former was concerned, attention was directed towards task-related and group-maintenance activities, whilst the latter was focused towards task and employee orientations.

Tannenbaum and Schmidt have suggested that the way in which leadership is affected is through the choice of a management style. To choose the most appropriate managerial style, the leader must consider the following:

(1) forces within the manager___background, knowledge, values, experience;

(2) forces within the subordinates___autonomy, responsibility, knowledge, experience;

(3) forces within the situation___organization, climate, nature of work group, nature of tasks, pressures of time.

While the insights provided by Tannenbaum and Schmidt have been developed and somewhat superseded in the course of the continuing debate that leadership has attracted, their work provides an important lesson for those with interests in quality management.

Participative Style of Leadership

Earlier it was noted that a complete consensus was lacking among the prescriptions offered by the gurus. However, there is a discernible consensus to be found in their writings on the concept of leadership in the form of top management; they all emphasize that commitment to a quality management initiative is essential. The reason is that, without this commitment, a quality initiative will be under-resourced and virtually impossible to sustain.

Tannenbaum and Schmidt do not restrict leadership to senior management but leave leadership as an organization-wide concept influenced by a common set of forces irrespective of where it is employed. Leadership, therefore, has to be all pervasive and not the particular preserve of those at the apex of the organization pyramid but a concept manifested through behaviour at all organizational levels.

What is not being claimed here is that identical sets of tasks have to be carried out in identical ways by those exhibiting leadership at different organizational levels. The form that leadership will take will be different at different levels at the same time but the same at the same level at all times. Thus, the style of leadership will become contingent upon the nature of the forces noted by Tannenbaum and Schmidt and the nature of the relationship between those forces; both factors will themselves be subject to change.

TQM[1] recognizes not only continuous quality improvement but also the assertion that people make quality. This tends to ensure that the style of leadership best suited to the introduction and sustainability of TQM is a participative style of leadership and, in consequence, encourages the involvement of those most closely linked to a process in the determination of that process. Potential benefits of the participative leadership[2] suggested by Tannenbaum and Schmidt are:

(1) people's involvement in decision-making improves the understanding of the issues involved;

(2) people are more committed to action where they have involved in the relevant decision-making;

(3) people are less competitive and more collaborative when they are working on joint goal;

(4) when people make decisions together, the social commitment to one another is greater and thus increases their commitment to the decision;

(5) several people deciding together make better decisions than one person alone.

A participative style of leadership can be seen to be essential in the building of a corporate vision. Yet all too often a vision is simply "handed down" from the few who occupy the higher echelons of the organizational structure and the expected, ready compliance to its exhortations from the many who occupy the lower rings of the organizational ladder. Hence, the need to build a sustainable and sustaining organizational context is imperative and the creation of a vision is a crucial element in that building process.

Integrated Approach to Leadership

Despite the important role that TQM assigns to vision, it does not leave that vision isolated but seeks to integrate it with other important contextual elements in order to ensure the sustainability of quality initiative. The other contextual elements that are fully interrelated with vision are mission, strategy, values and key issues. It is the task of leaders and the role of leadership at all levels of the organizational hierarchy to work actively to secure the fullest integration of the contextual elements. Collectively, they provide the macro dimension of TQM whilst other elements, which will be considered later, provide the micro, operational dimension.

It is in Kanji's *Business Excellence Model* that the importance of leadership becomes very clear. Leadership is not just one more criterion; it is the prime aspect of the model, showing that leadership is responsible for driving the organization in every area towards quality and excellence.

Considering the literature review on leadership in the context of organizations in general and, in particular, organizations committed to organizational excellence, the critical success factors that are believed to be necessary for leadership excellence were identified. These are the following:

(1) the existence of strong and shared organizational values (which provide the foundation for the identity of the organization and are reflected in its mission, vision, strategy and management practices);

(2) the development and communication of an inspiring vision;

(3) the definition of a mission that states what the organization represents;

(4) the development of a strategy aligned to the mission and vision and able to create a sustainable competitive advantage over the competitors;

(5) the establishment of an organizational structure and operational mechanisms that facilitate the implementation of the mission, vision and strategy.

Leadership excellence is thus the result of an outstanding performance of leaders in all these and other key issues, which, as the definition of critical success factors suggests, have the greatest impact on the competitive success of an organization.

The Need for a Vision

A sustainable and sustaining vision is not something that can be built by one person or a small group of persons in an organization. It is something that depicts the corporate future, which is something that cannot be achieved by the few but can only be accomplished with the synergy that emanates from the active participation of the many. The attainment of an organizational vision is dependent upon the mobilization of bias and the pursuit that mobilization must be of the many not of the few. This reflects the necessity for an organization to recognize that it can fulfill its role only if all staff work together on tasks that are beyond the capacity of one or two working alone.

The Characteristics of a Vision

(1) It indicates a change from the past and present to a new, dynamic future;

(2) It is a comprehensive view of the future;

(3) It holds out the real prospect of the vision being changed and adapted;

(4) It serves as a means to align corporate activities;

(5) It provides a rationale for action;

(6) It creates a context for individuals to locate their work schedules within a collective framework;

(7) It acts as a guide when dealing with uncertainty and complex events;

(8) It presents a standard against which to judge and make choices;

(9) It affords a means for overcoming employee inertia;

(10) It draws people together in pursuit of a superordinate goal.

While all visions should encompass the characteristics shown above, were they to do so it would not necessarily guarantee that the visions would be effective. For a vision to be effective, it must possess the following further characteristics.

(1) It unites and inspires people to make an extra effort in pursuit of collective and individual goals;

(2) It focuses energy on the outcome of collective effort and not simply upon the outcome of

individual effort;

(3) It creates a positive attitude that people can expand in their own immediate work environments;

(4) It depicts a whole, a totality, into which people can place themselves, their feelings and their attitudes;

(5) It meets the needs of the new, educated worker to be engaged in making a valued, individual contribution to a large, corporate effort.

The combined characteristics of an effective vision afford a context that gives both a role and shape to effective leadership behaviour.

Words & Expressions

1. voluminous	*a.*	大量的，多卷的，长篇的，著书多的
2. elite	*n.*	精英，精华，中坚分子
3. undifferentiated	*a.*	无差别的，一致的
4. discern	*v.*	识别，领悟，认识，看清楚，辨别
5. realm	*n.*	领域，范围，王国
6. isolate	*v.*	使隔离，使孤立，使绝缘
7. ascertain	*v.*	确定，查明，探知
8. whilst	*conj.*	然而，同时，时时，有时，当……的时候
9. autonomy	*n.*	自治，自治权
10. supersede	*v.*	取代，代替
11. consensus	*n.*	一致，舆论，合意
12. prescription	*n.*	药方，指示，惯例
13. guru	*n.*	领袖，专家
14. irrespective	*a.*	无关的，不考虑的，不顾的
15. pervasive	*a.*	普遍的，到处渗透的
16. apex	*n.*	顶点，尖端
17. contingent	*a.*	因情况而异的，不一定的，偶然发生的
18. assertion	*n.*	断言，声明，主张，要求，坚持
19. echelon	*n.*	梯形，梯次编队，梯阵，阶层
20. exhortation	*n.*	讲道词，训词，劝告
21. imperative	*a.*	必要的，势在必行的，命令的，紧急的
22. contextual	*a.*	上下文的，前后关系的
23. criterion	*n.*	标准，准则，规范，准据
24. depict	*v.*	描述，描画
25. synergy	*n.*	协同，协同作用，增效
26. emanate	*v.*	放射，发散
27. mobilization	*n.*	动员，运用
28. bias	*n.*	偏见，偏爱，斜纹

1. TQM：全面质量管理，是一个管理学概念，指的是以产品质量为核心，建立起一套科学、严密、高效的质量体系，以提供满足用户需要的产品或服务的全部活动。全面质量管理的基础是减少在生产或服务过程中产生的错误，提高客户满意度，优化供应链管理，追求现代化的设备，确保工人享有最高水平的培训。全面质量管理的主要目标是将错误限制在每生产的 100 万件产品中只有一件次品。

2. Participative leadership：参与型领导，指下属参与管理的一种民主型领导风格。其实质在于领导能够组织员工参与决策和管理，从而增强员工的主人翁意识，使员工更容易把个人目标融合于组织目标。该概念源于德国心理学家勒温有关领导风格的研究。后为许多学者所发展，从而形成一种普遍受欢迎的领导方式。

I. Match the words on the left with the meanings on the right.

1. voluminous   a. capable of filling a large volume or bulk
2. realm   b. to produce a smell, light, etc. or to show a particular quality
3. irrespective   c. a general area of knowledge, activity or thought
4. exhortation   d. used when saying that a particular fact has no effect on a situation and is not important
5. emanate   e. a communication intended to urge or persuade the recipients to take some action

II. Fill in the blanks with the following words and change the forms if necessary.

emanate	essential	isolate	future	concern

1. A voluminous literature has emerged concerned with those who led the organizations of yesterday, who lead them today and what is required of the leaders of the _____.
2. As far as the former was _____, attention was directed towards task-related and group-maintenance activities, whilst the latter was focused towards task and employee orientations.
3. A participative style of leadership can be seen to be _____ in the building of a corporate vision.
4. Despite the important role that TQM assigns to vision, it does not leave that vision _____ but

seeks to integrate it with other important contextual elements in order to ensure the sustainability of quality initiative.

5. A sustainable and sustaining vision is something that depicts the corporate future, which is something that cannot be achieved by the few but can only be accomplished with the synergy that _____ from the active participation of the many.

III. Decide whether the following statements are true (T) or false (F).

(   ) 1. Trying to discover what effective leaders do to achieve success is more important than trying to ascertain what makes effective leaders.

(   ) 2. Leadership function was focused towards task and employee orientations while leadership styles were directed towards task-related and group-maintenance activities.

(   ) 3. In Tannenbaum and Schmidt's opinion, leadership should be the particular preserve of those at the apex of the organization pyramid.

(   ) 4. The need to build a sustainable and sustaining organizational context is absolutely necessary and the creation of a vision is a key element in the building process of a corporate vision.

(   ) 5. A sustainable and sustaining vision is something that can be built by a small group of senior managers in an organization.

 Tips：专题介绍

领 导 行 为

1. 不同的权威观导致不同的领导行为

如图 5-1 所示，典型的领导作风可分为三类。

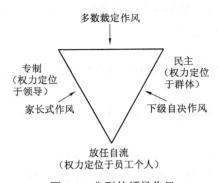

图 5-1 典型的领导作风

1）专制作风

专制作风的特点是专制的领导行为，独断专行，依靠发号施令推动工作，下级没有自由，权力只定位于领导者。这种领导行为来源于正式权限论。

2）民主作风

这是权威接受论所必然导致的领导行为，其特点是注重民主，注意倾听下级意见，吸收其参与决策过程；主要不是靠行政命令，而是靠个人的高尚品德和业务专长所形成的个人权威来推动工作，权力定位于群体。

3）放任作风

放任作风的特点是将权力分散于组织的每个成员手中，由每个人自己作出决策，一切措施也由下级摸索制定。领导者放弃权力，当然也就没有权威可言。这种情况并不多见。

社会心理学家勒温指出，在实际的领导过程中，极少存在三种极端的领导作风，而经常存在两种类型之间的混合型作风，即家长式作风、多数裁定作风、下级自决作风。

2. 不同的领导行为导致不同的下级行为

如图 5–2 所示，领导者的权威观（管理人员特征）、团体因素、下级特征、组织因素共同决定了领导行为，而领导行为又强有力地影响着下级的行为，不仅影响下级的满足度，而且影响对下级的激励程度，从而影响下级的劳动态度（出勤率、人员流动率）和劳动效果（劳动生产率）。

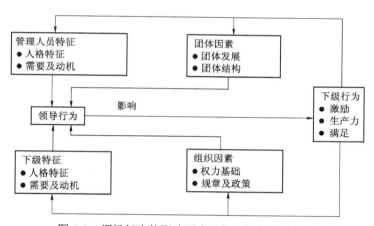

图 5-2　领导行为的影响因素及与下级行为的关系

具体而言，三种不同的领导行为导致的下级行为具有不同的特点。

（1）专制作风的领导通过严格的管理、重奖重罚，使组织完成工作目标，具有一定的工作效率，却往往造成组织成员的消极态度和对抗情绪，从而导致人员流动率高、出勤率低、不满事件增多、劳资纠纷严重、领导者与被领导者关系对立等。

（2）民主作风的组织工作效率最高，不仅能较好地达成工作目标，而且组织成员积极主动，表现出高度的主观能动性和创造精神。下级的物质需要和精神需要同时得到一定程度的满足，从而形成高出勤率、低流动率、劳资关系缓和、领导者与被领导者关系和谐的良好局面，其突出的表现是形成一定的团队精神。

（3）放任作风的工作效率最差。由于领导者对组织活动没有评判和规定，不关心组织成员的需要和态度，员工虽然有一定的士气（这种士气往往不是指向组织目标），但是工作效率低下，不能达成工作目标。下级群龙无首，各自为政，无序沟通，行为失控，恰似一盘散沙，丧失了组织凝聚力。

PART Ⅲ

Performance Management

Personnel Assessment

Text A

What Should You Know about Personnel Assessment?

导读：人力资源管理的核心是用人问题，而用人的关键则是识人和选人。人事测评作为人力资源管理的前沿技术，已经成为人力资源管理的重要课题。人事测评又叫人才测评或人员素质测评，主要是通过履历评判、答卷考试、心理测验、面试、情景模拟、评价中心技术、观察评定、业绩考核等多种手段，根据岗位需求及用人单位的组织特性，对受测者的知识水平、能力结构、个性特征、职业倾向、发展潜力等方面的素质进行综合测评的一种活动，其主要目的就是以最小的投入确保组织内部人力资源的合理配置，把合适的人放在合适的位置上。

Personnel assessment[1] refers to any method of collecting information on individuals for the purpose of making a selection decision. Selection decisions include, but are not limited to, hiring, placement, promotion, referral, retention, and entry into programs leading to advancement (e.g., apprenticeship, training, career development). Selecting qualified applicants is a critical step in building a talented and committed workforce, supporting an effective organizational culture, and enhancing the overall performance of the agency.

While many applicants may apply for any particular position, quantity does not guarantee quality. Assessment procedures can be a cost-effective tool in narrowing down large applicant pools. Assessment tools can also make the selection decision process more efficient because less time and fewer resources are expended dealing with applicants whose qualifications do not match what is needed by the agency.

Effective personnel assessment involves a systematic approach towards gathering information about applicants' job qualifications. Factors contributing to successful job performance (e.g., oral communication, problem solving) are identified using a process called job analysis. Job analysis identifies the duties performed on the job and the competencies needed for effective job performance. Basing personnel assessment closely on job analysis results makes the connection between job requirements and personnel assessment tools more transparent, thereby improving the perceived fairness of the assessment process.

What Are Personnel Assessment Tools?

Generally speaking, an assessment tool is any test or procedure administered to individuals to evaluate their job-related competencies, interests, or fitness for employment. The accuracy with which applicant assessment scores can be used to forecast performance on the job is the tool's most important characteristic, referred to as predictive validity.

Not all assessment tools are appropriate for every job and organizational setting. Agencies must consider a number of factors in determining the most appropriate assessment strategy for a particular situation. These considerations include timetables for filling positions, available staff and financial resources, number of positions to be filled, and the nature and complexity of the work performed in the positions to be filled.

Why Is Effective Personnel Assessment Important?

It is very simple — using effective assessment tools will reduce the degree of error in making hiring decisions. Well-developed assessment tools allow agencies to specifically target the competencies and skills they seek. This helps to ensure the time spent by both applicants and agency personnel adds value to the decision-making process. Selection errors have financial and practical impacts on organizations. The consequences of even a single selection error can create problems for an entire work unit. For example, managers may have to devote substantial time training and counseling the marginal employee and coworkers must often handle increased workloads as they correct or perform the employee's work. Some selection errors can have agency-wide consequences such as customer service complaints, increases in work-related accidents and injuries, high absenteeism, poor work quality, increased turnover, or damage to the reputation of the agency.

Good assessment will also benefit employees who experience greater organizational commitment and job satisfaction because they are matched to jobs for which they are well suited. In addition, using job-related assessment tools often results in more favorable applicant reactions to the selection process. Such perceptions have lasting consequences for the agency including promoting a positive image of the organization, increasing the likelihood of the applicant accepting a job offer, increasing the number of job referrals, and reducing the risk of selection system challenges and complaints.

What Is a Competency and What Is Competency-based Assessment[2]?

OPM[3] defines a competency as "A measurable pattern of knowledge, skills, abilities, behaviors, and other characteristics that an individual needs to perform work roles or occupational functions successfully." Competencies specify the "how" of performing job tasks, or what the person needs to do the job successfully. Competencies represent a whole-person approach to assessing individuals.

Competencies tend to be either general or technical. General competencies reflect the cognitive and social capabilities (e.g., problem solving, interpersonal skills) required for job performance in a variety of occupations. On the other hand, technical competencies are more specific as they are tailored to the particular knowledge and skill requirements necessary for a specific job. OPM has conducted a number of occupational studies to identify competencies for many federal occupations.

How Do I Determine Which Competencies Are Needed for the Position?

A job analysis identifies the job tasks, roles, and responsibilities of the incumbent performing the job, as well as the competencies required for performance, the resources used during performance, and the context (or environment) in which performance occurs. As such, a job analysis demonstrates the clear connection between job tasks and the competencies necessary to perform those tasks.

Conducting a job analysis involves collecting information from job experts. The term subject matter expert is properly applied to anyone who has direct, up-to-date experience of a job and is familiar with all of its tasks. The person might currently hold the job or supervise the job. SMEs[4] must provide accurate information and effectively communicate their ideas. SMEs should rate the job tasks and competencies for importance to successful job performance. Critical incidents (i.e., examples of particularly effective or ineffective work behaviors) are also developed in some cases to describe essential job functions. Documentation of the job analysis process and the linkages between job tasks, competencies, and selection tool content are essential to ensure an assessment strategy meets legal and professional guidelines.

Words & Expressions

1. selection decision		选拔决策
2. placement	*n.*	人员配置
3. referral	*n.*	举荐，被举荐的人
4. retention	*n.*	保留
5. apprenticeship	*n.*	学徒期
6. systematic	*a.*	系统的，体系的
7. perceive	*v.*	察觉
8. accuracy	*n.*	精确度，准确性
9. complexity	*n.*	复杂，复杂性
10. coworker	*n.*	同事，合作者

11. turnover	*n.*	人事流动率
12. absenteeism	*n.*	旷工，无故缺席
13. cognitive	*a.*	认知的，认识的
14. tailor	*v.*	剪裁，使合适
15. occupational	*a.*	职业的，占领的
16. incumbent	*n.*	在职者，现任者

1. Personnel assessment：人事测评，人事测评的方法包含在其概念自身中，即人才测量和人才评价。指通过一系列科学的手段和方法对人的基本素质及其绩效进行测量和评定的活动。

2. Competency-based assessment：能力本位评价，在人力资源管理学上，能力是指对一个人担任一个职位的一组标准化的要求，用以判断其是否称职。这包括其知识、技能及行为是否能够配合其工作。这种方式的根本点在于考核员工能力提高速度和幅度的相对值，而非绝对值。

3. OPM：美国联邦人事管理局（The Office of Personnel Management），是美国联邦政府下属的行政机构，其主要负责保持美国行政法律体系的独立性和中立性，同时还负责管理美国政府的安全调查事务。

4. SMEs：中小型企业（small and medium-sized enterprises），简称中小企业，是指在经营规模上较小的企业，雇用人数与营业额皆不大，此类企业通常是由单一个人或少数人提供资金组成，因此在经营上多半是业主直接管理而较少受外界干涉。"中小企业"的概念来自20 世纪 80 年代末期的"small business"概念。根据《中华人民共和国中小企业促进法》和《国务院关于进一步促进中小企业发展的若干意见》（国发〔2009〕36 号），中小企业划分为中型、小型、微型三种类型，具体标准根据企业从业人员、营业收入、资产总额等指标，结合行业特点制定。

I. Match the words on the left with the meanings on the right.

1. perceive   a. relating to the process of knowing, understanding and learning something

2. cognitive   b. the people you work with, especially those on the same job as you

3. occupational   c. the ability to do something in an exact way without making a mistake

4. coworker　　　　　d. to understand or think of something or someone in a particular way

5. accuracy　　　　　e. of or relating to the activity or business for which you are trained

II. Fill in the blanks with the following words and change the forms if necessary.

value	transparent	match	quality	qualify

1. Selecting _____ applicants is a critical step in building a talented and committed workforce, supporting an effective organizational culture, and enhancing the overall performance of the agency.

2. While many applicants may apply for any particular position, quantity does not guarantee _____.

3. Basing personnel assessment closely on job analysis results makes the connection between job requirements and personnel assessment tools more _____, thereby improving the perceived fairness of the assessment process.

4. Well-developed assessment tools allow agencies to specifically target the competencies and skills they seek. This helps to ensure the time spent by both applicants and agency personnel adds _____ to the decision-making process.

5. Good assessment will also benefit employees who experience greater organizational commitment and job satisfaction because they are _____ to jobs for which they are well suited.

III. Decide whether the following statements are true (T) or false (F).

(　　) 1. Selection decisions include, but are limited to, hiring, placement, promotion, referral, retention, and entry into programs leading to advancement such as apprenticeship, training and career development.

(　　) 2. Job analysis identifies the duties performed on the job and the competencies needed for effective job performance.

(　　) 3. Selection errors have financial and practical impacts on organizations, and some selection errors can have agency-wide consequences such as customer service complaints, increases in work-related accidents and injuries, low absenteeism, poor work quality, reduced turnover, or damage to the reputation of the agency.

(　　) 4. A job analysis identifies the job tasks, roles, and responsibilities of the incumbent performing the job, as well as the competencies required for performance, the resources used during performance, and the context (or environment) in which performance occurs.

(　　) 5. Conducting a job analysis involves collecting information from a psychologist, who is able to tell who has direct, up-to-date experience of a job and is familiar with all of its tasks.

Text B

Evaluating and Implementing Assessment Tools

导读：人才测评工具是指通过一系列科学的手段和方法对人的基本素质及其绩效进行测量和评定的活动。人才测评工具的具体对象不是抽象的人，而是作为个体存在的人的内在素质及其表现出的绩效。它的主要工作是通过各种方法对被试者加以了解，从而为企业的人力资源管理决策提供参考和依据。因此，在选择和评估某种测评工具时，我们应考虑其可靠性、有效性、技术性、法律环境及表面有效性，即求职者反馈。

An assessment tool is any test or procedure administered to individuals to evaluate their job-related competencies, interests, or fitness for employment. In selecting and evaluating an assessment tool, one must consider a number of important factors such as: (1) reliability; (2) validity; (3) technology; (4) legal context and (5) face validity (applicant reactions). Each of these issues that are discussed next concerns the design and effectiveness of selection systems.

Reliability

The term reliability refers to consistency. Assessment reliability is demonstrated by the consistency of scores obtained when the same applicants are reexamined with the same or equivalent form of an assessment. No assessment procedure is perfectly consistent. For example, if an applicant's keyboarding skills are measured on two separate occasions, the two scores are likely to differ.

Reliability reflects the extent to which these individual score differences are due to "true" differences in the competency being assessed and the extent to which they are due to chance, or random, errors. Common sources of such error include variations in:

(1) applicant's mental or physical state (e.g., the applicant's level of motivation, alertness, or anxiety at the time of testing);

(2) assessment administration (e.g., instructions to applicants, time limits, use of calculators or other resources);

(3) measurement conditions (e.g., lighting, temperature, noise level, visual distractions);

(4) scoring procedures (e.g., raters who evaluate applicant performance in interviews, assessment center exercises, writing tests).

A goal of good assessment is to minimize random sources of error. As a general rule, the smaller the amount of error, the higher the reliability.

Reliability is expressed as a positive decimal number ranging from 0 to 1.00, where 0 means the scores consist entirely of error. A reliability of 1.00 would mean the scores are free of any random error. In practice, scores always contain some amount of error and their reliability are less than 1.00. For most assessment applications, reliability above 0.70 are likely to be regarded as acceptable.

The practical importance of consistency in assessment scores is that they are used to make important decisions about people. As an example, assume two agencies use similar versions of a writing skills test to hire entry-level technical writers. Imagine the consequences if the test scores were so inconsistent (unreliable) that applicants who applied at both agencies received low scores on one test but much higher scores on the other. The decision to hire an applicant might depend more on the reliability of the assessments than his or her actual writing skills.

Reliability is also important when deciding which assessment to use for a given purpose. The test manual or other documentation supporting the use of an assessment should report details of reliability and how it was computed. The potential user should review the reliability information available for each prospective assessment before deciding which to implement. Reliability is also a key factor in evaluating the validity of an assessment. An assessment that fails to produce consistent scores for the same individuals examined under near-identical conditions cannot be expected to make useful predictions of other measures. Reliability is critically important because it places a limit on validity.

Validity

Validity refers to the relationship between performance on an assessment and performance on the job. Validity is the most important issue to consider when deciding whether to use a particular assessment tool because an assessment that does not provide useful information about how an individual will perform on the job is of no value to the organization.

There are different types of validity evidence. Which type is most appropriate will depend on how the assessment method is used in making an employment decision. For example, if a work sample test is designed to mimic the actual tasks performed on the job, then a content validity approach may be needed to establish the content of the test which matches in a convincing way the content of the job, as identified by a job analysis. If a personality test is intended to forecast the job success of applicant's for a customer service position, then evidence of predictive validity may be needed to show scores on the personality test are related to subsequent performance on the job.

The most commonly used measure of predictive validity is a correlation coefficient. Correlation coefficients range in absolute value from 0 to 1.00. A correlation of 1.00 (or−1.00) indicates two measures (e.g., test scores and job performance ratings) are perfectly related. In such a case, you could perfectly predict the actual job performance of each applicant based on a single assessment score. A correlation of 0 indicates two measures are unrelated. In practice, validity coefficients for a single assessment rarely exceed 0.50. A validity coefficient of 0.30 or higher is generally considered useful for most circumstances.

When multiple selection tools are used, you can consider the combined validity of the tools. To the extent the assessment tools measure different job-related factors (e.g., reasoning ability and honesty) each tool will provide unique information about the applicant's ability to perform the job. Used together, the tools can more accurately predict the applicant's job performance than either tool used alone. The amount of predictive validity one tool adds relative to another is often referred to as the incremental validity of the tool. The incremental validity of an assessment is important to know because even if an assessment has low validity by itself, it has the potential to add significantly to the prediction of job performance when joined with another measure.

Technology

The technology available is another factor in determining the appropriate assessment tool. Agencies that receive a large volume of applicants for position announcements may benefit from using technology to narrow down the applicant pool, such as online screening of resumes. Technology can also overcome distance challenges and enable agencies to reach and interview a larger population of applicants.

However, because technology removes the human element from the assessment process, it may be perceived as "cold" by applicants, and is probably best used in situations that do not rely heavily on human intervention, such as collecting applications or conducting applicant screening. Technology should not be used for final selection decisions, as these traditionally require a more individualized and in-depth evaluation of the candidate.

Legal Context

Any assessment procedure used to make an employment decision (e.g., selection, promotion, pay increase) can be open to claims of adverse impact based on subgroup differences. Adverse impact is a legal concept used to determine whether there is a "substantially different" passing rate between two groups on an assessment procedure. Groups are typically defined on the basis of race (e.g., blacks compared to whites), gender (i.e., males compared to females), or ethnicity (e.g., Hispanics compared to Non-Hispanics). Assessment procedures having an adverse impact on any group must be shown to be job-related.

What is a "substantially different" passing rate? The *Uniform Guidelines*[1] provide a variety of statistical approaches for evaluating adverse impact. The most widely used method is referred to as the 80% rule-of-thumb. The following is an example where the passing rate for females is 40% and the passing rate for males is 50%. The *Uniform Guidelines* lay out the following steps for computing adverse impact:

(1) Divide the group with the lowest rate (females at 40%) by the group with the highest rate (males at 50%);

(2) In this case, divide 40% by 50% (which equals 80%);

(3) Note whether the result is 80% or higher.

According to the 80% rule, adverse impact is not indicated as long as the ratio is 80% or higher. In this case, the ratio of the two passing rates is 80%, so evidence of adverse impact is not found and the passing rate of females is not considered substantially different from males.

Agencies are encouraged to consider assessment strategies to minimize adverse impact. When adverse impact is discovered, the assessment procedure must be shown to be job-related and valid for its intended purpose.

Face Validity(Applicant Reactions)

When applicants participate in an assessment process, they are not the only ones being evaluated; the agency is being evaluated as well. Applicants who complete an assessment process leave with impressions about the face validity and overall fairness of the assessment procedure. Their impressions can also be impacted by whether they believe they had a sufficient opportunity to display their job-related competencies. The quality of the interactions between the applicant and agency representatives can also affect applicant reactions. Agencies using grueling assessment procedures may end up alienating applicants. It is important to recognize applicants use the assessment process as one means to gather information about the agency. Failure to act on this fact can be very costly to agencies, particularly if top candidates are driven to look elsewhere for employment opportunities.

Designing a Selection Process

The design of an assessment strategy should begin with a review of the critical competencies identified from the job analysis results. Once you decide what to assess, you must then determine how to structure the personnel assessment process. In designing a selection process, a number of practical questions must be addressed, such as:

(1) How much money is available?

(2) What assessment tool(s) will be selected?

(3) If using multiple tools, in what order should they be introduced?

(4) Are trained raters needed, and if so, how many?

(5) How many individuals are expected to apply?

(6) What is the time-frame for filling vacancies?

For example, if your budget is tight, you will need to rule out some of the more expensive methods such as assessment centers or work simulation tests. If you are expecting to receive thousands of applications (based on projections from similar postings), you will need to develop an effective screening mechanism ahead of time. If you need to fill a vacancy and only have a few weeks to do so, then a multi-staged process will probably not be feasible. In working out answers to these questions, it is usually helpful to think in terms of the entire selection process, from beginning to end.

One key consideration is the number of assessment tools to include in the process. Using a variety of assessments tends to improve the validity of the process and will provide information on different aspects of an applicant's likely job performance. Using a single measure will tend to identify applicants who have strengths in a specific area but may overlook applicants who have high potential in other areas. Assessing applicants by using multiple methods will reduce errors because people may respond differently to different methods of assessment. For example, some applicants who excel at written tests may be too nervous to do well in interviews, while others who suffer from test anxiety may give impressive interviews. Another advantage of using a variety of assessment methods is that a multiple hurdle approach can be taken. The least expensive assessments can be used first to pare down the applicant pool. More labor-intensive and time-consuming procedures can be introduced at a later stage when there are fewer candidates to evaluate.

Considering which assessment methods best measure which competencies at which stage in the process should help you develop a process well suited to your agency's hiring needs.

Ensuring an Effective Assessment Process

Agencies are encouraged to standardize and document the assessment process through the following steps:

Treat all individuals consistently. This is most easily accomplished by adopting a standardized assessment and decision-making process. "Standardizing" means making a process uniform to ensure the same information is collected on each individual and is used in a consistent manner in employment decisions.

Ensure the selection tool is based on an up-to-date job analysis and is supported by a strong validity evidence. A validation study can verify applicants who score well on the selection device are more likely to do well on the job and contribute to organizational success. Agencies not familiar with validation research methodology are encouraged to consult a measurement expert.

To ensure applicants perceive the process as fair, agencies are encouraged to:

(1) offer applicants a realistic job preview before the assessment process;

(2) discuss with applicants the rationale for using the selection device, as well as what it assesses and why these competencies are important to the job;

(3) provide applicants the opportunity to ask questions about the job and the selection process;

(4) treat individuals with respect, sensitivity, and impartiality during the process;

(5) provide feedback about all hiring decisions in a timely and courteous manner;

(6) elicit feedback from applicants (those selected and those not selected) on the selection process;

(7) ensure all persons involved in the selection process (e.g., administrators, interviewers, assessors);

(8) understand their roles and responsibilities.

● Words & Expressions ●

1. consistency	n.	一致性
2. equivalent	a.	等价的，相等的
3. variation	n.	变化
4. distraction	n.	注意力分散，干扰
5. decimal number		十进制数

6. test manual   测验手册
7. identical   *a.*   同一的，完全相同的
8. mimic   *v.*   模仿，模拟
9. predictive validity   预测效度
10. correlation coefficient   相关系数
11. multiple selection   多重选取，多次选择
12. incremental validity   增值效度
13. general cognitive ability   一般认知能力
14. adverse impact   负面影响
15. time-frame   *n.*   时间期限
16. validation   *n.*   确认，批准，生效
17. elicit   *v.*   抽出，引出

Notes

1. Uniform Guidelines: 《美国员工招聘统一指南》，1978 年，美国公平就业机会委员会发布了关于员工选拔程序的统一指南。本指南旨在建立一套统一的选拔程序标准。公平就业机会委员会将本指南作为评估雇主雇佣行为的标准，以确保其遵守绩效原则。本指南既适用于在岗安置行动，也适用于外部招聘活动。

Exercises

I. Match the words on the left with the meanings on the right.

1. equivalent   a. to get information or reaction from someone
2. incremental   b. to draw someone's attention away from something
3. distraction   c. to increase gradually by regular degrees or additions
4. elicit   d. to be essentially equal to something
5. mimic   e. to imitate a person or manner, especially for satirical effect

II. Fill in the blanks with the following words and change the forms if necessary.

| demonstrate | reliable | relation | particular | impression |

1. Validity refers to the _____ between performance on an assessment and performance on the job.
2. Validity is the most important issue to consider when deciding whether to use a _____ assessment tool.
3. Assessment reliability is _____ by the consistency of scores obtained when the same applicants are reexamined with the same or equivalent form of an assessment.
4. The face validity refers to the _____ of the applicants about the validity and overall fairness of the assessment procedure.
5. In selecting and evaluating an assessment tool, one must consider a number of important factors such as _____, validity, technology, legal context, and face validity.

III. Decide whether the following statements are true (T) or false (F).

(   ) 1. In practice, scores always contain some amount of error and their reliability are more than 1.00.
(   ) 2. Validity coefficients for a single assessment usually exceed 0.50.
(   ) 3. Reliability reflects the extent to which these individual score differences are due to "true" differences in the competency being assessed and the extent to which they are due to chance, or random, errors.
(   ) 4. Reliability is the most important issue to consider when deciding whether to use a particular assessment tool because an assessment that does not provide useful information about how an individual will perform on the job is of no value to the organization.
(   ) 5. The potential user should review the reliability information available for each prospective assessment after deciding which to implement.

Tips：专题介绍

人才测评工具

　　人才测评工具是指通过一系列科学的手段和方法对人的基本素质及其绩效进行测量和评定的活动。人才测评工具的具体对象不是抽象的人，而是作为个体存在的人的内在素质及其表现出的绩效。人才测评工具的方法包含在其概念自身中，即人才测量和人才评价。人才测评工具的主要工作是通过各种方法对被试者加以了解，从而为企业的人力资源管理决策提供参考和依据。

　　人的素质有六个层面，分别是知识（knowledge）、技能（skill）、社会角色（social roles）、自我概念（self-concept）、特质（traits）及动机（motives）。"素质冰山模型"是美国著名心理学家麦克利兰于 1973 年提出的一个著名的模型，就是将人员个体素质的不同表现划分为表面的"冰山以上的部分"和深藏的"冰山以下的部分"。

　　"冰山以上的部分"包括基本知识、基本技能，是外在表现，是容易了解与测量的部分，相对而言也比较容易通过培训来改变和发展。这部分是对任职者基础素质的要求，但它不能把表现优异者与表现平平者区别开来，这一部分也称为基准性素质（threshold competence）。

　　"冰山以下部分"包括社会角色、自我概念、特质和动机，是人内在的、难以测量的部分。这部分不太容易通过外界的影响而得到改变，但却对人员的行为与表现起着关键性的作用。这一部分也称为鉴别性素质（differentiating competence）。它是区分绩效优异者与平庸者的关键因素；职位越高，鉴别性素质的作用比例就越大。

　　对此，麦克利兰创造性地运用"关键行为分析法"，通过观察个体在工作中的行为来推测和确定社会角色、自我概念、特质和动机等"冰山以下的部分"。

　　按照麦克利兰的方法，"选才"在个性测试板块整合了"SHL 岗位匹配度测试"及北京师范大学心理测量与评价研究所研发的"AOP 职场个性测试"，通过行为倾向挖掘个体潜能，并预测实际工作绩效。

　　"SHL 岗位匹配度测试"以全球取样对不同岗位任职者的行为做了访谈和现场观察后，将所有工作都可能会涉及的行为分为 8 大类、20 子类及 112 种具体行为。再通过 40 道职业行为测试题，测试应聘者与 8 大维度中最重要的 6 大维度之间的匹配程度，以此来评价应聘者潜能与应聘岗位的匹配程度。这种在国际上被广为认可的多维度人才测评题库资源的植入，为企业实现人岗匹配提供了保障。

　　"AOP 职场个性测试"作为专门为人才管理设计的诊断型工具，经过企业实践，发现并总结了与人才管理有关的一系列核心要素：目标导向、影响感召、耐心合作、精确服从等，再通过对这些方面的针对性评估，清晰勾勒出个体在职场中的各种特点，充分运用于企业经营管理的各个层面。

Unit 7

Performance Evaluation

Introduction of Performance Evaluation

导读： 业绩考核通常也称为业绩考评或"考绩"，是针对企业中每个职工所承担的工作，应用各种科学的定性和定量方法，对职工行为的实际效果及其对企业的贡献或价值进行考核和评价。它是企业人事管理的重要内容，更是企业管理强有力的手段之一。业绩考评的目的是通过考核提高每个个体的效率，最终实现企业的目标。

What Is It?

Performance evaluation[1] is a tool you can use to help enhance the efficiency of the work unit. This tool is a means to help ensure that employees are being utilized effectively. Employees can use it as a clear indication of what is expected of them before you tell them how well they are doing, and then as feedback of how well they did.

Purpose

Performance evaluation is a multi-purpose tool used to:

(1) measure actual performance against expected performance;

(2) provide an opportunity for the employee and the supervisor to exchange ideas and feelings about job performance;

(3) identify employee training and development needs, and plan for career growth;

(4) identify skills and abilities for purposes of promotion, transfer, and reduction in force;

(5) support alignment of organization and employee goals;

(6) provide the basis for determining eligibility for compensation adjustments based on merit;

(7) provide legal protection against lawsuits for wrongful termination.

The primary purpose of performance evaluation is to provide an opportunity for open communication about performance expectations and feedback. Most employees want feedback to understand the expectations of their employer and to improve their own performance for personal satisfaction. They prefer feedback that is timely and given in a manner that is not threatening.

Benefits

Many benefits result from the performance evaluation process:

(1) control of the work that needs to be done;

(2) enhancement of employee motivation, commitment, and productivity;

(3) identification of goals and objectives for the employee;

(4) satisfaction of the basic human need for recognition;

(5) identification of process improvement opportunities;

(6) identification of employee development opportunities.

Requirements

North Dakota Administrative Code (NDAC)[2] Chapter 4-07-10 contains requirements for performance management and evaluation:

4-07-10-02: Each agency, department, and institution shall adopt and use a program to provide for the development and management of the performance of each employee in a classified position.

4-07-10-03: Each employee in a classified position must be informed of the responsibilities assigned to the employee's position and of the level of performance needed to successfully perform the work.

4-07-10-04: Each agency, department, and institution shall use the criteria in one or the other of the following performance management program types:

1. Individual-based performance

(1) Performance reviews are conducted at least annually.

(2) Performance reviews are based on individual job-related requirements.

(3) A standard form or approach is used.

(4) Performance standards, or goals and objectives are used.

(5) The review includes a review of past performance.

(6) The review includes a discussion of how performance may be improved or how an employee's skills may be developed.

2. Team-based performance

(1) Performance reviews are conducted at least annually.

(2) Performance reviews are based on overall team performance and how the employee functions as part of a team.

(3) The emphasis of the program is on improving the quality of a service or product, constantly improving systems and processes, and on preventing problems and eliminating them.

(4) The program provides guidance for the education, training, and self-improvement of the employee.

Employee Involvement

Performance evaluation is most effective when employees are actively involved in open discussion about their own performance expectations and about how they are doing in meeting those expectations.

Involving the employee in the performance evaluation process will make it a meaningful, worthwhile experience for you, the employee, and the organization because employees need and want to have their voices heard, are more likely to consider the system as being fair if they have involvement and understand the process, and are more likely to demonstrate genuine commitment to goals and performance.

Ultimate benefits realized by the organization will be increased productivity, efficiency, job satisfaction, and morale and decreased turnover.

Strategies and Techniques

Not all performance evaluation methods work equally well in every organization — one size does not fit all! It is important to consider the categories of employees to be appraised (i.e. managers vs non-managers), the types of jobs performed, the nature of the relationship between employees and managers, the purpose(s) which the evaluation is intended to serve. Other factors are the availability of in-house expertise, developmental costs, and how easy it is to use.

At the core of all successful evaluation formats are clearly defined and explicitly communicated standards or expectations of employee performance. Employees must understand what is expected of them.

Words & Expressions

1. feedback	n.	反馈，成果，资料，回复	
2. supervisor	n.	监督人，管理人，检查员	
3. identify	v.	确定，识别，使参与	
4. alignment	n.	队列，成直线，校准，结盟	
5. eligibility	n.	适任，合格，被选举资格	
6. compensation	n.	补偿，报酬，赔偿金	
7. lawsuit	n.	诉讼（尤指非刑事案件），诉讼案	
8. termination	n.	结束，终止	
9. commitment	n.	承诺，保证，委托，承担义务，献身	
10. classified	a.	分类的，类别的，机密的	
11. assign	v.	分配，指派	
12. criteria	n.	标准，条件（criterion 的复数）	
13. emphasis	n.	重点，强调，加强语气	
14. eliminate	v.	消除，排除	

15. genuine	a.	真实的，真正的，诚恳的
16. ultimate	a.	最终的，极限的，根本的
17. morale	n.	士气，斗志
18. turnover	n.	营业额，流通量
19. explicit	a.	明确的，清楚的，直率的，详述的
20. representative	n.	代表，代理人，典型，众议员
21. in-house	a.	内部的，自身的

1. Performance evaluation：绩效考核，通常也称为业绩考评或"考绩"，是针对企业中每个职工所承担的工作，应用各种科学的定性和定量的方法，对职工行为的实际效果及其对企业的贡献或价值进行考核和评价。它是企业人事管理的重要内容，更是企业管理强有力的手段之一。

2. North Dakota Administrative Code：《北达科他州行政法典》，北达科他州行政法典立法委员会公开出版的这部行政法典编纂了国家行政机构的所有规则。这部行政法典最初于 1978 年 7 月 1 日出版，其内容每季度更新一次。

I. Match the words on the left with the meanings on the right.

1. feedback   a. to give someone a particular job or make him responsible for a particular person or thing

2. alignment   b. advice, criticism, etc. about how successful or useful sth. is

3. eligibility   c. the state of being arranged in line with sth. or parallel to sth.

4. assign   d. what happens at the end

5. ultimate   e. qualification for sth.

II. Fill in the blanks with the following words and change the forms if necessary.

efficient	appraise	satisfy	feedback	emphasize

1. Performance evaluation is a tool you can use to help enhance the _____ of the work unit. This

tool is a means to help ensure that employees are being utilized effectively.

2. Most employees want _____ to understand the expectations of their employer and to improve their own performance for personal satisfaction.

3. Ultimate benefits realized by the organization will be increased productivity, efficiency, job _____, and morale and decreased turnover.

4. The _____ of the program is on improving the quality of a service or product, constantly improving systems and processes, and on preventing problems and eliminating them.

5. It is important to consider the categories of employees to be _____, the types of jobs performed, the nature of the relationship between employees and managers, the purpose(s) which the evaluation is intended to serve.

III. Decide whether the following statements are true (T) or false (F).

(   ) 1. The primary purpose of performance evaluation is to provide an opportunity for identifying employee training and development needs, and planning for career growth.

(   ) 2. Providing the basis for determining eligibility for compensation adjustments based on merit is one of the benefits of the performance evaluation process.

(   ) 3. Not all employees in a classified position must be informed of the responsibilities assigned to the employee's position and of the level of performance needed to successfully perform the work.

(   ) 4. Performance evaluation is most effective when employees are actively involved in open discussion about their own performance expectations and about how they are doing in meeting those expectations.

(   ) 5. Not all performance evaluation methods work equally well in every organization — one size does not fit all!

Text B

Considerations for Your Performance Evaluation

导读：有效的业绩考核不仅能确定每位员工对组织的贡献或不足，还可以在整体上对人力资源的管理提供决定性的评估资料，从而改善组织的反馈机能，提高员工的工作业绩，激励员工士气，同时还可作为公平合理地酬赏员工的依据。而作为员工，面对一年一度的绩效考核，又可以做些什么呢？

If you are like most employees, you probably dread the annual performance evaluation process. It may seem as though you have no power to influence the outcome, so your strategy may be to just grin and bear it. In actuality, you probably have more power than you realize. Following are ten things to think about with regard to your performance evaluation. You may find that with a little foresight and a proactive approach you can make the evaluation process work for you.

Timetable

Most employers have a fixed schedule for employee performance evaluation. Usually, everyone is evaluated at the same time annually, or each employee is evaluated on the anniversary of his or her start date. Find out when your performance evaluation has been promised, and make sure your supervisor sticks to that timetable.

Purpose

The performance evaluation process should have a stated purpose. If the documents you receive do not contain a stated purpose, ask your supervisor to discuss this issue with you at the start of the evaluation process.

Anti-discrimination Laws[1]

Like every other aspect of your job, the performance evaluation process must comply with federal and state anti-discrimination laws. If you suspect noncompliance, you should document your concerns and bring them to your supervisor's attention immediately.

Privacy

You have a right to confidentiality of your performance evaluation. In most cases, only you and your supervisor will be involved in the evaluation process. Some companies may include a representative from the human resources department. Others take a team approach. If you suspect a breach of confidentiality, you should document your concerns and take them to your supervisor immediately.

Focus

Obviously, your workplace performance evaluation evaluates how well you are doing your job. You have a right not to be evaluated on factors unrelated to how well you do your job. For example, it is legal for your employer to assess your loyalty to the company, but it would be illegal to evaluate you based on your religious affiliation.

Compensation

Is the performance evaluation process tied directly to a compensation increase? If so, what factors determine whether employees get a raise? Find out whether raises are based on merit, cost of living, or some other factors.

Objective versus Subjective Criteria

Objective evaluation criteria include test results and other measurable goals, such as number of sales calls made. Subjective criteria, on the other hand, are those measured by the evaluator's personal assessment of the employee's performance, such as evaluating tasks on a scale from "extremely satisfactory" to "satisfactory" to "average", etc. A good performance appraisal form includes objective criteria for evaluation as well as subjective criteria for evaluating the employee's performance. If your evaluation form does not include some objective criteria, investigate whether you could suggest some objective criteria to add to the form.

Negative Appraisal

As a general matter, your performance evaluation should be specific, and this is especially important when you've been evaluated negatively. If your performance evaluation contains criticism, ask your supervisor to provide very specific examples to support the evaluation, and request specific suggestions for improvements.

Evaluate the Evaluator

Although it is rare, some courts have recognized an employee's cause of action against an employer for negligent performance of performance evaluation. In other words, your employer may owe you a duty to act in a reasonable manner in evaluating your performance. Thus, if you feel that the person in charge of evaluating your performance has not acted competently, you may wish to discuss it with human resources personnel, your union representative, or an employment law attorney.

Retain Records

Be sure to keep a copy of every performance evaluation, as well as informal assessments of your job performance, such as an e-mail message that commends you for a job well done. These records may be your insurance against arbitrary termination or demotion. Some courts have even ruled that performance appraisals create an implied contract of employment.

Words & Expressions

1. grin	v.	露齿而笑，咧着嘴笑
2. proactive	a.	有前瞻性的，先行一步的
3. anniversary	n.	周年纪念日
4. anti-discrimination		反歧视
5. comply	v.	遵守，顺从，遵从，答应
6. noncompliance	n.	不顺从，不服从
7. confidentiality	n.	机密，秘密
8. breach	n. & v.	违背，违反
9. affiliation	n.	加入，联盟，从属关系
10. negligent	a.	疏忽的，粗心大意的

11. attorney	n.	律师，代理人
12. retain	v.	保持，保留，记住
13. arbitrary	a.	任意的，武断的，专制的
14. termination	n.	结束，终止
15. demotion	n.	降级，降职
16. implied	a.	含蓄的，暗指的
17. foresight	n.	先见，远见，预见，深谋远虑

1. anti-discrimination laws：反歧视法，旨在防止歧视特定人群的立法。通常，这些类型的立法旨在防止就业、住房、教育和其他社会生活领域的歧视。反歧视法包括基于性别、年龄、种族、国籍、残疾、心理的群体保护等。反歧视法根植于平等原则，法院在确定某项行动或政策是否构成歧视时，可考虑其歧视性意图及其不同的影响。

I. Match the words on the left with the meanings on the right.

1. proactive a. a professional person authorized to practice law
2. comply b. not to take enough care of something that you are responsible for
3. breach c. to make things happen or change rather than react to events after they happen
4. negligent d. an action that breaks a law, rule or an agreement
5. attorney e. to do what you have to do or are asked to do

II. Fill in the Blanks with the following words and change the forms if necessary.

| compliance | foresee | appraise | supervise | loyal |

1. You may find that with a little _____ and a proactive approach you can make the evaluation process work for you.

2. If the documents you receive do not contain a stated purpose, ask your _____ to discuss this issue with you at the start of the evaluation process.

3. If you suspect _____, you should document your concerns and bring them to your

supervisor's attention immediately.

4. It is legal for your employer to assess your _____ to the company, but it would be illegal to evaluate you based on your religious affiliation.

5. A good performance _____ form includes objective criteria for evaluation as well as subjective criteria for evaluating the employee's performance.

III. Decide whether the following statements are true (T) or false (F).

(　　) 1. The performance evaluation process shouldn't have a stated purpose.

(　　) 2. In most cases, only you and your supervisor will be involved in the evaluation process. Some companies may include a representative from the human resources department.

(　　) 3. Subjective evaluation criteria include test results and other measurable goals, such as number of sales calls made.

(　　) 4. As a general matter, your performance evaluation should be specific, and this is especially important when you've been evaluated positively.

(　　) 5. Your employer may owe you a duty to act in a reasonable manner in evaluating your performance.

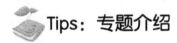 **Tips：专题介绍**

绩效考评体系

1. 绩效考评体系的特征

一种绩效考评体系是否具有有效的考查作用，可能是决定该体系是否令人满意的最为直接的方法。有效的绩效考评体系应具有以下特征。

1）与工作相关的标准

用来考核员工业绩的标准应该是与工作相关的，因此应通过工作分析来确定员工的工作绩效。一些主观因素，如主动性、热情、忠诚度和合作精神，虽然很重要，但在实际考核过程中，却难以界定和计量。因此，这些主观因素在正式的考核中一般不会被当作考核标准而采用。

2）业绩期望

在考核期到来之前，公司领导就应该清楚地表明他们对下属的业绩期望，建立和明确考核标准。否则，使用员工一无所知的标准来考核他们，显然是不合理的。

3）标准化

一方面，标准化是指对在同一负责人领导下从事同一种工作的员工来说，应使用同一种考核方法对其进行考核。对全体员工定期进行考核也很重要。此外，考核期应是相同的，虽然年度考核最为普遍，但许多具有前卫观念的企业所进行的考核还是较为频繁。

另一方面，标准化是指公司应该提供正规的考核文件。员工应在他们的考核结果上签字。如果员工拒绝签字，领导应为这种行为提供书面材料。

4）合格的考核者

考核员工业绩的责任应分配给至少能直接观察到工作业绩典型样本的人或一些人。通常，这个人是该员工的直接领导者。

为了确保连贯性，考核者必须受到良好的培训。

5）公开交流

大多数员工都渴望知道自己的业绩如何。一个好的考核体系会提供一种对员工这种渴望的持续性反馈。另外，绩效考核体系应允许领导直接了解其员工的有关信息。

6）让员工了解考核结果

对于许多被设计用来提高公司业绩的考核体系而言，不告知员工考核结果会产生一定的负面影响。允许员工审查考核结果，相当于允许他们发现任何可能已出现的错误。此外，部门领导应当对低于考核标准的员工给予必要的培训和指导，同时必须尽力挽救那些勉强合格的员工。

7）确定的考核步骤

确定的考核步骤也是非常重要的。如果一个公司没有确定的考核步骤，则应开发一个，用于处理当员工对他们认为不准确或不公平的考核结果提出诉讼时的情况。

同时，员工必须有一个能客观地提出抗议的平台。

2. 绩效考评体系的构建流程

1）绩效考评内容的确定标准

（1）符合企业文化和理念。绩效考评内容就是对员工工作行为、态度、业绩等方面的要求和目标。它是员工行为的导向，是企业文化和管理理念的具体化和形象化。所以，在绩效考评内容中必须明确企业鼓励什么和反对什么，绩效考评内容要能给员工以正确的指引。

（2）突出重点，不能面面俱到。绩效考评内容不可能包含岗位上的所有工作内容，为了提高绩效考评的效率，降低绩效考评成本，并且让员工清楚工作的关键点，应该选择岗位的主要工作内容进行绩效考评。这些主要内容实际上已经占据了员工 80%的工作精力和时间。

（3）明确绩效考评范围。绩效考评只是对员工的工作进行考评，而不是对员工的全面考查，对不影响工作的其他任何事情没必要进行绩效考评。例如，员工的生活习惯、行为举止、爱好等内容都不宜作为绩效考评的内容。

2）对绩效考评内容进行分类

为了使绩效考评更具有可靠性和可操作性，应该在对岗位的工作内容进行分析的基础上，根据企业的管理特点和实际情况，对绩效考评内容进行分类。例如，将绩效考评内容划分为"重要任务"绩效考评、"日常工作"绩效考评和"工作态度"绩效考评三个方面。

3. 编制绩效考评试题

1）编写绩效考评题目

在编写绩效考评题目时，要注意以下几个问题：

（1）题目内容要客观明确，语句要通顺流畅、简单明了，不会产生歧义。

（2）每个题目都要有准确的定位，题目与题目之间不要有交叉内容，同时也不应该有遗漏。

（3）题目数量不宜过多。

2）制定绩效考评尺度

绩效考评的尺度一般使用五类标准：极差、较差、一般、良好、优秀。也可以使用评分，如 0～10 分，10 分是最高分。制定绩效考评尺度时要注意以下几点：

（1）对于不同的项目，根据重要性的不同，需使用不同的分数区间。

（2）使用上述五类标准进行绩效考评时，在计算总成绩时也要使用不同的权重。

（3）为了提高绩效考评的可靠性，绩效考评的尺度应该尽量细化。

3）选择绩效考评方法

根据绩效考评内容的不同，绩效考评的方法也可以采用多种形式。采用多种方式进行绩效考评时，可以有效地减少绩效考评的误差，提高绩效考评的准确度。

为了减少绩效考评的误差，人力资源部门可以建议绩效考评人对被绩效考评人的"重要工作"和"日常工作"经常进行非正式的绩效考评，并记录关键事件。另外，在绩效考评时，绩效考评人应该对所有被绩效考评人的同一项目进行集中绩效考评，而不要以人为单位进行绩效考评。

4. 绩效考评制度化

人力资源部门在完成绩效考评内容选取、绩效考评题目编写、绩效考评方法选择及其他一些相关工作之后，就可以将这些工作成果进行汇总并系统化，以制定企业的绩效考评制度，作为企业人力资源管理关于绩效考评的政策文件。制定了绩效考评制度，就代表企业的绩效考评体系已经建立。

5. 绩效考评体系的设计原则

（1）全员参与，民主管理，得到广泛认同和支持。

（2）与公司战略和发展远景一致。

（3）与公司内、外部环境特征相适应。

（4）公平、公正、公开。

（5）相对准确性。

（6）可操作性。

PART Ⅳ

Benefits Management

Employee Welfare

Text A

Is Welfare Law a New HR Canon?

导读：福利是员工的间接报酬，一般包括健康保险、带薪假期、退休金等形式。这些奖励作为企业成员福利的一部分，奖给职工个人或者员工小组。福利必须被视为全部报酬的一部分，而总报酬是人力资源战略决策的重要方面之一。从管理层的角度看，福利可对以下若干战略目标做出贡献：协助吸引员工；协助维持员工数量；提高企业在员工和其他企业心目中的形象；提高员工对职务的满意度。与员工的收入不同，福利一般不需纳税。由于这一原因，相对于等量的现金支付，福利在某种意义上来说，对员工就具有更大的价值。针对员工福利制定的法律条例对公司人力部门有着重要影响。

Changes to legislation and government strategy around issues such as age discrimination and welfare reform are resulting in evolution in the group risk benefits arena, with additional requirements driving new product design and perks provision. One such change is the government's *Welfare Reform Act 2007*, which received Royal Assent[1] on 3 May and is intended to reduce the number of people claiming incapacity benefit[2] by encouraging them back into the workplace. The government hopes that this help raise the employment level to 80%.

This will be achieved by introducing a revised payment system for those claiming incapacity benefits. Once the legislation comes into effect, the date of which has yet to be finalized, claimants will have to undergo a personal assessment to determine if they have a genuine problem and then a second test to identify what type of work they are able to carry out, if they are fit to do so. Those that are deemed eligible for support following the first assessment are expected to receive a payment of equivalent value to the existing job-seekers allowance, although the government has yet to confirm the finer detail of the second allowance for those who are considered unfit to work. Steve Smythe, health and risk consultant at Jardine Lloyd Thompson, says: "It's a cultural change. It will take time for the new way of thinking to be adopted but it will make the idea of rehabilitation more accepted."

If claimants are judged fit enough to carry out some kind of work, then when they return to the workplace, their employers could receive assistance to help support them, such as funding to help cover the cost of providing items such as voice-activated technology, suitable furniture or to help transport employees between their home and place of work.

It is anticipated that these reforms could have consequences for the group risk market. Wojciech Dochan, head of commercial marketing at Unum, explains: "Currently, group income protection limits take incapacity benefits into account so they may need to be altered for the new system."

The government, alongside its welfare reform programme, is also placing a greater focus on rehabilitation, which could have an impact on both employers and the benefits market. On 18 June this year, Lord McKenzie announced the creation of a new vocational task group made up of representatives from government, business, customers and insurers, to help those who are ill, or injured, return to, or remain in, work. Employers are likely to be encouraged to do more to support their staff.

The task group will firstly identify the services currently available and any wider provision and also determine why organizations do not provide more support for staff and what needs to be done to increase their understanding. It will then publish an initial report on these points later this year and a further report with proposals for mechanisms, tools and incentives to encourage employers' wider take-up of occupational health and vocational rehabilitation services for their employees, next year.

It is not yet fully clear what effect both the *Welfare Reform Act 2007* and McKenzie's reports will have on the group risk market, although both employers and providers may well have to review their provision in this area. Most group income protection schemes, for example, are currently structured so that they top up the amount staff receive through incapacity benefits. As this amount is likely to vary more widely between individuals under the terms of the new reforms, however, employers may have to review how their plan is structured, particularly in terms of its administration.

There will also be greater scope for employers that offer group income protection to spell out why it is worth taking either as a core benefit or as an option through a flexible benefits scheme, as staff will no longer feel that they will be able to rely on the state for assistance if they become unable to work.

The focus on rehabilitation, however, is also thought likely to drive new product design. Smythe says that insurers are already adapting plans to incorporate more support for employees and he believes there is an opportunity for providers to offer this type of rehabilitation and case management service on a standalone basis.

But these are not the only changes to affect the group risk benefits market in the past year. The *Employment Equality (Age) Regulations 2006*, which came into effect on 1st October 2006, require employers to treat all employees the same regardless of their age.

From a group risk perspective, this meant that employers had to alter their contracts to provide cover beyond any retirement age that was previously in place, typically shifting cover from age 60 to age 65 years and, in some cases, beyond.

Clearly this has cost implications. "The increase has had little effect on group life and critical illness premiums but it has meant more significant increases for group income protection contracts. Depending on the profile of the workforce and whether there are members aged under or over 60 years, premiums have increased by anything from around 15%-20% to as much as 100% to reflect the increased liability", explains Dochan.

Faced with this increased cost, employers have taken different approaches to dealing with this additional requirement. Matthew Lawrence, practice head for risk at Aon Consulting, explains: "Some employers decided to extend the group income protection policy and paid the additional premium while others, especially the larger ones, have opted for self-funding to pick up this additional liability. Where they do go for self-funding, their insurer will often agree to be a claims adjudicator for employees not covered by the contract. Depending on the scheme, this can either be negotiated into the premium or charged as an additional fee when they deal with a claim."

Insurers were initially cautious about taking on additional risk, but many have now relaxed their position on the age up to which they will write cover. "There was an element of caution from the insurers initially but we're seeing a lot more of them adapting to the new requirements. While quotes initially went up to 65 years or, in some cases, 70 years, we're now seeing more of them quoting up to age 75 years," says Smythe.

For instance, Unum will now automatically accept schemes up to age 70 years and will often consider extending cover beyond this if the circumstances enable it. But while insurers may now be happier to offer cover to these older lives, there are still issues to resolve.

Heyday, an organization which represents people who are in or nearing retirement, is taking a case to the European Court of Justice to challenge the UK government's interpretation of the age discrimination legislation. It believes that, by implementing the rule to request continued employment from age 65 years rather than have an automatic right to continue to work, the UK is not fully implementing the European Directive[3] on age discrimination. As a consequence, it would like to see the government forced to amend the legislation so that workers over aged 65 years have the same protection as their younger counterparts.

While it might, in theory, be possible for employers to honour such an interpretation. Bob Cheesewright, group risk marketing manager at Friends Provident, says that in practice it would throw up major difficulties for them in funding group income protection benefits. "If this was the case, anyone who was claiming could continue to receive benefit indefinitely. If this is allowed to happen, it makes premiums astronomically expensive," he explains.

Cheesewright believes there is room for a more measured approach when it comes to group income protection. "The legislation states that different treatment is permitted where there is a good reason for it and this could be argued for group income protection. The insurance exists to protect the younger person with a family rather than the older person who could draw their pension. I'm sure, especially where budgets are limited, older colleagues would accept a different benefit that is more relevant to their circumstances rather than see the scheme withdrawn altogether. This would also protect employers from effectively writing a blank cheque for cover," he explains.

Whether or not group income protection is afforded this interpretation, premiums will have to remain significantly higher than before the legislation was introduced. One possible solution to this may be to include income protection within flexible benefits schemes, where employees can select their own perks. This would enable employers to offer the same value of benefit rather than the same level of cover so there wouldn't be any discrimination.

Alternatively, new types of group income protection contracts might come into play. In particular, limited-term contracts, which pay for a set period of up to five years, cap liability and make premiums as much as 40% cheaper than the traditional cover. Lawrence says: "There has been interest in these types of contracts, but this hasn't turned into sales yet." Changes to employment contracts, and the perceived meanness associated with reducing a benefit could be behind this. Employers may also be loath to provide a benefit that stops paying, just when it is needed most.

Words & Expressions

1. canon	n.	标准，教规
2. evolution	n.	演变，进化论，进展
3. arena	n.	舞台，竞技场
4. perk	n.	小费，额外收入，额外津贴（-s）
5. incapacity benefit		丧失工作能力福利，丧失工作能力补贴
6. finalize	v.	使……结束，把……最后定下来
7. genuine	a.	真实的，真正的，诚恳的
8. eligible	a.	合格的，合适的，符合条件的，有资格当选的
9. rehabilitation	n.	复原
10. voice-activated	a.	声控的，通过声音启动的
11. anticipate	v.	预期，期望
12. vocational	a.	职业的，行业的
13. incentive	n.	动机，刺激
14. occupational	a.	职业的，占领的
15. incorporate	v.	包含，吸收，体现，把……合并
16. standalone	a.	单独的
17. perspective	n.	观点，远景，透视图
18. premium	n.	保险费，额外费用，奖金
19. profile	n.	侧面，轮廓，外形

20.	liability	*n.*	责任，债务，倾向
21.	adjudicator	*n.*	评判员，裁定者
22.	astronomically	*ad.*	天文学上地，天文数字般地
23.	loath	*a.*	勉强的，不情愿的

1. Royal Assent：（国王对国会决议的）御准权，在英国，经下议院、上议院一致同意（或者依照法律可以不经上议院同意）的议案呈交君主御准，君主给予正式的同意，议案因此成为法案。御准日期（Date of Royal Assent），即君主同意议案，成为法案的日期。

2. incapacity benefit：丧失工作能力福利，英国的国家福利，用以支付给因疾病或残疾而不能工作且已经缴纳国民保险的达到国家退休年龄的国民，该福利由工作和养老金部的执行机构 Jobcentre Plus 管理。

3. European Directive：欧盟指令，是欧盟的一项立法行动，它要求各会员国在不陈述行动方法的情况下取得特别的成效。它区别于欧盟各国内部执行的规则，不需要任何执行措施。指令通常会使会员国有一定的回旋余地，以便采取具体的规则。根据不同的主题，可以通过各种立法程序采用欧盟指令。

I. Match the words on the left with the meanings on the right.

1. canon   a. a standard, rule or principle that is believed by a group of people to be right and good

2. perk   b. teaching or relating to the skills you need to do a particular job

3. vocational   c. the cost of insurance, especially the amount that you pay each year

4. premium   d. to be unwilling to do something

5. loath   e. an incidental benefit awarded for certain types of employment

II. Fill in the blanks with the following words and change the forms if necessary.

premium	rehabilitate	incorporation	eligibility	genuine

1. Once the legislation comes into effect, the date of which has yet to be finalized, claimants will

have to undergo a personal assessment to determine if they have a _____ problem and then a second test to identify what type of work they are able to carry out, if they are fit to do so.

2. Those that are deemed _____ for support following the first assessment are expected to receive a payment of equivalent value to the existing job-seekers allowance, although the government has yet to confirm the finer detail of the second allowance for those who are considered unfit to work.

3. It will then publish an initial report on these points later this year and a further report with proposals for mechanisms, tools and incentives to encourage employers' wider take-up of occupational health and vocational _____ services for their employees, next year.

4. Some employers decided to extend the group income protection policy and paid the additional _____ while others, especially the larger ones, have opted for self-funding to pick up this additional liability.

5. Smythe says that insurers are already adapting plans to _____ more support for employees and he believes there is an opportunity for providers to offer this type of rehabilitation and case management service on a standalone basis.

III. Decide whether the following statements are true (T) or false (F).

(   ) 1. An initial report and a further report with proposals for mechanisms, tools and incentives to encourage employers' wider take-up of occupational health and vocational rehabilitation services for their employees will be published next year.

(   ) 2. Although both employers and providers may well have to review their provision in this area, it is not yet fully clear what effect both the *Welfare Reform Act 2007* and McKenzie's reports will have on the group risk market.

(   ) 3. Insurers were continuously cautious about taking on additional risk and cannot adapt to the new requirements.

(   ) 4. Employers will fund group income protection benefits to honour the new interpretation of law in practice.

(   ) 5. Premiums will have to remain significantly higher than before the legislation was introduced, no matter whether group income protection is afforded this interpretation.

Text B

Medical Insurance

导读： 医疗保险是由社会或企业提供必要的医疗服务或物质帮助的社会保险。医疗保险具有保险的两大职能：风险转移和补偿转移。即把个体身上的由疾病风险所致的经济损失分摊给所有受同样风险威胁的成员，用集中起来的医疗保险基金来补偿由疾病所带来的经济损失。

Private medical insurance (PMI)[1] has long been an attractive benefit among employees. On-going negative press about the National Health Service (NHS)[2] means that PMI's popularity is unlikely to wane any time soon. According to Bupa's *Health* of the national survey, published last month, PMI is now the second most sought after benefit, falling only behind pensions. But aside from providing an attractive benefit for employees, there is an added dimension to health care in that employers are increasingly feeling they have to look after staff welfare. This is just one of a number of factors that can affect the usage and cost of PMI. Thomas van Every, chief medical officer of PatientChoice, says: "Employers are having to consider the lifestyles of their employees rather than just their acute health. For example, obesity, smoking cessation, and stress management are areas where employers are starting to provide services."

A further change in the market is that employers are also becoming increasingly aware of the benefits for their organization in providing for the health of their staff. This is particularly important when called upon to demonstrate the return on their investment.

David Priestley, sales manager at PruHealth, says: "Employers are increasingly focusing on the broader health implications across their business, not purely about managing the costs of the PMI scheme. It is about managing their workforce to improve performance. There is more focus on sickness absence which costs the UK approximately £ 13 billion a year in lost time and productivity and, as a consequence, employers are investing in the health and well-being services for their employees."

Duty of Care

Investing in well-being services to complement PMI schemes, can help employers to meet duty-of-care obligations towards their workforce. Mandy Blanks, PR manager at Standard Life Healthcare, says, "Employers should be aware of the duty of care to their employees."

Related legislative developments such as the workplace smoking ban should also be a welcome tool for employers hoping to encourage employees to quit such bad habits even outside the workplace. It may be a while before the impact of this legislation on employee health can be fully seen, however, there has been speculation that improved staff health and well-being could help to reduce employees' need for benefits such as PMI for any illnesses or conditions relating to employees' lifestyle choices such as diet or smoking.

Cost is very much at the heart of employers' decision to provide PMI and, in a competitive market, insurers are clamoring for corporate business. "It is much easier to switch plans these days. There is no need to stay with a product or provider you're not completely satisfied with, as some companies are now offering easy switching, often on continuous underwriting terms," says Blanks.

But while it is true that consumers are usually encouraged to shop around when it comes to renewing their car and house insurance, this may not always be the best approach for employers unless they have valid reasons for switching insurers other than a desire to cut the cost of premiums at each move.

Charlie MacEwan, head of communications at WPA[3], explains: "There are some insurers out there going for great growth and others competing with some seriously competitive premiums in the corporate health care trust market, which is fine but it will not sustain the market in the long term."

"Employers moving on price are always going to move on price. Some companies that left WPA a few years ago have asked to come back and we have had to say no because all they are going to do is move on price. We are looking for sustainable business and clients who are going to work with us in the long run."

WPA works on a system of shared responsibility through self insurance, which MacEwan acknowledges is taking a while to obtain general acceptance from employers. "It is tough to ask employees to work in partnership with you because they see it as a diminishing benefit. But, on the other hand, it is the employer who is paying the bill and if there is any control on costs that has to be for the better," he explains.

Health Care Trusts

This move towards self insurance by employers, where they set up a corporate health care trust fund to pay for medical costs, is also having an effect on the market. "It is something employers should look at. Directors want to sleep at night so there is an insurance element to a corporate health care trust but it is at a significantly lower cost," says MacEwan.

To encourage employees to take a greater interest in their own health, insurers are continuing to add to their product propositions. PatientChoice, for example, has introduced its priority product combining PMI with sickness absence compensation for employers. This works by covering staff for private medical care, but provides cash benefits for employers if the employee uses the NHS instead of opting for private care.

PruHealth, meanwhile, has relaunched its gym membership offering, which is part of its vitality proposition in which all members are eligible for cheaper gym membership, but now the more they go to the gym, the less they pay for membership. The company has also introduced vitality funding, which helps employers to reduce PMI premiums by 15%-20%. This reduction is effectively passed on to employees, because if they engage with the vitality programme, for example, by exercising, eating well or stopping smoking, PruHealth will give them that 15%-20% back in a cash reimbursement at the end of the year.

In a further move, Bupa has launched a mole checking service, which can be offered as part of its PMI product.

There has also been some growth towards more bespoke tailored PMI products for employers. According to research carried out by Standard Life Healthcare, 57% of employers are looking for packages where modules can be tailored to suit their company. To meet this need, Standard Life Healthcare has launched its business health care product for the SME market. Through the package, staff can build a scheme to suit their needs from four main modules: core health care, dental cover, health care cash plan and travel cover.

So while PMI may not be the cheapest of the health care benefits on the market, it can be an added bonus on the road to building a healthy workforce.

Words & Expressions

1. wane	*v.*	衰落，变小，退潮，消逝
2. seek after		追求，探索
3. dimension	*n.*	维度，尺寸，容积
4. obesity	*n.*	肥大，肥胖
5. cessation	*n.*	停止，中止，中断
6. speculation	*n.*	投机，推测，思索，投机买卖
7. clamor	*v.*	吵闹，大声地要求
8. underwriting	*n.*	保险业，保险，证券包销
9. renew	*v.*	使更新，续借，复兴，重申
10. valid	*a.*	有效的，有根据的，正当的
11. sustain	*v.*	维持，支撑，承担，忍受，供养
12. diminishing	*a.*	逐渐缩小的，衰减的
13. proposition	*n.*	命题，提议，主题，议题
14. compensation	*n.*	补偿，报酬，赔偿金
15. opt	*v.*	选择
16. relaunch	*v.*	重新上市，重新开张
17. vitality	*n.*	活力，生气，生命力，生动性
18. reimbursement	*n.*	退还，偿还，赔偿
19. mole	*n.*	痣
20. bespoke	*a.*	定做的，预订的
21. bonus	*n.*	奖金，红利，额外津贴

Notes

1. medical insurance：医疗保险，又称健康保险，是将多种渠道筹集的经费（保险费）集中起来形成基金（医疗保险基金），用以补偿个人（被保险人）因病或其他损伤所造成的经济损失的一种保险。

2. National Health Service：NHS，英国国家医疗服务体系，这个体系一直承担着保障英国全民公费医疗保健的重任，遵循救济贫民的原则，并提倡普遍性原则。凡有收入的英国公民都必须参加社会保险，按统一的标准缴纳保险费，按统一的标准享受有关福利，福利系统由政府统一管理实行。

3. WPA：公共事业振兴署（Works Progress Administration），美国总统罗斯福在大萧条时期实施新政时建立的一个政府机构，以助解决当时大规模的失业问题，是新政时期（以及美国历史上）兴办救济和公共工程的政府机构中规模最大的一个。

I. Match the words on the left with the meanings on the right.

1. renew   a. the magnitude of something in a particular direction
2. proposition   b. compensation paid (to someone) for damages or losses or money already spent
3. clamour   c. to utter or proclaim insistently and noisily
4. dimension   d. to reestablish on a new, usually improved, basis or make new or like new
5. reimbursement   e. a proposal offered for acceptance or rejection

II. Fill in the blanks with the following words and change the forms if necessary.

proposition	partnership	obligate	valid	lifestyle

1. Employers are having to consider the _____ of their employees rather than just their acute health. For example, obesity, smoking cessation, and stress management are areas where employers are starting to provide services.

2. Investing in well-being services to complement PMI schemes, can help employers to meet duty-of-care _____ towards their workforce.

3. This may not always be the best approach for employers unless they have _____ reasons for switching insurers other than a desire to cut the cost of premiums at each move.

4. To encourage employees to take a greater interest in their own health, insurers are continuing to add to their product _____.

5. It is tough to ask employees to work in _____ with you because they see it as a diminishing benefit.

III. Decide whether the following statements are true (T) or false (F).

(   ) 1. PruHealth has also introduced vitality funding, which helps employers to reduce PMI premiums by 15%-20%.

(　　) 2. PMI is now the most sought after benefit, falling only behind pensions.

(　　) 3. It is the employer who is paying the bill and if there is any control on costs that has to be for the better

(　　) 4. Thomas van Every says that Employers are increasingly focusing on the broader health implications across their business, not purely about managing the costs of the PMI scheme.

(　　) 5. There has been speculation that improved staff health and well-being could help to reduce employees' need for benefits such as PMI for any illnesses or conditions relating to employees' lifestyle choices such as diet or smoking.

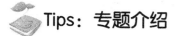 Tips：专题介绍

员工福利的类型

公司福利的类型五花八门、不胜枚举。每个公司除了法律政策规定的福利以外，还可以提供任何有利于公司和员工发展的福利项目。

下面是公司经常选用的一些福利项目。

1. 公共福利

公共福利是指法律规定的一些福利项目。主要有以下几种。

1）医疗保险

这是公共福利中最主要的一种福利，公司必须为每一位正式员工购买相应的医疗保险，确保员工患病时能得到一定的经济补偿。

2）失业保险

失业是市场经济的必然产物，也是经济发展的必然副产品。为了使员工在失业时有一定的经济支持，公司应该为每一位正式员工购买规定的失业保险。

3）养老保险

员工年老时，将失去劳动能力，因此公司应该按规定为每一位正式员工购买养老保险。

4）工伤保险

员工可能由于种种意外事故，受伤致残，为了使员工在受伤致残时得到相应的经济补偿，公司应该按规定为每一位正式员工购买工伤保险。

2. 个别福利

个别福利是指公司根据自身的发展需要和员工的需要选择提供的福利项目，主要有以下几种。

1）养老金

养老金又称退休金，是指员工为公司工作了一定年限，到了一定年龄后，公司按规章制度及公司效益提供给员工的金钱，可以每月提取，也可以每季度或每年提取。根据各地的生活指数，养老金有最低限度。如果公司已为员工购买了养老保险，养老金可以相应减少。

2）储蓄

储蓄又称互助会，是指由公司组织、员工自愿参加的一种经济互助组织，员工每月储蓄若干金钱，当员工经济发生暂时困难时，可以申请借贷以渡过难关。

3）辞退金

辞退金是指公司由于种种原因辞退员工时，支付给员工一定数额的辞退金。一般来说，辞退金的多少主要由员工在公司工作时间的长短来决定，在聘用合同中也应该明确规定。

4）住房津贴

住房津贴是指公司为了使员工有一个较好的居住环境而提供给员工的一种福利，主要包括以下几种：根据岗位不同每月提供住房公积金；公司购买或建造住房后免费或低价租给或卖给员工；为员工的住所提供免费或低价装修；为员工购买住房提供免息或低息贷款；全额或部分报销员工租房费用。

5）交通补助

交通补助主要包括以下几种：公司派专车到员工家接送上下班；公司派专车按一定的路线行驶，上下班员工到一些集中点等候乘车；公司按规定为员工报销上下班交通费；公司每月发放一定数额的交通补助费。

6）工作午餐

工作午餐是指公司为员工提供的免费或低价的午餐。有的公司虽然不直接提供工作午餐，但提供一定数额的工作午餐补助费。

Social Security

Text A

Social Security in the United States

导读： 美国社会保障制度在美国经济发展中发挥着非常重要的作用，它也有一个产生、发展和逐步完善的过程，这个过程贯穿着近现代美国经济的发展史。它是美国经济发展的保护器、安全阀、调节剂。面对当前社会保障中的困难和问题，美国社会保障制度也在发生着一些变化。

In the United States, social security refers to the federal old-age, survivors, and disability insurance (OASDI) program. The original *Social Security Act* (1935) and the current version of the Act, as amended encompass several social welfare and social insurance programs. The larger and better known programs are:

(1) federal old-age (retirement), survivors, and disability insurance;

(2) unemployment benefits;

(3) temporary assistance for needy families;

(4) health insurance for aged and disabled (medicare);

(5) grants to states for medical assistance programs (medicaid);

(6) state children's health insurance program (SCHIP);

(7) supplemental security income (SSI);

(8) patient protection and affordable care act.

Social security is a social insurance program that is primarily funded through dedicated payroll taxes called *Federal Insurance Contributions Act* (FICA) tax. Tax deposits are formally entrusted to the Federal Old-Age and Survivors Insurance Trust Fund, the Federal Disability

Insurance Trust Fund, the Federal Hospital Insurance Trust Fund, or the Federal Supplementary Medical Insurance Trust Fund.

The main part of the program is sometimes abbreviated OASDI (old age, survivors, and disability insurance) or RSDI (retirement, survivors, and disability insurance). When initially signed into law by President Franklin D. Roosevelt[1] in 1935 as part of his New Deal[2], the term social security covered unemployment insurance as well. The term, in everyday speech, is used to refer only to the benefits for retirement, disability, survivorship, and death, which are the four main benefits provided by traditional private-sector pension plans. In 2004, the U.S. social security system paid out almost $500 billion in benefits.

By dollars paid, the U.S. social security program is the largest government program in the world and the single greatest expenditure in the federal budget, with 20.8% for social security, compared to 20.5% for discretionary defense and 20.1% for medicare/medicaid. Social security is currently the largest social insurance program in the U.S. where in 2003 combined spending for all social insurance programs constituted 37% of government expenditure and 7% of the gross domestic product. Social security is currently estimated to keep roughly 40 percent of all Americans age 65 or older out of poverty. The Social Security Administration is headquartered in Woodlawn, Maryland, just to the west of Baltimore.

The 2011 annual report by the program's Board of Trustees noted the following: in 2010, 54 million people were receiving social security benefits, while 157 million people were paying into the fund; of those receiving benefits, 44 million were receiving retirement benefits and 10 million disability benefits. In 2011, there will be 56 million beneficiaries and 158 million workers paying in. In 2010, total income was $781.1 billion and expenditures were $712.5 billion, which meant a total net increase in assets of $68.6 billion. Assets in 2010 were $2.6 trillion, an amount that is expected to be adequate to cover the next 10 years. In 2023, total income and interest earned on assets are projected to no longer cover expenditures for social security, as demographic shifts burden the system. By 2035, the ratio of potential retirees to working age persons will be 37 percent — there will be less than three potential income earners for every retiree in the population. The trust fund would then be exhausted by 2036 without legislative action.

Proposals to privatize social security recently became part of the social security debate during the Bill Clinton and George W. Bush presidencies.

Benefits

The largest component of OASDI is the payment of retirement benefits. Throughout a worker's career, the Social Security Administration keeps track of his or her earnings. The amount of the monthly benefit to which the worker is entitled depends upon that earnings record and upon the age at which the retiree chooses to begin receiving benefits. For the entire history of social security, benefits have been paid almost entirely by using revenue from payroll taxes. This is why social security is referred to as a pay-as-you-go system. Around 2017, payroll tax revenue is projected to be insufficient to cover social security benefits and the system will begin to withdraw money from the Social Security Trust Fund. The existence and economic significance of the Social Security Trust Fund is a subject of considerable dispute because its assets are special treasury bonds; i.e. the money in the trust fund has been lent back to the federal government to pay for other expenses.

Joining and Quitting

Obtaining a social security number for a child is voluntary. Further, there is no general legal requirement that individuals join the social security program. Although the *Social Security Act* itself does not require a person to have a social security number (SSN)[3] to live and work in the United States, the *Internal Revenue Code* does generally require the use of the social security number by individuals for federal tax purposes.

Importantly, most parents apply for social security numbers for their dependent children in order to include them on their income tax returns as a dependent. Everyone filing a tax return, as taxpayer or spouse, must have a social security number or taxpayer identification number (TIN) since the IRS[4] is unable to process returns or post payments for anyone without an SSN or TIN.

The FICA taxes are imposed on all workers and self-employed persons. Employers are required to report wages for covered employment to social security for processing Forms W-2 and W-3. There are some specific wages which are not a part of the social security program (discussed below). *Internal Revenue Code* provisions Section 3101 imposes payroll taxes on individuals and employer matching taxes. Section 3102 mandates that employers deduct these payroll taxes from workers' wages before they are paid. Generally, the payroll tax is imposed on everyone in employment earning "wages" as defined in 3121 of the *Internal Revenue Code* and also taxes net earnings from self-employment.

Trust Fund[5]

Social security taxes are paid into the Social Security Trust Fund maintained by the U.S. Treasury. Current year expenses are paid from current social security tax revenues. When revenues exceed expenditures, as they have in most years, the excess is invested in special series, non-marketable U.S. government bonds, thus the Social Security Trust Fund indirectly finances the federal government's general purpose deficit spending. In 2007, the cumulative excess of social security taxes and interest received over benefits paid out stood at $2.2 trillion. The trust fund is regarded by some as an accounting trick which holds no economic significance. Others argue that it has specific legal significance because the treasury securities it holds are backed by the "full faith and credit" of the U.S. government, which has an obligation to repay its debt.

The Social Security Administration's authority to make benefit payments as granted by Congress extends only to its current revenues and existing trust fund balance, i.e., redemption of its holdings of treasury securities. Therefore, social security's ability to make full payments once annual benefits exceed revenues depends in part on the federal government's ability to make good on the bonds that it has issued to the Social Security Trust Fund. As with any other federal obligation, the federal government's ability to repay social security is based on the power to tax and the commitment of the Congress to meet its obligations.

In 2009, the Office of the Chief Actuary of the Social Security Administration calculated an unfunded obligation of \$15.1 trillion for the social security program. The unfunded obligation is the difference between the present value of the cost of social security and the present value of the assets in the trust fund and the future scheduled tax income of the program. In the actuarial note explaining the calculation, the Office of the Chief Actuary wrote that "The term obligation is used in lieu of the term liability, because liability generally indicates a contractual obligation (as in the case of private pensions and insurance) that cannot be altered by the plan sponsor without the agreement of the plan participants."

International Agreements

People sometimes relocate from one country to another, either permanently or on a limited-time basis. This presents challenges to businesses, governments, and individuals seeking to ensure future benefits or having to deal with taxation authorities in multiple countries. To that end, the Social Security Administration has signed treaties, often referred to as *Totalization Agreements*, with other social insurance programs in various foreign countries.

Overall, these agreements serve two main purposes. First, they eliminate dual social security taxation, the situation that occurs when a worker from one country works in another country and is required to pay social security taxes to both countries on the same earnings. Second, the agreements help fill gaps in benefit protection for workers who have divided their careers between the United States and another country.

Words & Expressions

1. encompass	*v.*	围绕，包括
2. amend	*v.*	修正，改进
3. entrust	*v.*	信赖，委托
4. demographic	*a.*	人口统计学的
5. headquarter	*v.*	总部设于
6. relocate	*v.*	重新安置，迁移
7. calculate	*v.*	计算，考虑
8. contractual	*a.*	契约的，合同的
9. eliminate	*v.*	剔除，排除
10. sponsor	*n.*	赞助人，发起人
11. cumulative	*a.*	累积的
12. mandate	*n.&v.*	命令，要求

1. Franklin D. Roosevelt：富兰克林·罗斯福，史称"小罗斯福"，是美国第 32 任总统，美国历史上唯一连任四届的总统，是第二次世界大战期间同盟国阵营的重要领导人之一。1941 年珍珠港事件发生后，罗斯福力主对日本宣战，并引进了价格管制和配给。罗斯福以租借法案使美国转变为"民主国家的兵工厂"，使美国成为同盟国主要的军火供应商和融资者，也使得美国国内产业大幅扩张，实现充分就业。 罗斯福曾多次被评为美国最佳总统，被美国的权威期刊《大西洋月刊》评为影响美国的 100 位人物第 4 名。

2. New Deal：新政，指 1933 年富兰克林·罗斯福任美国总统后实行的一系列经济政策，主要包括三个核心：救济（relief）、复兴（recovery）和改革（reform），也称"3R 新政"。新政增加了政府对经济的直接或间接干预，缓解了大萧条带来的经济危机与社会矛盾，还通过国会制定了《紧急银行法令》《全国工业复兴法》《农业调整法》《社会保障法案》等法案。

3. SSN：社会保障号，是美国联邦政府社会安全局发给公民、永久居民、临时（工作）居民的一组九位数字号码。社会保障号以前多用来进行报税，等纳税人退休后用来领取退休金。但是目前，社会保障号的功能已被大大地扩大了，它不仅用于报税，还被一般人看成能否在美国工作的一种凭据。

4. IRS：美国国内税务局（Internal Revenue Service）。1862 年，林肯总统及当时的国会为支付战争费用，创立了国内税务局，隶属于财政部。

5. Trust fund：信托基金，也叫投资基金，是一种"利益共享、风险共担"的集合投资方式，是指通过契约或公司的形式，借助发行基金券的方式，将社会上不确定的多数投资者不等额的资金集中起来，形成一定规模的信托资产，交由专门的投资机构按资产组合原理进行分散投资，获得的收益由投资者按出资比例分享，并承担相应风险的一种集合投资信托制度。

I. Match the words on the left with the meanings on the right.

1. entrust
2. contractual
3. demographic
4. sponsor
5. mandate

a. information about the people living in a certain area

b. agreed in contract

c. an official instruction given to a person or an organization

d. to make someone responsible for doing something important

e. a person or company that pays for an event in exchange for advertisement at that event

II. Fill in the blanks with the following words and change the forms if necessary.

significant	employ	primary	budget	private

1. Social security is a social insurance program that is _____ funded through dedicated payroll taxes called *Federal Insurance Contributions Act* (FICA) tax.
2. By dollars paid, the U.S. social security program is the largest government program in the world and the single greatest expenditure in the federal _____.
3. Proposals to _____ social security recently became part of the social security debate during the Bill Clinton and George W. Bush presidencies.
4. The existence and economic _____ of the Social Security Trust Fund is a subject of considerable dispute because its assets are special treasury bonds.
5. Employers are required to report wages for covered _____ to social security for processing Forms W-2 and W-3.

III. Decide whether the following statements are true (T) or false (F).

(   ) 1. In the United States, social security refers to the federal old-age, survivors, and disability insurance (OASDI) program.

(   ) 2. Retirement, disability, survivorship, and birth are the four main benefits provided by traditional private-sector pension plans.

(   ) 3. Social security is currently the largest social insurance program in the U.S.

(   ) 4. For the entire history of social security, benefits have been paid almost entirely by using revenue from payroll taxes. This is why social security is referred to as a pay-as-you-go system.

(   ) 5. Further, there is some general legal requirement that individuals join the social security program.

Text B

Keep Social Security Strong

导读：美国在社会保障方面可谓是给其他国家做足了榜样，很多国家都想仿照美国建立具有本国特色的社会保障制度。难道美国的社会保障制度就完美无缺吗？其实，美国应该继续改进其社会保障制度，使之更加坚挺有力，并造福于后代。

For more than 50 years, AARP[1] has been fighting to protect and strengthen social security. Now, we're launching a conversation about how to strengthen it so future generations will receive the benefits they've earned when they're ready to retire. With shrinking pensions, dwindling savings and longer life expectancies, we know that future generations will depend on social security even more.

Strengthening Social Security

For more than 75 years, Americans have been paying into social security and collecting earned benefits when they retire. Without any changes, social security will be able to pay 100 percent of benefits for the next 25 years. After that, it will still be able to pay 75 percent of promised benefits, but that's not good enough. With gradual and modest changes, however, we can ensure that future generations get the benefits they've earned.

Social Security Values

Throughout the debate over how to strengthen social security, AARP is going to fight to ensure that any final plan is based on these critical values:

(1) You will receive the benefits you've earned over a lifetime of hard work if you pay into social security.

(2) Your guaranteed social security benefit will keep up with inflation as long as you live.

(3) Your spouse will be protected and you will receive a benefit if you become disabled and can no longer work.

(4) Your family will be protected if you die.

Retirement Security

Social security's guaranteed benefits are a rock-solid commitment to American families. Companies can go out of business. Pensions can be terminated. The stock market can take a nose dive. Social security benefits are there in good times and bad.

Americans earn and pay for social security's guaranteed retirement benefits by making contributions out of each and every paycheck throughout their working lives. Today, the average retirement benefit is about $1,200 per month and is adjusted annually to keep pace with inflation.

On average, social security benefits replace $4 out of every $10 dollars a person earns while working.

In addition to providing benefits to retirees, social security also protects workers who become disabled and the families of workers who die. Among seniors, 20% of married couples and about 41% of singles rely on social security for 90% or more of their income. For middle income seniors, social security provides 54 percent of their family income.

The Wrong Conversation

Some people in Washington, D.C., are talking about cutting social security to balance the budget. Social security is self-financed by payroll tax contributions, which are separate from the rest of the budget, and has not created the current fiscal mess. It shouldn't be used to fix a deficit it didn't cause.

Instead of putting our children and grand-children's retirement in jeopardy, AARP believes Congress should find ways to solve our nation's budget problems without making dangerous cuts to social security.

Social Security: More Than You Might Think

Many people do not realize how valuable social security is to them. On average, an individual would have to save an additional $300,000 while working to replace the benefits social security provides in retirement. Independent investments, pensions, individual retirement accounts and 401(k)[2] accounts are all important parts of retirement savings, but social security is the guaranteed base of retirement security for most Americans. In fact, couples on average can expect about $22,000 per year in social security benefits.

Social security is the most successful program in our nation's history, and we need to make the modest changes necessary to strengthen the guaranteed benefit for both current and future generations.

Keep Social Security Strong for Future Generations

Social security has been keeping its promise all those years as a strong foundation for financial security in retirement.

That's worth remembering as the oldest baby boomers reach traditional retirement age, younger boomers start to anticipate it, and future generations ask what retirement security will mean for them. It's also worth remembering as the bipartisan federal deficit commission considers cuts to social security as one solution to our country's fiscal straits.

Pardon me if I don't agree.

The fact is that social security hasn't contributed one thin dime to our country's perennial budget deficits or accumulated debt. Rather, social security is now and always has been fully paid for by hardworking Americans who deserve a return on their contributions. It should be off-limits to the deficit commission.

As a matter of fact, social security has been taking in more than it's paid out for the last 25 years, and the accumulated difference is now worth $2.5 trillion. Combined with social security payroll taxes, that's enough to pay full benefits to every beneficiary through 2037.

Is it fair to cut social security benefits that working people have earned in order to fix a problem that social security didn't cause? This isn't an abstract argument. It's about hardworking people who've paid into social security all their working lives and built their retirement security around it. It's also about the surviving spouses and children of workers who die or become disabled, for whom social security is an irreplaceable lifeline.

Let me share some statistics.

Social security paid benefits to 1.12 million hoosiers in 2008, including 165,000 workers with disabilities and 84,000 children. The average monthly benefit was $1,104, slightly below the national average of $1,168. That relatively small sum is especially important because the other foundations of retirement security — pensions, savings and investments — have taken some pretty big hits between the long bear market of 2000-2003 and our current deep recession.

At the market bottom in 2009, in fact, Americans' 401(k) and IRA[3] investments had lost an estimated $2.8 trillion in value. While many funds have recouped some of those losses, most second-quarter investment statements show that we're still treading water. As for pensions, it's not at all clear that younger generations will even have them, whether they work in the public or private sectors.

Now it's true that social security needs some long-term changes so it can continue to pay promised benefits to future generations. But there's time and opportunity to make incremental changes — nothing drastic — to keep social security strong for our children and grandchildren. That's been social security's enduring legacy and promise.

Let me add just a few words about the trust fund, which some people deride as just a bunch of IOUs[4]. True, the trust fund isn't cash. It's an accounting mechanism that tracks social security revenues and expenditures over time. But it's also a promise and an obligation of the federal government to everyone who's paid into social security, both now and in the future.

Today, social security is financially strong and in no immediate danger of "going broke." But long-term changes will be needed to keep it that way. That's why AARP fully supports a search for solutions so that social security endures another 75 years. But AARP strongly opposes any "solutions" that involve unfair benefit cuts or risky proposals such as private accounts that put everyone's retirement at greater risk.

Americans have counted on social security for 75 years. Let's strengthen and protect it for at least 75 more.

Words & Expressions

1. shrink	v.	退缩，收缩	
2. dwindle	v.	减少，缩小	
3. modest	a.	谦虚的，适度的	
4. rock-solid	a.	坚硬如岩石的，毫不动摇的	
5. terminate	v.	终止，结束	
6. jeopardy	n.	危险	
7. foundation	n.	根基，基础	
8. pardon	v.	原谅，宽恕	
9. mechanism	n.	机制，原理	
10. incremental	a.	增加的，增值的	

1. AARP：美国退休者协会（American Association of Retired Persons），是一个非营利组织，是美国年代最久和规模最大的为老年人呼吁倡议的群体。协会的座右铭是"服务，而不是被服务"，工作目标是帮助美国老年人获得独立、尊严和自主的命运。

2. 401(k)：401(k)计划，也称401(k)条款，始于20世纪80年代初，是一种由雇员、雇主共同缴费建立起来的完全基金式的养老保险制度。20世纪90年代迅速发展，逐渐取代了传统的社会保障体系，成为美国诸多雇主首选的社会保障计划。

3. IRA：个人退休账户（individual retirement account），也称个人退休金账户，是美国商业银行1974年为没有参加"职工退休计划"的个人创设的一种新型的储蓄存款账户。

4. IOUs：欠条（I owe you），美国俚语，通常指欠条、借据。

I. Match the words on the left with the meanings on the right.

1. shrink   a. too special to be replaced by anything

2. modest   b. to become smaller

3. mechanism   c. not very big or small

4. terminate   d. a system that is intended to achieve sth.

5. irreplaceable   e. completely end

II. Fill in the blanks with the following words and change the forms if necessary.

solution   annually   base   strengthen   incremental

1. Social security is the guaranteed _____ of retirement security for most Americans.

2. We need to make the modest changes necessary to _____ the guaranteed benefit for both current and future generations.

3. Today, the average retirement benefit is about $1,200 per month and is adjusted _____ to keep pace with inflation.

4. There's time and opportunity to make _____ changes to keep social security strong for our children and grandchildren.

5. Instead of putting our children and grand-children's retirement in jeopardy, AARP believes Congress should find ways to _____ our nation's budget problems without making dangerous

cuts to social security.

III. Decide whether the following statements are true (T) or false (F).

(　　) 1. Social security will be able to pay 100 percent of benefits for the next 25 years if there are not any changes.

(　　) 2. Americans earn and pay for Social Security's guaranteed retirement benefits by making contributions out of each and every paycheck throughout their working lives.

(　　) 3. For middle income seniors, Social Security provides 50 percent of their family income.

(　　) 4. Independent investments, pensions, individual retirement accounts and 401(k) accounts are all important parts of retirement savings, but Social Security is the guaranteed base of retirement security for most Americans.

(　　) 5. AARP strongly opposes any "solutions" that involve unfair benefit cuts or risky proposals such as private accounts that put everyone's retirement at greater risk.

Tips 专题介绍

我国的社会保障制度

　　基本养老保险、失业保险、基本医疗保险、工伤保险、生育保险等社会保险，是广大劳动者在遇到某些困难情况下基本生活和安全的最后保险。一系列社会保障制度，在原先的计划经济条件下，都是由企业直接负担的。市场经济的改革将其逐步社会化，但由于这个改革的过程相当漫长，所以尚在不断发展之中。

　　当前，我国的社会保险制度框架基本确立，已覆盖大部分城镇职工。我国在这方面也已有很多立法，如《失业保险条例》《社会保险费征缴暂行条例》等。劳动保障监察制度也基本建立，全国县级以上劳动和社会保障行政部门普遍建立了监察执法机构，配备了监察人员，全面开展了监察执法工作。劳动和社会保障行政执法监督工作也取得了较大的进展。

　　我国企业当前主要存在的问题是欠缴保险费，因此影响了职工社会保障经费的落实。亏损的企业欠缴保险费，有些盈利的企业也将社会保险费看作企业的额外负担，能拖则拖。这方面，企业管理者应有正确的认识，意识到这些费用是企业给员工工作回报的一部分，同时也是企业为社会应尽的义务。

　　社会保障方面最新的发展，反映了我国将逐步消除城乡二元结构的社会保障建设，将农民纳入社会劳动统计及社会保障体系之内。这样做，可以使失业保险涵盖这一部分人口，这就意味着我国的失业保险覆盖面将逐步变宽。

PART V
Career Design & Development

10

Career Design

Text A

More Feast, Less Famine

导读： 在当前经济全球化的大环境下，竞争压力越来越大，工作压力越来越大，失业率也越来越高。如何能让更多的人就业，而不是靠政府救济金维持生存甚至流落街头，已经成为越来越多的国家所关注的问题。政府应为国民营造更好的就业环境，刺激就业，同时作为求职者本身也应该更好地提高自身素质，学习更多对将来就业有用的技能，这样才能在全球化市场中立于不败之地。

Work today is about far more than economics. More even than when Theodore Roosevelt[1] extolled its virtues, people the world over want work not just to put food on the table and money in the bank, but as a means of gaining personal satisfaction. The changes now under way stand to make the world as a whole significantly better off and allow many more people to win the prize of being able to work hard at something worth doing. Yet, as this report has explained, there are many people who are not winning the prize and for whom the outlook is grim, even in rich countries where getting a decent job had been taken for granted.

Globalization[2] and other pro-market reforms were sold as a package deal. Opening up a country's markets, the argument went, would increase overall wealth in every country, and policies for internal redistribution would help the inevitable losers — or else their personal misery could have serious social consequences for everyone else. That is why jobs are rightly at the top of the political agenda the world over.

Where unemployment is currently higher than usual, there is enormous pressure on politicians to spend money they have not got on quick fixes that almost certainly would not work. But almost everywhere, what is needed from government are the sort of fundamental reforms that can make a big difference in the long run, beyond the next electoral cycle.

The mismatch between the skills demanded by employers and those available in the market is a reflection both of bad choices by students, who have not thought hard enough about what will help them find a good job, and of education systems that are too often indifferent to the needs of the labour market and too slow to change even if they try. It is not just Egypt where the universities provide training for public-sector jobs that are no longer abundant yet fail to equip students with what they need to thrive in a market economy. Out of necessity, India is emerging as a model for tackling these problems, both because its companies have become expert in turning useless graduates into useful ones and because it has allowed industry to take the lead in creating a huge new programme to tackle skills shortages.

A second challenge is for governments to create the right conditions for businesses to create more jobs. That means running sustainable macroeconomic policies[3], so that firms need not fear that their investments will be undermined by another economic crisis; sensible regulation; and a tax system that is both competitive, with low marginal rates, and does not distort business decisions in arbitrary ways. Given the importance of job creation, it would make sense to shift some of the burden of taxation permanently away from employment towards consumption or carbon emissions. And since entrepreneurship plays a big part in creating jobs, especially in the phase when young businesses expand rapidly, government should do all it can to encourage more of it though in view of its poor track record in this area, that should be mainly a matter of supporting (rather than obstructing) private-sector-led initiatives.

The goal of creating flexible labour markets should not be abandoned, but in future the ways in which inflexible labour markets are loosened up should be given more thought. The countries with the biggest youth-unemployment problems tend to be those where either there is no flexibility (as in much of the Middle East) or where flexibility applies only to newcomers to the jobs market, whereas older incumbents have continued to enjoy the protection that made the labour market inflexible in the first place (as in Spain). The political attractions of leaving the incumbents' privileges untouched are obvious, but so, by now, are the social consequences of making the young bear most of the costs of flexibility.

Long-term unemployment often turns into permanent unemployment, so governments should aim to keep people in work, even if that sometimes means continuing to pay them benefits as they work. Health care and pension systems should be (re-)designed to allow workers as much flexibility as possible, not least in deciding when to retire. In the rich world these welfare systems were built on the assumption that men with lifetime nine-to-five jobs were the main breadwinners. In emerging markets that are introducing social protection for those unable to earn a living, the systems should be designed in ways that do not discourage work.

There is no excuse for delay in starting to put in place these long-term solutions. Jeff Immelt of GE may well be right to think that in America "ultimately we will get it sorted," but he is also right that political dysfunction in Washington, DC, has "an opportunity cost. It is not like the rest of the world that has stopped while we are going through this." The same is true in many other countries where reform has stalled or is not even on the agenda yet.

And while individuals wait for their governments to get their acts together, there is plenty that they can do to give themselves the best chance of surviving and thriving in the new world of work. They need to clean up their image on the Internet, get in touch with their entrepreneurial DNA and brush up on their serial mastery, and form their very own posse.

Words & Expressions

1. extol	*v.*	赞美，颂扬
2. unemployment	*n.*	失业，失业率，失业人数
3. electoral	*a.*	选举的，选举人的
4. mismatch	*n.*	错配，不协调
5. indifferent	*a.*	漠不关心的，无关紧要的，中性的，中立的
6. tackle	*v.*	处理，抓住，固定，与……交涉
7. sustainable	*a.*	可以忍受的，足可支撑的，养得起的
8. macroeconomic	*a.*	宏观经济的，总体经济的
9. undermine	*v.*	破坏，渐渐破坏，挖掘地基
10. sensible	*a.*	明智的，明显的，意识到的，通晓事理的
11. distort	*v.*	扭曲，使失真，曲解
12. arbitrary	*a.*	任意的，武断的，专制的
13. entrepreneurship	*n.*	企业家精神
14. incumbent	*n.*	在职者，现任者
15. pension	*n.*	退休金，抚恤金，津贴
16. breadwinner	*n.*	负担家计的人，养家糊口的人
17. dysfunction	*n.*	功能紊乱，机能障碍
18. posse	*n.*	一队，民防团
19. initiative	*n.*	主动权，首创精神

Notes

1. Theodore Roosevelt：西奥多·罗斯福，被称为"老罗斯福"，美国军事家、政治家、外交家，1901 年成为美国总统，时年 42 岁，是美国历史上最年轻的在任总统。他因成功调停了日俄战争，获得 1906 年的诺贝尔和平奖，是第一个获得此奖项的美国总统。

2. Globalization：全球化，是一种概念，也是一种人类社会发展的过程。全球化目前有诸多定义，通常意义上的全球化是指全球联系不断增强，国与国之间在政治、经济贸易上互相依存。20 世纪 90 年代后，随着全球化对人类社会影响层面的扩张，其已逐渐引起各国政治、教育、社会及文化等学科领域的重视，纷纷开展研究热潮。对于全球化的观感是好是坏，目前仍是见仁见智。

3. Macroeconomic policies：宏观经济政策，指国家或政府为了增进整个社会经济的福利，改进国民经济的运行状况，达到一定的政策目标而有意识和有计划地运用一定的政策工具而制定的解决经济问题的指导原则和措施，它包括综合性的国家或地区发展战略和产业政策、国民收入分配政策、价格政策、物资流通政策等。

I. Match the words on the left with the meanings on the right.

1. globalization   a. a result or effect of something

2. sustainable   b. money paid regularly by the government or company to someone who does not work any more because of retirement or illness

3. consequence   c. the process of making sth. operate in countries around the world

4. arbitrary   d. able to continue for a long period

5. pension   e. to decide or change without any reason or plan

II. Fill in the blanks with the following words and change the forms if necessary.

fix privilege tax significant abundance

1. The changes now under way stand to make the world as a whole _____ better off and allow many more people to win the prize of being able to work hard at something worth doing.

2. Where unemployment is currently higher than usual, there is enormous pressure on politicians to spend money they have not got on quick _____ that almost certainly would not work.

3. It is not just Egypt where the universities provide training for public-sector jobs that are no longer _____ yet fail to equip students with what they need to thrive in a market economy.

4. Given the importance of job creation, it would make sense to shift some of the burden of _____ permanently away from employment towards consumption or carbon emissions.

5. The political attractions of leaving the incumbents' _____ untouched are obvious, but so, by now, are the social consequences of making the young bear most of the costs of flexibility.

III. Decide whether the following statements are true (T) or false (F).

( ) 1. Opening up a country's markets would increase overall wealth in every country.

( ) 2. What is needed from government are the sort of fundamental reforms that can make a big difference in the short run, beyond the next electoral cycle.

(　　) 3. It is only Egypt where the universities provide training for public-sector jobs that are no longer abundant yet fail to equip students with what they need to thrive in a market economy.

(　　) 4. A second challenge is for governments to create the right conditions for businesses to create more jobs.

(　　) 5. While individuals wait for their governments to get their acts together, they can do many things to give themselves the best chance of surviving and thriving in the new world of work.

Text B

The Jobless Young Left Behind

导读： 严重的失业率不仅会给各国政府带来巨大压力，而且会对广大百姓，尤其是年轻人产生极其负面的影响。年轻人因为失业不仅就业信心大受打击，而且人口流动性也大大增强，在职业的选择上也更加困惑，举棋不定。同时，年轻人的失业也会给社会带来很多不稳定的因素。

Maria Gil Ulldemolins is a smart, confident young woman. She has one degree from Britain and is about to conclude another in her native Spain. And she feels that she has no future.

Ms Ulldemolins belongs to a generation of young Spaniards who feel that the implicit contract they accepted with their country — work hard, and you can have a better life than your parents — has been broken. Before the financial crisis, Spanish unemployment, a perennial problem, was pushed down by credit-fueled growth and a prolonged construction boom: in 2007 it was just 8%. Today it is 21.2%, and among the young a staggering 46.2%. "I trained for a world that doesn't exist," says Ms Ulldemolins.

Spain's figures are particularly horrendous. But youth unemployment is rising perniciously across much of the developed world. It can seem like something of a side show; the young often have parents to fall back on; they can stay in education longer; they are not on the scrapheap for life. They have no families to support nor dire need of the medical insurance older workers may lose when they lose their jobs. But there is a wealth of evidence to suggest that youth unemployment does lasting damage.

In the past five years, youth unemployment has risen in most countries in the OECD[1], a rich-country club. One in five under-25s in the European Union labour force is unemployed, with the figures particularly dire in the south. In America, just over 18% of under-25s are jobless; young blacks, who make up 15% of the cohort, suffer a rate of 31%, rising to 44% among those without a high-school diploma (the figure for whites is 24%). Other countries, such as Switzerland, the

Netherlands and Mexico, have youth unemployment rates below 10%: but they are rising.

The Costs Mount up

In tough times young people are often the first to lose out. They are relatively inexperienced and low-skilled, and in many countries they are easier to fire than their elders. This all goes to make them obvious targets for employers seeking savings, though their low pay can redress things a little. In much of the OECD, youth-unemployment rates are about twice those for the population as a whole. Britain, Italy, Norway and New Zealand all exceed ratios of three to one; in Sweden the unemployment rate among 15- to 24-year-olds is 4.1 times higher than that of workers aged between 25 and 54.

Not only is the number of underemployed 15- to 24-year-olds in the OECD higher than at any time since the organization began collecting data in 1976. The number of young people in the rich world who have given up looking for work is at a record high too. Poor growth, widespread austerity programs and the winding up of job-creating stimulus measures threaten further unemployment overall. The young jobless often get a particular bounce in recoveries: first out, they are often also first back in. But the lack of a sharp upturn means such partial recompense has not been forthcoming this time round. In America, the jobs recovery since 2007 has been nearly twice as slow as in the recession of the early 1980s, the next-worst in recent decades — and from a worse starting-point. In some countries a rigging of the labour market in favour of incumbents and against the young makes what new jobs there are inaccessible.

Youth unemployment has direct costs in much the same way all unemployment does: increased benefit payments; lost income-tax revenues; wasted capacity. In Britain, a report by the London School of Economics (LSE)[2], the Royal Bank of Scotland and the Prince's Trust[3] puts the cost of the country's 744,000 unemployed youngsters at £155 million ($247 million) a week in benefits and lost productivity.

Some indirect costs of unemployment, though, seem to be amplified when the jobless are young. One is emigration: ambitious young people facing bleak prospects at home often seek opportunities elsewhere more readily than older people with dependent families. In Portugal, where the youth unemployment rate stands at 27%, some 40% of 18- to 30-year-olds say they would consider emigrating for employment reasons. In some countries, such as Italy, a constant brain-drain[4] is one more depressing symptom of a stagnant economy. In Ireland, where discouragement among young workers has shot up since 2005, migration doubled over the same period, with most of the departed between 20 and 35. This return of a problem the "Celtic tiger" once thought it had left behind is treated as a national tragedy.

It's Personal

Another cost is crime. Attempts to blame England's recent riots on youth unemployment were overhasty. But to say there is no link to crime more generally looks unduly optimistic. Young men are already more likely to break the law than most; having more free time, more motive and less to lose. Some researchers claim to have identified a causal link between increased youth unemployment and increases in crime, specifically property crime (robbery, burglary, car theft and damage) and drug offence. No such link is seen for overall unemployment. If the crime leads to prison, future employment prospects will fall off a cliff.

And then there are the effects on individuals. "Young people are hit particularly hard by the economic and emotional effects of unemployment," says Jonathan Wadsworth, a labour economist at the LSE. The best predictor of future unemployment, research shows, is previous unemployment. In Britain, a young person who spends just three months out of work before the age of 23 will on average spend an additional 1.3 months in unemployment between the ages of 28 and 33 compared with someone without the spell of youth joblessness. A second stint of joblessness makes things worse.

Research from the United States and Britain has found that youth unemployment leaves a "wage scar" that can persist into middle age. The longer the period of unemployment, the bigger the effect is. Take two men with the same education, literacy and numeracy scores, places of residence, parents' education and IQ. If one of them spends a year unemployed before the age of 23, ten years later he can expect to earn 23% less than the other. For women the gap is 16%. The penalty persists, though it shrinks; at 42 it is 12% for women and 15% for men. So far, the current crisis has not led to these long-term periods of youth unemployment rising very much; almost 80% of young people in the OECD who become unemployed are back in work within a year. But that could well change.

The scarring effects are not necessarily restricted to the people who are actually unemployed. An American study shows that young people graduating from college and entering the labour market during the deep recessions of the early 1980s suffered long-term wage scarring. Graduates in unlucky cohorts suffer a wage decline of 6%-7% for each percentage-point increase in the overall unemployment rate. The effect diminishes over time, but is still statistically significant 15 years later.

After a period of unemployment, the temptation to take any work at all can be strong. Wage scarring is one of the reasons to think this has lasting effects, and policies designed to minimize youth unemployment may sometimes exacerbate them. Spain, which has developed a scheme for rolling over temporary contracts to provide at least some chances of employment to the young, should pay heed to the experience of Japan in the early 2000s. Young people unemployed for a long time were channeled into "non-regular" jobs where pay was low and opportunities for training and career progression few. Employers seeking new recruits for quality jobs generally preferred fresh graduates (of school or university) over the unemployed or underemployed, leaving a cohort of people with declining long-term job and wage prospects: "youth left behind", in the words of a recent OECD report. Japan's "lost decade" workers make up a disproportionate share of depression and stress cases reported by employers.

Unemployment of all sorts is linked with a level of unhappiness that cannot simply be explained by low income. It is also linked to lower life expectancy, higher chances of a heart attack in later life, and suicide. A study of Pennsylvania workers who lost jobs in the 1970s and 1980s found that the effect of unemployment on life expectancy is greater for young workers than for old. Workers who joined the American labour force during the Great Depression suffered from a persistent lack of confidence and ambition for decades.

There are other social effects, too, such as "full-nest syndrome". In 2008, 46% of 18- to 34-year-olds in the European Union lived with at least one parent; in most countries the stay-at-homes were more likely to be unemployed than those who had moved out. The effect is particularly notable in the countries of southern Europe, where unemployment is high and declining fertility means small families. A recent study by CGIL, an Italian trade-union federation, found that more than 7 million Italians aged between 18 and 35 were still living with their parents. Since 2001 one in four British men in their 20s, and one in six women, have "boomeranged" home for a period. This sort of change will, for good or ill, ripple on down the generations which may, if young people live longer and longer at home, become more spread out.

Words & Expressions

1. Spaniard	n.	西班牙人
2. perennial	a.	常年的，四季不断的，常在的，反复的
3. horrendous	a.	可怕的，惊人的
4. perniciously	ad.	有害地，有毒地
5. scrapheap	n.	废物堆，废料堆
6. dire	a.	可怕的，悲惨的，极端的
7. cohort	n.	一群，支持者
8. redress	v.	救济，赔偿，纠正，重新调整
9. austerity	n.	紧缩，朴素，苦行，严厉
10. bounce	n.	弹跳，弹起
11. upturn	n.	情况好转
12. recompense	n.	赔偿，报酬
13. forthcoming	a.	即将来临的
14. rigging	n.	索具，绳索，装备，绑定
15. stagnant	a.	停滞的，不景气的，污浊的，迟钝的
16. riot	n.	暴乱，放纵，蔓延
17. overhasty	a.	太急速的，过于草率的，过于匆忙的
18. unduly	ad.	过度地，不适当地，不正当地
19. stint	n.	节约，定额，定量
20. numeracy	n.	计算能力，识数
21. heed	n.	注意，留心
22. fertility	n.	多产，肥沃，生育力
23. ripple	v.	在……上形成波痕

1. OECD：经济合作与发展组织（the Organization for Economic Co-operation and Development），简称经合组织（OECD），成立于 1961 年，目前成员国总数达 36 个，总部设在巴黎。旨在共同应对全球化带来的经济、社会和政府治理等方面的挑战，并把握全球化带来的机遇。

2. LSE：伦敦政治经济学院（the London School of Economics and Political Science），创立于 1895 年，为伦敦大学联盟成员，是英国久负盛名的世界顶尖公立研究型大学。与牛津大学、剑桥大学、伦敦大学学院、帝国理工学院并称 "G5 超级精英大学"，也是英国金三角名校和罗素大学集团成员。

3. The Prince's Trust：王子信托基金，是一家英国慈善机构，由查尔斯·威尔士亲王创立于 1976 年，旨在帮助年轻人。该机构为处于弱势地位的年轻人设置一系列培训项目，提供辅导服务及资金支持，以帮助其树立信心。

4. Brain-drain：人才流失，指在一单位内，对其经营发展具有重要作用，甚至是关键性作用的人才非单位意愿的流走，或失去其积极作用的现象。人才流失有显性流失与隐性流失之分，前者是指单位的人才因某种原因离开该单位另谋他就，给该单位的人力资源管理造成困难，从而影响其经营发展。隐性人才流失则是指单位内的人才因激励不够或其他原因而失去工作积极性，其才能没有发挥出来，从而影响单位的经营发展。

I. Match the words on the left with the meanings on the right.

1. pernicious　　　a. a pile of unwanted things, especially pieces of metal

2. scrapheap　　　b. to correct something that is wrong or unfair

3. redress　　　　c. bad economic conditions in which people do not have much money to spend

4. austerity　　　d. not changing or making progress for a long period

5. stagnant　　　e. something very harmful or evil

II. Fill in the blanks with the following words and change the forms if necessary.

suffer　　austerity　　recession　　support　　unemployment

1. They have no families to _____ nor dire need of the medical insurance older workers may lose when they lose their jobs.

2. Poor growth, widespread _____ programs and the winding up of job-creating stimulus measures threaten further unemployment overall.

3. A young person who spends just three months out of work before the age of 23 will on average spend an additional 1.3 months in _____ between the ages of 28 and 33 compared with someone without the spell of youth joblessness.

4. An American study shows that young people graduating from college and entering the labour market during the deep _____ of the early 1980s suffered long-term wage scarring.

5. Workers who joined the American labour force during the Great Depression _____ from a persistent lack of confidence and ambition for decades.

III. Decide whether the following statements are true (T) or false (F).

(   ) 1. One in five under-25s in the European Union labour force is unemployed, with the figures particularly dire in the north.

(   ) 2. In America, the jobs recovery since 2007 has been nearly twice as slow as in the recession of the early 1980s, the worst in recent decades.

(   ) 3. Some researchers claim to have identified a causal link between increased youth unemployment and increases in crime, specifically property crime such as robbery, burglary, car theft and damage, and drug offence.

(   ) 4. The scarring effects of unemployment are not necessarily restricted to the people who are actually unemployed.

(   ) 5. A study of Pennsylvania workers who lost jobs in the 1970s and 1980s found that the effect of unemployment on life expectancy is greater for old workers than for young.

Tips：专题介绍

职业生涯周期的阶段和任务

阶段	角色	任　务
1. 成长、幻想、探索 （0～21 岁）	学生、候选人、申请人	1. 发展和发现自己的需要和兴趣； 2. 发展和发现自己的能力和才干； 3. 学习职业方面的知识，寻找现实的角色模式； 4. 从测试和咨询中获取最大限度的信息； 5. 查找有关职业和工作角色的可靠信息源； 6. 发展和发现自己的价值观、动机和抱负； 7. 作出合理的教育决策； 8. 在校品学兼优，以保持尽可能开放的职业选择； 9. 在体育活动、业余爱好和学校的各项活动中寻找机会进行自我测试，以发现一种现实的自我意象； 10. 寻找实习和兼职工作的机会，测试早期的职业决策。
2. 进入工作世界 （16～25 岁）	应聘者、新学员	1. 学会如何寻找工作，如何申请工作，如何进行工作面试； 2. 学会如何评估一项工作和一个公司的信息； 3. 通过简历挑选和测试； 4. 作出现实和有效的第一项工作选择。

续表

阶段	角色	任　务
3. 基础培训 （16～25 岁）	实习生、新员工	1. 克服缺乏经验带来的不安全感，培养一种责任感； 2. 理解公司文化，尽快了解工作内容； 3. 学会与第一个上级或培训者相处； 4. 学会与其他受训者相处； 5. 接受肄业仪式和其他与做一名新员工有关的仪式，从中学到东西； 6. 接受、承认和熟悉公司的制服、徽章、身份证、停车证、公司手册等。
4. 正式成员资格，职业早期 （17～25 岁）	正式成员	1. 有效地工作，学会如何处事，改善处事的方式； 2. 承担部分责任； 3. 接受自己的附属状态，学会如何与上司和自己的同事相处； 4. 在有限的工作范围内发展进取心和现实水平的主动性； 5. 寻求良师和保护人； 6. 根据自己的才干和价值观，以及公司内部的机会和约束，重新评估自己当初决定追求的这一工作种类； 7. 准备作出长期工作承诺和一定时期的最大贡献，或者转向一个新的岗位和公司； 8. 学会应对第一项工作中的成功感或失败感。
5. 正式成员资格，职业中期 （25 岁以上）	正式成员、任职者、终身成员、主管、经理	1. 取得一定程度的独立； 2. 取得自己的实际成绩，相信自己的决策； 3. 慎重评估自己的动机、才干和价值观，依此决定要达到的专业化程度； 4. 慎重评估公司和职业机会，依此制定下一步的有效决策； 5. 解除自己与良师的关系，准备成为他人的良师； 6. 在家庭、自我和工作事务之间取得一种适当的平衡； 7. 如果成绩平平，任职被否定，或失去挑战力，学会应对失败情绪。
6. 职业中期危机 （35～45 岁）	—	1. 开始意识到个人的职业锚——个人的才干、动机和价值观； 2. 现实理解个人的职业锚对个人前途的暗示； 3. 就接受现状或争取看得见的前途作出具体选择； 4. 围绕所作出的具体选择，与家人达成新的平衡； 5. 建立与他人的良师关系。
7. 非领导角色的职业后期 （40 岁～退休）	骨干成员、有贡献的个人或管理部门的成员、有效贡献者、碌碌无为者	1. 保持技术上的竞争力，或者学会用以经验为基础的智慧代替直接的技术能力； 2. 发展必备的人际和群体交往技能； 3. 发展必备的监督和管理技能； 4. 学会在一种政治环境下制定有效的决策； 5. 学会应对崭露头角的年轻人的竞争和进取； 6. 学会应对中年危机和家庭的"空巢"问题； 7. 为高级领导角色做准备。
8. 领导角色的职业后期	总经理、官员、高级合伙人、企业家、资深幕僚	1. 从主要关心自我，转向更多地为公司利益承担责任； 2. 肩负操作公司机密和资源的重任； 3. 学会操控公司内部和公司/环境边界两方面的高水平的政治局面； 4. 学会在持续增长的职业承诺与家庭特别是配偶的需求之间谋求平衡； 5. 学会高水平地行使权利和义务，而不是软弱无力或意气用事。
9. 衰退和离职	—	1. 在业余爱好、家庭、社交和社区活动、非全日制工作等方面，寻找新的满足源； 2. 学会如何与配偶亲密地生活； 3. 评估完整的职业，着手退休。
10. 退休	—	1. 在失去全日制工作或公司角色后，保持一种认同感和自我价值观； 2. 在某些活动中依然倾心尽力； 3. 运用自己的智慧和经验； 4. 回首过去的一生，有自我实现的满足感。

Job Promotion

Text A

Promotion and Employee Motivation

导读：企业职务晋升制度有两大功能，一是选拔优秀人才，二是激励现有员工的工作积极性。企业从内部提拔优秀的员工到更高、更重要的岗位上，对员工或对企业发展都具有重要意义。对个人来讲，职务晋升是员工个人职业生涯发展的重要途径。对企业来讲，内部职务晋升相对于其他激励措施（如货币激励），可以鼓励组织成员的长期行为，并能使与企业同甘共苦、一起成长的员工受惠于企业发展的成果。另外，内部晋升不仅能让被晋升者得到更多的机会，也能给未晋升者或新入职者带来职业发展的期望，使员工将个人职业发展与企业的长期发展结合起来，从而增强员工对企业的归属感与忠诚度。

More talented workers are usually more productive higher up in organizational hierarchies. Promotions assign workers to jobs better suiting their abilities and quickly move up talented workers. They can be used to reward past employee efforts, promote investments in specific human capital and lower job turnover.

Promotion to Different Kinds of Employees

This requires recruits to accept lower paid port-of-entry jobs. This early period of employment is a screening process. Good performance leads to promotion. When promotion ladders are used as deferred compensation[1], almost all junior workers who prove themselves are promoted. The prospect of promotion encourages the good workers to stay and invest in specific human capital. Job seekers will self-select by limiting their applications to the type of jobs where they expect to succeed and be promoted out of the less well paid port-of-entry jobs.

Older workers may have reached a career peak in their wages and accumulated human capital[2]. This may reduce their access to jobs that use promotions as incentives. Promotions as motivators for additional effort may not be as effective for older workers because they may not wish to wait in lower paid port-of-entry jobs that are the precursor to some promotions once performance is proven. To the extent that the lure of promotions is designed to encourage recruits to invest in specific human capital, promotion ladders may not work as effectively with workers with shorter payback horizons on new skill investments and who have a preference for harvesting their existing human capital. This may reduce access to jobs that use promotions to reward investments in specific capital.

Older job changers may prefer jobs whose compensation is made up mostly of wages and less of promises of promotion and on-the-job human capital. Younger rival applicants, both internal and external, may find the promise of more on-the-job human capital and promotions to be attractive given the length of their remaining working lives and may trade this for higher wages. This may lengthen job searches for older job seekers because they may want jobs with different wage and promotion components to comparable younger workers. Job packages with the preferred mixes may be fewer and further between.

Promotions as Prizes

There is no need for tasks, responsibilities and output rates to differ between pre- and post-promotion jobs for firms to profit from promotions. Workers can be promoted because those left behind are motivated to supply more effort and invest in hard to verify specific human capital by the prospect of a wage rise upon their own promotion later on.

Workers enter at one level and are promoted if they win a promotion tournament. The promotions are similar to prizes in sports tournaments. The promotions are prizes for past efforts, not future potential. Even if individual output and specific human capital investments cannot be measured with any precision, it is often possible to identify who is the best worker with relative performance evaluation, which is a common reason for running promotion tournaments. Observing the actions and the outputs of competing employees performing similar tasks provides information to employers on what has been done and what could be done. There can be a gap between the contribution of the best worker and that of the next best, and so on, that is large enough to be perceived without being quantifiable. These gaps are indicators of who is exerting most effort and investing more in the specific human capital, albeit often otherwise unverifiable human capital is needed to underpin success. To induce greater employee effort and human capital investment, the best performer (highest scorer) is promoted to a better paid job. In addition to motivating workers promoted to the higher level, the prospect of future promotion is a prize to motivate those left behind at the lower levels.

To effectively encourage workers to work harder, there must be a fair but not overly generous chance of promotion and a reasonable pay rise or a lower chance of promotion and a much larger pay rise. Higher level jobs may be handsomely paid not because of a higher output, but to act as a prize to encourage effort at the lower levels. There must be regular job turnover so that follow-up promotions keep hope alive among the junior workers. The pay rise must not be so large that the required level of effort puts workers off and they go elsewhere or workers do not co-operate when teamwork is required and employees engage in non-productive industrial politics.

Incentives and Recruitment versus Promotions

The need for regular job turnover and rising stars may disadvantage older workers seeking jobs with firms that use promotion tournaments. The wage structure of a firm must be seen as a whole. Competition for promotions has large effects on employee incentives. Promotion systems balance the allocation of talent across jobs and the corporate hierarchy, the rewarding of team and individual effort provision and the accumulation of human capital. It is the structure of wages within the firm rather than individual current wages and productivity that can be important to the overall productivity of the firm.

Promotions are regular prizes offered to encourage more effort at the lower levels, properly reward the promoted and sort employees into more senior jobs that better match their relative abilities and accumulated human capital. Promotion ladders and promotion tournaments supplement theories of careers that are built on the accumulation of general and specific human capital by introducing implicit contracts that commit workers to higher levels of effort and employers to reward this with pay rises and periodic promotions later in careers.

Promotion systems complicate the hiring of older workers because they often perform different tasks and organizational roles to younger workers. Older workers appear in most types of jobs up and down the entire job ladder. Young workers cluster into port-of-entry jobs. Prime age workers are rising through the ranks. Older workers earn significantly more than younger workers in all countries studied. Older workers as a group have more human capital so they can compete for middle level and senior vacancies that younger employees aspire to now or in the future. Who is hired has incentive repercussions beyond the vacancy at hand.

Hiring an outsider when an insider can be promoted undercuts the incentive effect of promotions. Workers are hired both for their productivity and the incentive effect on co-workers of seeing them rise to successively higher levels. Firms that use promotions retain their older staff because, in addition to profiting from their specific human capital, these workers made their way up from below. Internal candidates who have risen through the ranks should be of proven ability and have extensive firm-specific human capital. The global incentive effect of promotions of long-standing employees is reinforcing, because their rise through the ranks will motivate younger workers at lower levels to do the same.

Hiring an outsider with superior ability may reduce the long-run profits of the firm. Internal candidates are favoured because of incentive effects on all employees. By promising a promotion system that favors internal candidates, this increases the effort levels of young workers and the possibility of receiving the higher wage in the future, reduces the wage required to initially attract young workers into the firm. Older outside applicants are disadvantaged because, as a group, they would be applying for vacancies that required more human capital, experience or seniority.

These are the positions in which employers promise a favourable treatment to younger internal applicants.

If the firm regularly hires outsiders for higher positions, anticipation of this employer behaviour by current employees has adverse effects in prior periods on worker effort and on hard to verify employee investments in specific human capital. Filling a vacancy internally will also save on the fixed costs of hiring such as firm-specific training for recruits.

Outside hiring may be profitable if the external candidate is significantly better. Employers also open up competition to outsiders to reduce collusion and industrial politics among internal candidates and to absorb external talent. The morale, work effort and productivity of internal candidates can be preserved by implicitly setting a higher bar for outsiders to keep the promise to offer junior employees careers. Internal applicants are already advantaged because of their large accumulations of firm-specific capital. Favouritism implies that senior positions are filled internally more often than not because outside applicants must have a significant margin of superiority to succeed against internal candidates.

Words & Expressions

1.	hierarchy	*n.*	阶层，层级，等级制度
2.	assign	*v.*	分配，指派
3.	incentive pay		奖励工资，激励工资
4.	ladder	*n.*	阶梯，途径，梯状物
5.	screening process		筛选过程，过虑程式
6.	compensation	*n.*	报酬
7.	precursor	*n.*	先驱，前导
8.	lure	*n.*	诱惑
9.	lengthen	*v.*	使延长，加长
10.	tournament	*n.*	比赛
11.	precision	*n.*	精确
12.	quantifiable	*a.*	可以计量的
13.	albeit	*conj.*	虽然，即使
14.	unverifiable	*a.*	无法核实的
15.	underpin	*v.*	巩固，加强……的基础
16.	allocation	*n.*	分配，配置
17.	cluster	*v.*	群聚，聚集
18.	repercussion	*n.*	反响，影响
19.	favouritism	*n.*	徇私，偏爱

1. Deferred compensation：递延酬劳，它是一种安排，在此安排中，雇员的一部分收入在实际收入后的某个日期支付。它主要包括养老金、退休计划和股票期权。大多数递延酬劳的主要好处是将税款推迟到雇员实际收到收入的日期。

2. Human capital：人力资本，是指存在于人体之中的具有经济价值的知识、技能和体力（健康状况）等质量因素之和。20 世纪 60 年代，美国经济学家舒尔茨和贝克尔首先创立了比较完整的人力资本理论，这一理论有两个核心观点：一是在经济增长中，人力资本的作用大于物质资本的作用；二是人力资本的核心是提高人口质量，教育投资是人力投资的主要部分。

I. Match the words on the left with the meanings on the right.

1. incentive   a. something that encourages you to work harder
2. assign   b. something that happened or existed before something else and influenced its development
3. precursor   c. to treat one person or group better than others in an unfair way
4. favouritism   d. the effects of an action or event, especially bad effects that continue for some time
5. repercussion   e. to give someone a particular job or make him responsible for a particular person or thing

II. Fill in the blanks with the following words and change the forms if necessary.

capital	preserve	reward	motivate	hierarchical

1. Promotions can be used to _____ past employee efforts, promote investments in specific human capital and lower job turnover.

2. Promotions as _____ for additional effort may not be as effective for older workers because they may not wish to wait in lower paid port-of-entry jobs that are the precursor to some promotions once performance is proven.

3. Workers can be promoted because those left behind are motivated to supply more effort to verify specific human _____ by the prospect of a wage rise upon their own promotion later on.

4. Promotion systems balance the allocation of talent across jobs and the corporate _____, the rewarding of team and individual effort provision and the accumulation of human capital.

5. The morale, work effort and productivity of internal candidates can be _____ by implicitly setting a higher bar for outsiders to keep the promise to offer junior employees careers.

III. Decide whether the following statements are true (T) or false (F).

(　　) 1. The prospect of promotion encourages the good workers to stay and invest in specific human capital. While to job seekers, they will apply for any type of jobs where they expect to get high port-of-entry pay even when the promotion prospect is low.

(　　) 2. Older job changers may prefer jobs whose compensation is made up mostly of promises of promotion and on-the-job human capital. Younger rival applicants, both internal and external, may find the promise of wages to be attractive.

(　　) 3. Workers enter at one level and are promoted if they win a promotion tournament. The promotions are similar to prizes in sports tournaments. The promotions are prizes for future potential, not past efforts.

(　　) 4. To effectively encourage workers to work harder, there must be a very generous chance of promotion and a reasonable pay rise or a lower chance of promotion and a much larger pay rise.

(　　) 5. Older workers as a group have more human capital so they can compete for middle level and senior vacancies that younger employees aspire to now or in the future.

Text B

Commonly Practiced Promotion Systems

导读： 为了提升员工的个人素质和能力，充分调动全体员工的主动性和积极性，并在公司内部营造公平、公正、公开的竞争机制，规范公司员工的晋升、晋级工作流程起着至关重要的作用。我们较为熟悉的晋升制度有按工作表现晋升、按投入程度晋升、按年资晋升等。不同的企业或组织所适用的制度也有所不同，比如在工作表现可以用若干标准衡量的企业中，人力资源经理可以依据员工工作表现是否合乎既定标准来决定其是否升迁。按年资晋升在表面上只看资历，实际上是资历与能力相结合，在获得可晋升的资历之后，究竟能否晋升，完全依据对其工作的考核。这种制度承认员工经验的价值，给予大家平等竞争的机会。

Promotion systems affect almost all aspects of organizational lives. This is particularly evident from studies of human resources management[1] and internal labor markets[2], to name just a few. Given the importance of promotion systems in organizations, it is surprising that few studies have attempted to examine the role of various environmental, organizational and job factors on the effectiveness of promotion systems. This paper attempts to fill some of the void and explore the organizational impact of a variety of important promotion systems commonly practiced in organizations including up-or-out systems[3], absolute merit-based systems[4], relative merit-based systems, and seniority-based systems.

Theoretical Background of the Paper

Traditionally, students of human resources management have placed the study of promotion and recruitment under the rubric of employee selection. Selection is the process of matching workers to jobs to maximize organizational productivity and performance. Promotion and recruitment are linked because the HR practitioner is supposedly indifferent to whether that candidate is recruited from inside or outside the organization. However, promotion proves to be the more pervasive phenomenon. Empirical studies[5] reveal that around 75% of vacancies are filled by promotions from within the organization.

While the reliance on an internal labor market is characteristic of most organizations, there is considerable variation in the mechanisms used to select candidates for promotion. Universities, professional service firms, and the military often use up-or-out models of promotion, where junior employees must make the grade within a specified period of time or exit the organization. Many other organizations rely on some form of merit or rank-order system, where those receiving the highest performance evaluations in a given cohort are promoted while those missing the cut remain at their current level. Seniority has also been widely used as a basis for promotion in many industries (particularly in public administration) but has fallen from favor in recent years.

Types of Promotion Systems

A useful discussion on promotion systems can be found in the organizational economics literature. According to economists, a promotion system serves two fundamental purposes. First, it selects more able individuals for positions of greater responsibility and, secondly, it motivates employees at one level to strive harder to reach the next one. In this study, we deliberately chose to model only the job assignment or matching function of promotion systems. We did this for three reasons:

(1) The incentive effect of promotion systems has received little or no coverage in the HRM literature. Promotion is seen as simple job assignment not as a tool for potentially motivating all workers (whether promoted or not).

(2) Motivation is extremely difficult to model. Motivation impacts productivity and turnover, waxes and wanes over an employee's tenure, and fluctuates in response to organizational events (such as being passed over for promotion). There is little reliable data concerning the magnitude of these motivational effects. Any attempt to provide a credible model of motivation is likely to be met with howls of derision for some perceived error of omission or commission.

(3) Procedural rules for promotion are easy to model. For instance, if seniority is the basis for

promotion, it is a simple matter to identify the most senior employee in a given cohort or group. The rules are so transparent and uncontroversial that, in effect, the process is self-validating.

For the purposes of the study, we focus on four commonly practiced promotion systems.

Absolute and Relative Merit-based Systems

The most common form of promotion system is the merit-based system (MBS), which can be further subdivided into its relative and absolute forms. In an absolute MBS, the candidate must perform above some arbitrary cutoff level in past, current or projected future performance to become eligible for promotion. In a relative MBS, candidates are ranked according to performance and the highest-ranked candidates are promoted regardless of their absolute performance level while those at the bottom tend to face some negative disciplinary actions.

While it may seem that candidates have an incentive to shirk and reduce their performance to a uniformly low level in a relative MBS, the opposite may actually be true. The desire for promotion and uncertainty over the final cutoff point create an intense competition between candidates that has been likened to a rat-race or sports tournament. However, as we have elected to set aside incentive effects in the current study, the issue becomes the relative ability of each system to select talented candidates for higher-level positions.

In a relative MBS, there is always a chance that a cohort will be totally comprised of negative performers. In this case, selecting the best performer for promotion may still result in negative performance outcomes for the organization. This can be contrasted with an absolute MBS that will not promote candidates unless their performance exceeds some minimum threshold level. An absolute MBS will only select from the best "qualified" performers. Thus, while a relative MBS will always have a candidate to promote, an absolute MBS will always ensure that a negative performer will not be promoted: a classic case of the trade-off between a sin of commission versus a sin of omission.

Up-or-out Systems

Up-or-out systems (UOS) are commonly found in universities, professional service firms, and the military. In the traditional UOS, candidates are evaluated after a set period of time. The performers above certain performance criteria in a cohort are promoted while those failing to make the grade are dismissed from the organization. In theory, the system could also include a middle group of candidates that are neither promoted nor dismissed but this is seldom seen in practice.

An up-or-out approach combines the rat-race-like incentive effects of merit-based approaches with the additional threat of job loss for inadequate results. Interestingly, UOS are mainly used for junior employees. Organizations typically revert to a merit-based system after one or two rounds of up-or-out pressure.

As a matching system, UOS combines the benefits of a merit-based system with the ability to drop poor performers from the candidate pool. As a result, an UOS samples more often from the candidate population than a merit-based system. Increased sampling from the candidate population improves the probability that a superior performer will be available for promotion. Thus, this over-sampling may improve the performance of the organization relative to a merit-based system.

Seniority-based Systems

Seniority-based systems promote the candidate in a cohort with either: (1) the most experience in the job; (2) the most experience in the organization; or (3) the most experience in the industry. For this study we focus on the second category, i.e., the experience in the organization as a criterion for seniority. Seniority-based systems offer clear career paths and succession planning[6], low turnover, and objectivity in the promotion process. However, if learning rate is heterogeneous, then a seniority system cannot guarantee that the best performer will be promoted. In this situation, seniority is a weak selection device. In the current model the ability of all agents is held constant but differential learning is possible.

Words & Expressions

1. void	n.	空虚, 空隙, 空白处
2. theoretical	a.	理论的, 理论上的
3. rubric	n.	红字标题, 红色印刷, 题目
4. practitioner	n.	开业者, 从业者
5. pervasive	a.	普遍的
6. empirical study		实证研究, 经验研究
7. cohort	n.	一群
8. literature	n.	文献
9. incentive	a.	激励的
10. wax and wane		月圆月缺, 兴衰成败
11. tenure	n.	任期
12. magnitude	n.	大小
13. derision	n.	嘲笑
14. self-validating	a.	自行生效的, 自行证实的
15. subdivide	v.	再分, 细分
16. arbitrary	a.	任意的
17. eligible for		合格, 够资格
18. cutoff point		分界点
19. rat-race	n.	事业竞争, 商业竞争
20. trade-off	n.	权衡, 折中
21. omission	n.	疏忽, 遗漏
22. revert	v.	恢复, 使恢复原状
23. succession planning		接班人计划, 继任计划
24. heterogeneous	a.	多样化的, 不均匀的

1. Human resources management：人力资源管理，指企业的一系列人力资源政策及相应的管理活动。这些活动主要包括企业人力资源战略的制定、员工的招募与选拔、培训与开发、绩效管理、薪酬管理、员工流动管理、员工关系管理、员工安全与健康管理等，亦指企业运用现代管理方法，对人力资源的获取（选人）、开发（育人）、保持（留人）和利用（用人）等方面所进行的计划、组织、指挥、控制和协调等一系列活动，最终达到实现企业发展目标的一种管理行为。

2. Internal labor market：内部劳动力市场，指的是存在于企业内部的劳动力市场，它实际上也是企业内部的各种劳动合约与就业安排的制度总和。这一概念的提出表明：在现今发达的市场经济国家，劳动市场并不是新古典理论所描述的那种单一的外部市场供求调节模式，而是内部市场与外部市场相并存的二元结构。

3. Up-or-out system："不晋则退"制度，这一制度在大学、专业服务公司和军队中普遍实行。在这一传统的制度下，候选人在设定的某段时间内接受评估。在某一群体中，绩效标准高于某一特定绩效标准的员工被提拔，而那些未能达标的员工则被开除出该组织。从理论上讲，该制度还可能包括一群既不被提拔也不被解雇的中层候选人，但在实践中很少见到这种情况。

4. Merit-based system（MBS）：基于绩效的制度，它可以进一步细分为相对的形式和绝对的形式。在绝对绩效制中，候选人必须在过去、当前或未来的表现中，拥有较高的绩效水平，才有资格获得晋升。在相对绩效制中，根据表现对候选人进行排名，而排名最高的候选人，无论其绝对表现水平如何，都会受到提拔，而排名靠后的则会受到负面的纪律处分。

5. Empirical study：实证研究，是一种通过直接和间接观察或经验获取知识的方法。经验证据可以定量地或定性地分析。通过量化证据或以定性的形式对其进行理解，研究者可以回答经验性的问题，这些问题应该与收集到的证据（通常称为数据）进行明确的定义和回答。研究设计因场地和被调查的问题而有所不同。许多研究人员将定性和定量分析相结合，以更好地回答无法在实验室环境中进行研究的问题，尤其是在社会科学和教育领域。

6. Succession planning：接班人计划，又称管理继承人计划，是指公司确定和持续追踪关键岗位的高潜能人才，并对这些高潜能人才进行开发的过程。高潜能人才是指那些公司相信他们具有胜任高层管理位置潜力的人。企业接班人计划就是通过内部提升的方式系统、有效地获取组织人力资源，它对公司的持续发展有至关重要的意义。

I. Match the words on the left with the meanings on the right.

1. void   a. an exchange that occurs as a compromise
2. derision   b. an empty area or space
3. trade-off   c. published writings in a particular style on a particular subject
4. literature   d. spreading or spread throughout
5. pervasive   e. the act of treating with contempt

II. Fill in the blanks with the following words and change the forms if necessary.

common   heterogeneity   aspect   examine   void

1. Promotion systems affect almost all _____ of organizational lives.
2. However, it is surprising that few studies have attempted to _____ the role of various environmental, organizational and job factors on the effectiveness of promotion systems.
3. This paper attempts to fill some of the _____ and explore the organizational impact of a variety of important promotion systems commonly practiced in organizations including up-or-out systems, absolute merit-based systems, relative merit-based systems, and seniority-based systems.
4. The most _____ form of promotion system is the merit-based system (MBS), which can be further subdivided into its relative and absolute forms.
5. However, if learning rate is _____, then a seniority system cannot guarantee that the best performer will be promoted.

III. Decide whether the following statements are true (T) or false (F).

(   ) 1. Seniority has also been widely used as a basis for promotion in many industries (particularly in public administration) but has fallen from favor in recent years.

(   ) 2. Promotion and recruitment are linked because the HR practitioner is supposedly indifferent to whether that candidate is recruited from inside or outside the organization.

(   ) 3. Promotion is seen as a tool for potentially motivating all workers (whether promoted or not).

(   ) 4. Empirical studies reveal that more than 75% of vacancies are filled by promotions from the organization.

(   ) 5. Given the importance of promotion systems in organizations, it is surprising that few studies have attempted to examine the role of various environmental, organizational and job factors on the effectiveness of promotion systems.

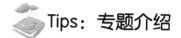

Tips：专题介绍

有效的激励方式

所谓激励，就是组织通过设计适当的外部奖酬形式和工作环境，以一定的行为规范和惩罚性措施，借助信息沟通激发、引导、保持和归化组织成员的行为，以有效地实现组织及其成员个人目标的系统活动。人力资源管理中常用的几种激励方式如下。

1. PRP 计划

PRP 计划是近年来西方比较流行的一种雇员工资管理计划，被称为"与业绩相关的收入"，简称"业绩报酬"或"业绩工资收入"（pay-for-performance）。PRP 计划是企业激励计划（incentive plans）的一个组成部分，其设计不仅基于降低生产成本，而且从理念上视雇员为企业的合伙人，依据他们对企业的贡献和业绩状况支付报酬。

一般来说，PRP 计划比较适用于各项成本支出容易计算、雇员的工资绩效与工作数量之间有直接的联系、工作程序标准和运行有规律、很少出现误工现象、容易控制工作质量及能够准确计算劳动消耗的工作。

更重要的是，PRP 计划的实施需要一个良好的企业文化氛围和劳资关系，在计划实施过程中，一定要让雇员了解计划的目的、意义和评定标准，尽可能得到雇员的理解和支持，并将计划的重点放在对雇员的超额业绩激励上，而不是通过扣减雇员的基本工资，来达到降低生产成本的目的。

2. 全公司奖励计划

1）利润分享计划（profit sharing plans）

当公司达到利润目标时对员工予以经济奖励。但这些奖励和基本工资、生活费用调整或永久增加业绩工资无关。人力资源专业人员常用以下三种方式中的一种来决定利润分享的金额。

（1）固定比例法：公司根据成功达到目标的情况决定一个百分比，把这一百分比的税前或税后年利润作为利润分享的奖金。例如，一个公司可能会决定把 7%的利润用于利润分享。

（2）比例升级法：通过增加分享金额的办法，激励员工为超额利润目标而努力。例如，公司可以决定，800 万美元以内的利润，3%用于利润分享；超过 800 万美元的利润，6%用于利润分享。

（3）获利界限法：只有在公司利润超过事先定好的最低标准并且低于最高标准的时候才进行利润分享。公司建立最低标准是为了在把利润分给员工之前保证公司对股东的回报。建立最高标准是因为公司创造超过该标准的利润的因素不是员工生产力或创造力，而是诸如技术革新这类因素。

2）员工持股计划（employee stock option plans）

员工持股计划属于一种特殊的报酬计划，是指为了吸引、保留和激励公司员工，通过让员工持有股票，使员工享有剩余索取权的利益分享机制和拥有经营决策权的参与机制。员工持股计划本质上是一种福利计划，适用于公司所有雇员，由公司根据工资级别或工作年限等因素分配本公司股票。

3. 巨授计划

企业一次性发放 3～5 年的所有股票期权，而这些期权的执行价均由期权最初发放时的价格决定。经营者和员工备受激励以提高业绩和创造价值，使之成为更有效但具风险的激励策略。

巨授计划是具有最大杠杆效应的期权计划。它事先确定了期权数量，也锁定了行权价。通常，第一年就一次性授予在另外两种计划下几年授予的期权总和。但当股价下跌时，可能会失去激励作用。

在这一计划下，经营者持有的股票期权的价值随着公司经营业绩的提高而提高，相对来说，这一计划的诱因最强，有吸引人才的魅力，通常在中小型高科技公司中运用较多。但是，在股价变动率剧烈的高科技行业，股价激烈上涨，经营者可能萌生提早退休的念头，相反股价暴跌，将丧失对经营者的诱因，会产生重新评估股票期权计划的必要。

PART Ⅵ

Organizational Management & Development

Labor Relations

Text A

What Is Labor Relations

导读： 劳资关系，是指劳工和资方之间的权利和义务关系，这种关系通过劳资双方所签订的劳动契约和团体协约而成立。劳资关系又称为劳雇关系，一方是受雇主雇用从事工作获得工资的人，另一方是雇用劳工的事业主、事业经营之负责人或代表事业主处理有关劳工事务之人，彼此间的关系即属劳雇关系。劳资关系所牵涉的范围甚广，劳资关系良好与否关系到生产秩序、社会安定及国家安全等。

Labor relations is a broad field encompassing all the countless interchanges between employers and employees. While labor relations is most often used to discuss this exchange as it belongs to unionized employees, it may also refer to non-union employees as well. Labor relations are dictated in a large part by the government of a nation and the various regulations it provides to industry regarding the treatment of employees.

In the United States, labor relations gained a huge boost with the passage of the *National Labor Relations Act*[1] in 1935. This act covered a wide range of labor rights, including the right to strike, the right to bargain as a union, and a general right to protest and take action to achieve their desires. The *National Labor Relations Act*, also known as the *Wagner Act*, gave most employees these rights. It was upheld by the Supreme Court in 1937.

Labor relations has three faces: science building, problem solving, and ethical. In the science building face, labor relations is part of the social sciences, and it seeks to understand the employment relationship and its institutions through high-quality, rigorous research. In this vein, industrial relations scholarship intersects with scholarship in labor economics, industrial sociology, labor and social history, human resources management, political science, law, and other areas. In the problem solving face, labor relations seeks to design policies and institutions to help the employment relationship work better. In the ethical face, labor relations contains strong normative principles about workers and the employment relationship, especially the rejection of treating labor as a commodity in favor of seeing workers as human beings in democratic communities entitled to human rights. "The term human relations refers to the whole field of relationship that exists because of the necessary collaboration of men and women in the employment process of modern industry." It is that part of management which is concerned with the management of enterprise — whether machine operator, skilled worker or manager. It deals with either the relationship between the state and employers and workers' organization or the relation between the occupational organizations themselves.

　　Labor relations scholarship assumes that labor markets are not perfectly competitive and thus, in contrast to mainstream economic theory, employers typically have greater bargaining power than employees. Labor relations scholarship also assumes that there are at least some inherent conflicts of interest between employers and employees (for example, higher wages versus higher profits) and thus, in contrast to scholarship in human resources management and organizational behavior, conflict is seen as a natural part of the employment relationship. Industrial relations scholars therefore, frequently study the diverse institutional arrangements that characterize and shape the employment relationship — from norms and power structures on the shop floor, to employee voice mechanisms in the workplace, to collective bargaining arrangements at company, regional or national level, to various levels of public policy and labor law regimes, to "varieties of capitalism".

　　When labor markets are seen as imperfect, and when the employment relationship includes conflicts of interest, then one cannot rely on markets or managers to always serve workers' interests, and in extreme cases to prevent worker exploitation. Labor relations scholars and practitioners therefore support institutional interventions to improve the workings of the employment relationship and to protect workers' rights. The nature of these institutional interventions, however, differs between two camps within industrial relations. The pluralist camp sees the employment relationship as a mixture of shared interests and conflicts of interests that are largely limited to the employment relationship. In the workplace, pluralists, therefore, champion grievance procedures, employee voice mechanisms such as works councils and labor unions, collective bargaining, and labor-management partnerships. In the policy arena, pluralists advocate for minimum wage laws, occupational health and safety standards, international labor standards, and other employment and labor laws and public policies. These institutional interventions are all seen as methods for balancing the employment relationship to generate not only economic efficiency, but also employee equity and voice. In contrast, the Marxist-inspired critical camp sees employer-employee conflicts of interest as sharply antagonistic and deeply embedded in the social-political-economic system. From this perspective, the pursuit of a balanced employment relationship gives too much weight to employers' interests, and instead deep-seated structural reforms are needed to change the sharply antagonistic employment relationship that is inherent within capitalism. Militant trade unions are thus frequently supported.

History

Labor relations has its roots in the industrial revolution which created the modern employment relationship by spawning free labor markets and large-scale industrial organizations with thousands of wage workers. As society fought with these massive economic and social changes, labor problems arose. Low wages, long working hours, monotonous and dangerous work, and abusive supervisory practices led to high employee turnover, violent strikes, and the threat of social instability. Intellectually, labor relations was formed at the end of the 19th century as a middle ground between classical economics and Marxism, with Sidney Webb and Beatrice Webb's *Industrial Democracy* (1897) being the key intellectual work. Industrial relations thus rejected the classical econ.

Institutionally, labor relations was founded by John R. Commons when he created the first academic labor relations program at the University of Wisconsin in 1920. Early financial support for the field came from John D. Rockefeller, Jr. who supported progressive labor-management relations in the aftermath of the bloody strike at a Rockefeller-owned coal mine in Colorado. In Britain, another progressive industrialist, Montague Burton, endowed chairs in industrial relations at Leeds, Cardiff and Cambridge in 1929-1930, and the discipline was formalized in the 1950s with the formation of the Oxford School by Allan Flanders and Hugh Clegg.

Industrial relations was formed with a strong problem-solving orientation that rejected both the classical economists' laissez-faire[2] solutions to labor problems and the Marxist solution of class revolution. It is this approach that underlies the New Deal legislation in the United States, such as the *National Labor Relations Act* and the *Fair Labor Standards Act*.

Theoretical Perspectives

Labor relations scholars have described three major theoretical perspectives or frameworks, that contrast in their understanding and analysis of workplace relations. The three views are generally known as unitarism, pluralism and radical school. Each offers a particular perception of workplace relations and will, therefore, interpret such events as workplace conflict, the role of unions and job regulation differently. The radical perspective is sometimes referred to as the "conflict model", although this is somewhat ambiguous, as pluralism also tends to see conflict as inherent in workplaces. Radical theories are strongly identified with Marxist theories.

Unitary Perspective

In unitarism, the organization is perceived as an integrated and harmonious whole with the ideal of "one happy family", where management and other members of the staff all share a common purpose, emphasizing mutual cooperation. Furthermore, unitarism has a paternalistic approach where it demands loyalty of all employees, being predominantly managerial in its emphasis and application.

Consequently, trade unions are deemed as unnecessary since the loyalty between employees and organizations are considered mutually exclusive, where there can't be two sides of industry. Conflict is perceived as disruptive and the pathological result of agitators, interpersonal friction and communication breakdown.

Pluralist Perspective

In pluralism the organization is perceived as being made up of powerful and divergent sub-groups, each with its own legitimate loyalties and with their own set of objectives and leaders. In particular, the two predominant sub-groups in the pluralistic perspective are the management and trade unions.

Consequently, the role of management would lean less towards enforcing and controlling and more toward persuasion and coordination. Trade unions are deemed as legitimate representatives of employees, and conflict is dealt by collective bargaining and is viewed not necessarily as a bad thing and, if managed, could in fact be channeled towards evolution and positive change.

Marxist/Radical Perspective

This view of industrial relations looks at the nature of the capitalist society, where there is a fundamental division of interest between capital and labor, and sees workplace relations against this background. This perspective sees inequalities of power and economic wealth as having their roots in the nature of the capitalist economic system. Conflict is therefore seen as inevitable and trade unions are a natural response of workers to their exploitation by capital. While there may be periods of acquiescence, the Marxist view would be that institutions of joint regulation would enhance rather than limit management's position as they presume the continuation of capitalism rather than challenge it.

Labor Relations Today

By many accounts, labor relations today is in crisis. In academia, its traditional positions are threatened on one side by the dominance of mainstream economics and organizational behavior, and on the other by postmodernism. In policy-making circles, the industrial relations' emphasis on institutional intervention is trumped by a neoliberal emphasis on the laissez-faire promotion of free markets. In practice, labor unions are declining and fewer companies have industrial relations functions. The number of academic programs in industrial relations is, therefore, shrinking, and scholars are leaving the field for other areas, especially human resources management and organizational behavior. The importance of work, however, is stronger than ever, and the lessons of industrial relations remain vital. The challenge for industrial relations is to re-establish these connections with the broader academic, policy, and business worlds.

Words & Expressions

1. unionize	*v.*	统一，使成立联合组织
2. dictate	*v.*	命令，指挥
3. ethical	*a.*	伦理的，道德的
4. rigorous	*a.*	严格的，苛刻的
5. intersect	*v.*	贯穿，交叉
6. normative	*a.*	标准的，规范的
7. rejection	*n.*	拒绝
8. assume	*v.*	假定，设想
9. mainstream	*n.*	主流
10. contrast	*n.*	对比
11. diverse	*a.*	不同的，多种多样的
12. exploitation	*n.*	剥削
13. intervention	*n.*	干预
14. pluralist	*n.*	多元论者
15. grievance	*n.*	委屈，抱怨
16. advocate	*v.*	提倡，主张
17. Marxist	*n.*	马克思主义者
18. antagonistic	*a.*	对抗性的，敌对的
19. equity	*n.*	公平，公正
20. militant	*n.*	激进分子
21. economics	*n.*	经济学
22. progressive	*a.*	进步的，先进的，革新的
23. endow	*v.*	赋予
24. unitarism	*n.*	单一主义
25. paternalistic	*a.*	家长式作风的
26. agitator	*n.*	煽动者
27. divergent	*a.*	分开的，分歧的

Notes

1. *National Labor Relations Act*：《国家劳资关系法案》，又称《华格纳法案》，是由议员华格纳提出，于 1935 年颁布的国家劳工关系法。该法案规定赋予工人以组织工会和与企业家签订合同的权利；雇主不能采用任何方式禁止工人罢工或破坏工会组织。

2. Laissez-faire：自由放任政策，又称自由放任主义或无干涉主义，意思就是政府放手让商人自由进行贸易。这一词首先出现在 18 世纪重农主义的字典里，以反对政府对贸易的干涉。到了 19 世纪早期和中期，该词成为自由市场经济学的同义词。自由放任主义反对政府对经济的干涉，并且反对政府征收除了足以维持和平、治安和财产权以外的税赋。在欧洲和美国早期的经济学理论中，自由放任的经济政策通常与反面的重商主义经济政策做比较。

I. Match the words on the left with the meanings on the right.

1. concern   a. the act of not accepting

2. vigorous   b. to support sth publicly

3. rejection   c. to affect sb; to involve sb

4. advocate   d. very different from each other and of various kinds

5. diverse   e. very active, determined or full of energy

II. Fill in the blanks with the following words and change the forms if necessary.

ethical   assume   account   exploitation   broad

1. By many _____ , labor relations today is in crisis.

2. It is a _____ field encompassing all the countless interchanges between employers and employees.

3. Labor relations has three faces: science building, problem solving, and _____ .

4. Labor relations scholarship _____ that labor markets are not perfectly competitive and thus, in contrast to mainstream economic theory, employers typically have greater bargaining power than employees.

5. When labor markets are seen as imperfect, and when the employment relationship includes conflicts of interest, then one cannot rely on markets or managers to always serve workers' interests, and in extreme cases to prevent worker _____ .

III. Decide whether the following statements are true (T) or false (F).

(   ) 1. Labor relations has three faces: science building, problem solving, and ethical.

(   ) 2. In the problem solving face, labor relations seeks to design policies and institutions to help the employment relationship work better.

(   ) 3. The term human relations refers to the whole field of relationship that exists because of the necessary collaboration of men and women in the employment process of modern industry.

(   ) 4. Conflict is not seen as a natural part of the employment relationship.

(   ) 5. The pluralist camp sees the employment relationship as a mixture of shared interests and conflicts of interests that are largely limited to the employment relationship.

Text B

Michigan Lawyers' Question: Whether National Labor Relations Board's Decisions Protect Workers or Labor Organizations

导读：劳资关系一直以来都备受人们的关注，因为这一关系涉及劳资双方的切身利益及其利益的平衡。

In a last flurry of decisions before the National Labor Relations Board's Chairman Wilma Liebman's term ended and she stepped down, the NLRB released 20 decisions that labor and employment lawyers are describing as union-friendly.

While employers, unions and their lawyers aren't surprised by the pendulum swing from pro-labor to pro-employer and back again, there is one decision—Specialty Healthcare and Rehabilitation Center of Mobile—that overrules the 20-year-old decision in Park Manor, a decision that hadn't been changed since the President George H.W. Bush administration.

In that decision, released Aug. 30, the NLRB adopted a new approach to determine what makes an appropriate bargaining unit in non-acute care hospitals such as nursing homes and rehabilitation centers.

In the 3-1 ruling, the board found that certified nursing assistants[1] (CNAs) may comprise an appropriate unit without including all other nonprofessional employees. It overruled 1991's Park Manor, which had adopted a test for bargaining unit determinations.

Now, employees at non-acute facilities are subject to the same "community of interest" standard the board has traditionally applied at other workplaces.

The upshot, according to Jeffrey J. Fraser, employment lawyer at Miller, Johnson, Snell & Cummiskey, P.L.C. in Grand Rapids, is that it will be easier for unions to convince workers to organize.

"It's easier to get to a majority of 50 percent plus one if the unit is much smaller," he said.

Fraser added that he wasn't surprised by most of the NLRB decisions during Liebman's last days on the board, but Specialty Healthcare was a bit alarming.

"There is a political agenda here, and that agenda is that unions are good," he said.

The decision comes at a time when the need for CNAs will be growing rapidly as the baby boomers age, because they are the backbone of many nursing homes.

"These workers are especially important for unions because that kind of work can't be outsourced. And unions are losing membership as other work is outsourced, so they're moving into areas of work that can't be moved away," Fraser said.

The challenge is that, instead of dealing with just one union for nonprofessional staff, employers could wind up having to negotiate with the eight different categories of workers — such as receptionists, clerks and social service assistants — that the NLRB grouped together 20 years ago.

"That added burden of bargaining with the union and the added expense, those are things my clients would be concerned about," he said.

Brandon W. Zuk of Fraser Trebilcock Davis & Dunlap, P. C. in Lansing represents unions who work for the public sector, and employers who are in the private sector.

He said that Specialty Healthcare's rationale is "broad enough it could be spread to other employers".

Zuk also said he thinks that the current board — which is still generally split 2-1, with a union-friendly majority — might take up a case that applies the same standard in acute care hospitals, which are governed by separate rules.

In addition to Specialty Healthcare, decisions in Lamons Gasket Co. and in UGL-UNICCO Service Company came out during the same week.

In those decisions, the NLRB overruled decisions from 2007 and 2002, respectively, addressing how long the union-employer relationship should be protected in new unions and in companies where there is a new owner.

Lamons Gasket focuses on the new bargaining relationship created by an employer's voluntary recognition of a union based on a showing of support by a majority of employees. In its 2007 decision in Dana Corp., the board allowed for an immediate challenge to the union's status by 30 percent of employees or a rival union.

But Lamons Gasket overruled that, and barred challenges to a union's status for a "reasonable period", which the board said is six to 12 months.

Kurt M. Graham, of Clark Hill PLC's Grand Rapids office, will likely advise employers to not voluntarily recognize the union, because that could add another year to the three years during which union contracts are protected by a one-year certification bar after an election and a contract bar for one to three years after a contract is completed.

"Most, but not all employers were forcing a ballot election," Graham said.

"Sometimes, employers may believe that they need to recognize a union shop because they have customers that also have union shops, and it is in their best business interests to do so in order to maintain that relationship," he said.

But he noted that, for 80 years, the NLRB has considered secret ballot elections the bedrock of union elections. The majority said that in 1,900 certification elections, only 1.2 percent resulted in employees voting against organizing, but Graham said that where a secret ballot followed a voluntary recognition, 25 percent of elections resulted in decertification.

UGL-UNICCO addresses the period after a change in ownership at companies with union workers. Prior to UGL, the rule was 2002's MV Transportation, which created a 45-day window immediately after a sale or merger for employees to challenge a union's status.

If 30 percent of employees agreed to the challenge, the union could be decertified. The UGL decision protects the union's relationship with the new employer for a "reasonable period", also defined as six to 12 months.

"Basically, all this decision did was to take the workers out of the equation," Graham said. "The NLRB is supposed to protect workers, not employers and not unions."

Words & Expressions

1. flurry	n.	骚动，慌张
2. pendulum	n.	摆钟，摇摆不定的事态
3. rehabilitation	n.	复兴
4. backbone	n.	脊骨，骨气，骨干，中坚
5. receptionist	n.	接待员
6. overrule	v.	驳回，否决
7. respectively	ad.	分别地，各自地
8. voluntarily	ad.	自愿地，自发地
9. equation	n.	相等，平衡
10. ballot	n.	投票
11. union	n.	联盟，工会

Notes

1. certified nursing assistant：助理护士，简称 CNA，相当于中国医院里的护理员。工作内容主要为照顾患者的个人生活，提供住院护理，比如洗澡、更换床单、测量生命体征、协助护士做简单的伤口包扎等。美国的助理护士需要通过专业培训，包括理论课程和临床实践，并通过考试获得证书，在注册护士的指导下进行工作。

Exercises

I. Match the words on the left with the meanings on the right.

1. swing   a. a way of dealing with sb/sth

2. comprise   b. in the same order as the people or things already mentioned

3. respectively   c. to admit or to be aware that sth exists or is true

4. approach   d. to move backwards or forwards or from side to side while hanging from a fixed point

5. recognize   e. to have sb/sth as parts or members

II. Fill in the blanks with the following words and change the forms if necessary.

concern	interest	equation	subject	negotiate

1. Basically, all this decision did was to take the workers out of the _____ .

2. Employees at non-acute facilities are _____ to the same "community of interest" standard the board has traditionally applied at other workplaces.

3. The challenge is that, instead of dealing with just one union for nonprofessional staff, employers could wind up having to _____ with the eight different categories of workers.

4. The added burden of bargaining with the union and the added expense are things my clients would be _____ about.

5. Sometimes, employers may believe that they need to recognize a union shop because they have customers that also have union shops, and it is in their best business _____ to do so in order to maintain that relationship.

III. Decide whether the following statements are true (T) or false (F).

(　　) 1. There is one decision that overrules the 20-year-old decision in Park Manor that had been changed since the President George Bush administration.

(　　) 2. In its 2007 decision in Dana Corp., the board took into account an immediate challenge to the union's status by 20 percent of employees or a rival union.

(　　) 3. The challenge is that employers could not negotiate with the eight different categories of workers.

(　　) 4. In order to maintain that relationship employers think that they need to recognize a union shop.

(　　) 5. Employees at non-acute facilities are subject to the same "community of interest" standard the board has traditionally applied at other workplaces.

Tips：专题介绍

劳 动 关 系

劳动关系又称为劳资关系。《中华人民共和国劳动法》对劳动关系作了明确的界定，劳动关系是指劳动者与所在单位之间在劳动过程中发生的关系。《劳动法》从法律的角度确立和规范了劳动关系，是调整劳动关系及与劳动关系有密切联系的其他关系的法律规范。

1. 劳动关系的法律特征

《劳动法》中所规范的劳动关系，主要包括以下三个法律特征：

（1）劳动关系是在现实劳动过程中所发生的关系，与劳动者有着直接的联系。

（2）劳动关系的双方当事人，一方是劳动者，另一方是提供生产资料的劳动者所在单位。

（3）劳动关系的一方劳动者，要成为另一方所在单位的成员，要遵守单位内部的劳动规则及有关制度。

2. 劳动关系的基本内容

（1）劳动者与用人单位之间在工作事件、休息时间、劳动报酬、劳动安全、劳动卫生、劳动纪律及奖惩、劳动保护、职业培训等方面形成的关系。

（2）劳动行政部门与用人单位、劳动者在劳动就业、劳动争议及社会保险等方面的关系。

（3）工会与用人单位、职工之间因履行工会的职责和职权，代表和维持职工合法权益而发生的关系。

3. 正确处理企业劳动关系应遵循的原则

（1）兼顾各方利益原则。

（2）协商为主的解决原则。

（3）以法律为准则。

（4）劳动争议预防为主。

4. 企业改善内部劳资关系的途径

（1）立法。

（2）发挥工会及党组织的作用。

（3）培训主管人员。

（4）提高职工的工作生活质量。

（5）职工参与民主管理。

5. 劳动关系的分类

1）按实现劳动过程的方式来划分

（1）直接实现劳动过程的劳动关系，即用人单位与劳动者建立劳动关系后，由用人单位直接组织劳动者进行生产劳动的形式，当前这一类劳动关系居绝大多数。

（2）间接实现劳动过程的劳动关系，即劳动关系建立后，通过劳务输出或借调等方式由劳动者为其他单位服务实现劳动过程的形式，这一类劳动关系目前居少数，但今后会逐年增多。

2）按劳动关系的具体形态来划分

（1）常规形式，即正常情况下的劳动关系。

（2）停薪留职形式。

（3）放长假的形式。

（4）待岗形式。

（5）提前退养形式。

（6）应征入伍形式。

3）按用人单位性质划分

（1）国有企业劳动关系。

（2）集体企业劳动关系。

（3）三资企业劳动关系。

（4）私营企业劳动关系。

4）按劳动关系规范程度划分

（1）规范的劳动关系，即依法通过订立劳动合同建立的劳动关系。

（2）事实劳动关系，即未订立劳动合同，但劳动者事实上已成为企业、个体经济组织的成员，并为其提供有偿劳动的情况。

（3）非法劳动关系，如招用童工和无合法证件人员；无合法证照的用人单位招用劳动者等情形。

6. 劳动关系与劳务关系的联系与区别

当劳务关系的平等主体是两个，而且一方是用人单位，另一方是自然人时，它的情形与劳动关系很相近，从现象上看都是一方提供劳动力，另一方支付劳动报酬，因此两者很容易混淆。还有一种派遣劳务人员或借用人员的情形，致使两个单位之间的劳务关系与派出或借出单位与劳动者之间的劳动关系紧密地交叉在一起。

在劳动关系中，时常遇到劳动关系与劳务关系并存的情况，弄清两者的区别，对于做好劳动人事工作、正确适用法律、妥善处理各类纠纷显得特别重要。从整体上看，劳动关系与劳务关系的区别主要有 5 点：

1）主体不同

劳动关系的主体是确定的，即一方是用人单位，另一方必然是劳动者。而劳务关系的主体是不确定的，可能是两个平等主体，也可能是两个以上的平等主体；可能是法人之间的关系，也可能是自然人之间的关系，还可能是法人与自然人之间的关系。

2）关系不同

劳动关系两个主体之间不仅存在财产关系即经济关系，还存在人身关系，即行政隶属关系。也就是说，劳动者除提供劳动之外，还要接受用人单位的管理，服从其安排，遵守其规章制度等。劳动关系双方当事人的法律地位虽然是平等的，但实际生活中的地位是不平等的。这就是我们常说的用人单位是强者，劳动者是弱者。而与劳动关系相近的劳务关系两个主体之间只存在财产关系，或者说是经济关系，即劳动者提供劳务服务，用人单位支付劳务报酬。彼此之间不存在行政隶属关系，而是一种相对于劳动关系当事人，主体地位更加平等的关系。

3）劳动主体的待遇不同

劳动关系中的劳动者除获得工资报酬外，还有保险、福利待遇等；而劳务关系中的自然人，一般只获得劳动报酬。

4）适用的法律不同

劳动关系适用《劳动法》，而劳务关系则适用《合同法》。

5）合同的法定形式不同

劳动关系用劳动合同来确立，其法定形式是书面的。而劳务关系须用劳务合同来确立，其法定形式除书面之外，还可以是口头和其他形式的。

Cross-cultural Management

Text A

The Combination of Diversified Cultures

导读： 由于全球化和国际竞争的日趋激烈，越来越多的公司都选择跨国合资的经营模式以求得效率和利益的最大化。日本电子大亨 Sony（索尼）就是其中的成功典范。索尼涉足中国市场，并以其独到的经营模式和跨文化的管理模式在中国的电子产业中拥有一席之地。

The success of Sony[1] in China has shown us a good example of diversified enterprise culture management.

Sony Co., Ltd. in China is a foreign enterprise growing up in the concept of international management. It does not only have the advantages of the meticulous and rigorous Japanese culture, but also have the "open-minded" European and American management styles. Indeed, it prospers in the Chinese market.

Qualifications Useless Theory

Like many internationally renowned enterprises, Sony incorporates knowledge and good business background when choosing employees, in addition to the standard of talent superior wisdom, and it emphasizes more on the responsibility for their positions, innovative concepts and pragmatic attitudes in work. Sony Corporation is an enterprise advocating "creating new ways of life", "innovation" — this word is reflected not only in its world-class technological development areas, but also in the concept of employment. In the recruitment session, Akio Morita, one of the founders of Sony, promoted the "qualifications useless theory" slogan, which is still impressive today. As for the incentive mechanism, breaking stereotypes, encouraging innovation, and giving full play to the personality have been included in the corporate culture. Sony seems to have become a master in the R&D[2] sector. Many people in Sony regard "self-realization" as their target, and throw themselves into work. All this is based on a simple and plain truth — each employee is required to have self-confidence and positive attitude to cope with the unsteady situation. Sony encourages innovation, and also stresses pragmatism. "Innovation can make people be full of passion and fighting spirit, while it must be accompanied by pragmatism. Efficiency can play best."

The Unique View about the "Job-hopping"

It has a unique view about the "Job-hopping" phenomenon. Relatively stable working environment does not mean the flowing stagnation of talented people. The frequent movement of employees does not only appear in state-owned enterprises[3]. To be more precise, it should be accepted as the product of the talented people market today. At present, many enterprises are facing the problem of frequent movement of the staff. In fact, from another perspective, it reflects a new phenomenon in which various kinds of talents are moving into the competitive market, and some are in development. As for the enterprises, their different stages of development need employees good at different skills. It is very important for a company to make full use of their current staff members to advocate its innovation or transformation. Generally speaking, it is a good opportunity for companies to improve their core competence.

Make Full Use of Trivialness

The staff should make full use of trivialness to improve their abilities. Sony strongly encourages college students to engage in some social activities when they have spare time. Learning to be self-reliant is a manifestation of "independence" capability, and we can enrich our knowledge and understanding of the society. To some degree, if someone can throw himself into the trivialness, he will do a job well. In foreign companies, this is especially important.

The Current Situation of Cross-culture Management[4] in Today's Era

Cross-cultural management does not only mean differences, but also means similarities. During the cultural integrating process, managers should lay equal emphasis on cultural differences and cultural similarities.

For quite a long time, governments encourage the micro-mode of cross-cultural management. This management mode is also called cultural infiltration management mode or localization management model. The key point of this model is to integrate the local cultural theory with the management styles. The product-positioning process, product innovation, brand creation and marketing of multinational enterprises have become more consistent with native conditions. Through cross-cultural management, enterprises can achieve mutual communication and fusion, and finally eliminate cultural barriers. These cultural barriers depend mainly on the employees from various nations. Therefore, the cross-cultural management level has directly affected the actions of corporate members, thereby affecting the business strategy. The establishment of micro-mode of cross-cultural management calls us to raise attention to the awareness and coordination of cultural differences.

Cross-culture refers to two basic meanings. First, it is the "mutual understanding". To understand another culture better, we must learn about the development, changes, advantages and disadvantages of their culture, so that we can make a good combination among them. Second, it is the search of conjunction of different cultures. This requires managers, to some extent, to get out of the native cultural constraints, and to see them in a different view. It is a very effective way to seek the integration points between the native culture and other cultures. During the process of "minimizing cultural differences", the managers should use the formal or informal, tangible or intangible ways to build cross-cultural communication organizations or cross-cultural communication channels. Through cross-cultural training program, they can establish high-quality management teams and enable trainees to know better about the different cultural backgrounds and eliminate prejudices.

In fact, many cross-cultural businesses have shown that the formation of a unified value system in the host country, based on a highly efficient, cohesive leadership, leads to the success of enterprise culture management. Native drive also refers to the business organization layers and the allocation of posts. Take our country for example, foreign enterprises choose Chinese in another nationality as managers to settle cross-cultural issues. By using more local community staff, managers can increase the cohesion of the enterprise, eliminate cross-cultural problems, and enhance management efficiency.

However, with the business expansion around the world, this kind of cross-cultural management mode is gradually exposing its shortcomings — the culture of foreign-funded enterprises in China can not raise a quantitative change to qualitative changes, the corporate decision-making rights are still in the hands of foreigners, the staff cannot distinguish the exact advantages and disadvantages of different cultures, etc. So cultural conflicts in foreign-funded enterprises still exist, and many employers take various ways (bribery) to avoid paying the taxation after knowing about the Chinese cultures. In order to eliminate these defects, governments of many countries are calling for a new cross-cultural management mode.

The world economy is on the trend of integration. Economic integration is always based on market, financial environment and business scales on the international level. There is no country having the ability to produce all the goods and services they need. Economic integration is an inevitable way to satisfy their needs.

Today, a popular way of enterprise culture is called macro-mode of cross-cultural management. This management mode is also called cultural integration model, which is the senior form of cross-cultural management. It is now on the stage of exploration and innovation, and requires various states to reach further integration on the basis of culture infiltration. In the integration process, companies should absorb the classic features of different nations, and pay attention to the mutual interests of employers and employees. This model advocates managers to seek effective ways of management from the same or similar points of various management styles.

Words & Expressions

1. meticulous	*a.*	一丝不苟的
2. rigorous	*a.*	严格的，严厉的，严密的，严酷的
3. incorporate	*v.*	包含，吸收，体现，把……合并
4. pragmatic	*a.*	实际的，实用主义的
5. recruitment	*n.*	补充，人才招聘
6. slogan	*n.*	标语，呐喊声
7. stereotype	*n.*	陈词滥调，老套，铅版
8. stagnation	*n.*	停滞，滞止
9. manifestation	*n.*	表现，显示，示威运动
10. infiltration	*n.*	渗透，渗透物
11. conjunction	*n.*	结合，连接词
12. constraint	*n.*	约束，局促，态度不自然，强制
13. tangible	*a.*	有形的，切实的，可触摸的
14. cohesion	*n.*	凝聚，结合
15. defect	*n.*	缺点，缺陷，不足之处
16. integration	*n.*	集成，综合
17. bribery	*n.*	贿赂，受贿，行贿
18. job-hopping	*n.*	换工作，跳槽

Notes

1. Sony：索尼，总部位于日本东京，是世界视听、电子游戏、通信产品和信息技术等领域的先导者，世界最早便携式数码产品的开创者，世界最大的电子产品制造商之一，世界电子游戏业三大巨头之一，美国好莱坞六大电影公司之一。

2. R&D：研究与开发，指在科学技术领域，为增加知识总量（包括人类文化和社会知识的总量），以及运用这些知识去创造新的应用而进行的系统的、创造性的活动，包括基础研究、应用研究、试验发展三类活动。国际上通常采用 R&D 活动的规模和强度指标反映一国的科技实力和核心竞争力。一国的 R&D 水平体现一国的政治经济实力，一个企业的 R&D 水平体现一个企业的竞争力。

3. State-owned enterprises：国有企业，是指国家对其资本拥有所有权或者控制权，政府的意志和利益决定了国有企业的行为。作为一种生产经营组织形式，同时具有商业类和公益类的特点，其商业性体现为追求国有资产的保值和增值，其公益性体现为国有企业的设立通常是为了实现国家调节经济的目标，起着调节国民经济各个方面发展的作用。按照国有资产管理权限划分，国有企业分为中央企业（由中央政府监督管理的国有企业）和地方企业

（由地方政府监督管理的国有企业）。对于个别中央企业在国家社会经济发展过程中所承担的责任较为特殊，归属于国务院直属管理，这些中央企业属于正部级。

4. Cross-culture Management：跨文化管理，又称为"交叉文化管理"，即在全球化经营中，对子公司所在国的文化采取包容的管理方法，在跨文化条件下克服任何异质文化的冲突，并据以创造出企业独特的文化，从而形成卓有成效的管理方式。

I. Match the words on the left with the meanings on the right.

1. cohesion   a. a situation in which people or things combine well to form a unit

2. pragmatic   b. to include something as a part of an arrangement or a document

3. enterprise   c. to deal with problems in a practical way

4. barrier   d. a business company or organization

5. incorporate   e. anything that prevents progress or makes it difficult to achieve sth

II. Fill in the blanks with the following words and change the forms if necessary.

emphasis	cohesion	absorb	coordinate	stagnation

1. Relatively stable working environment does not mean the flowing _____ of talented people.

2. The establishment of micro-mode of cross-cultural management calls us to raise attention to the awareness and _____ of cultural differences.

3. In addition to the standard of talent superior wisdom, Sony _____ more on the responsibility for their positions, innovative concepts and pragmatic attitudes in work.

4. In the integration process, companies should _____ the classic features of different nations, and pay attention to the mutual interests of employers and employees.

5. Many cross-cultural businesses have shown that the formation of a unified value system in the host country, based on a highly efficient, _____ leadership, leads to the success of enterprise culture management.

III. Decide whether the following statements are true (T) or false (F).

(   ) 1. As for the incentive mechanism, breaking stereotypes, encouraging innovation, and giving full play to the personality have been included in the corporate culture.

(   ) 2. Cross-cultural management does only mean differences.

(   ) 3. Cross-culture refers to two basic meanings. First, it is the "mutual understanding" and second it is integration.

(   ) 4. By using more local community staff, managers can increase the cohesion of the enterprise, eliminate cross-cultural problems, and enhance management efficiency.

(   ) 5. The macro-mode of cross-cultural is now on the stage of investigation and research.

Text B

Face Value — Bold Fusion

导读：联想公司是一家在全球化进程中成功进驻国际市场的中国品牌，联想的营销理念正是跨文化的沟通，这点在联想首席执行官 William Amelio 与联想中国总裁杨元庆的默契合作与沟通中也得以充分体现。

William Amelio believes that cross-cultural thinking will turn Lenovo[1] into China's first successful global brand.

"ONE thing about being an English speaker is we are a little lazy when it comes to learning other languages," confesses William Amelio, who, unlike his six-year-old son, can barely manage a word of Mandarin. Fortunately for the chief executive of Lenovo, a Chinese computer firm on a mission to conquer the world, the language barrier has not been too troublesome. His Chinese colleagues, he says, understand that to thrive in a multinational company they have to "speak the global language of business, which is English". That includes Lenovo's chairman, Yang Yuanqing, who in less than two years has progressed from hesitant to fluent English, giving presentations and cracking jokes in his adopted tongue.

Mr. Amelio views the communication between himself and Mr. Yang — a Bill Gates[2] with Chinese characteristics — as a measure of how well Lenovo is putting together two very different business cultures. In 2004 Lenovo bought the personal-computer business of IBM, to pursue Mr. Yang's dream of building China's first successful global brand. To win his board's backing for this deal, after some ill-fated attempts at growing organically abroad, Mr. Yang agreed to hire an experienced American as chief executive. But the first choice, Steve Ward of IBM, was forced out in December 2005 following a difficult start to the merger.

When the Texas Pacific Group[3], a private-equity firm with a large stake in Lenovo, contacted Mr. Amelio, he might have spurned the job as a poisoned chalice. Instead, he saw it as a "pioneering opportunity" and a "great fit". It helped that he had spent 18 years at IBM, before spells at AlliedSignal, Honeywell, NCR and, finally, five years in charge of the Asian operations of Lenovo's arch-rival, Dell.

Mr. Amelio's relations with Mr. Yang, with whom he had been competing head-to-head, and who is hardly the sort to take the backseat, might easily have been difficult — especially with that initial language barrier. Instead, he says, he has a "great alignment with the chairman", whom he meets every couple of weeks for a couple of hours. The division of labour was immediately decided: Mr. Yang runs the board of directors and sets the strategic direction and Mr. Amelio has operational control.

Mr. Amelio prizes focus and self-discipline — and has a black belt in karate to prove it. He tries to apply to business the philosophy he learned from his Japanese coach: "I have been competitive all my life," he says. "He taught me to compete against myself, not others." The coach also inspired Mr. Amelio to visit Japan, in the late 1980s, and then China, sparking a continuing interest in Asia. Mr. Amelio now lives in Singapore, partly because it is an easy base from which to travel in the region.

Mr. Amelio talks a lot about "effective execution", something he says he came to understand while working with Larry Bossidy at Honeywell. Execution is especially pressing at Lenovo because the company's strategy is already settled. Nothing could be as novel as its attempt to meld what he calls "two uniquely different cultures".

The Chinese part of the firm, beset by deeply hierarchical and deferential behaviour, needs to get people to talk more openly to each other — even if that means confronting a superior. An "Executive Expressions" course helps Chinese managers learn how to put their message across and oppose their colleagues. The importance of straight talk in meetings, not afterwards, is constantly emphasized to all workers.

These cross-cultural lessons are needed if Lenovo is to accomplish the four main parts of its strategy.

First, it wants to cultivate its Chinese sales model in the rest of the world. In most countries Lenovo sells chiefly to big businesses and governments, with which good long-term relations are crucial. In China, by contrast, it makes lots of one-off sales to small businesses and individuals, and as a result has by far the largest market share, of around 36%. In an effort to repeat this success in America, Lenovo has just reached a deal to sell more computers through Best Buy[4], a retail chain.

Second, Lenovo wants to make its businesses outside China more competitive — not least by adopting the same efficient, low-cost manufacturing techniques.

Third, and closely related, it wants to improve its supply chain — the firm's greatest weakness outside China, according to Mr. Amelio. In China, Lenovo can deliver "pretty much anywhere" within eight working days 95% of the time, he says; in the rest of the world it had until recently been doing so only 40% of the time, though it has now improved that figure to 60%.

A better supply chain should also help the company attain its fourth goal of a credible global brand. Lenovo only has until 2010 to make free use of the trusted IBM name, before having to switch to its own, less esteemed label.

Lenovo's shares tumbled recently on news that IBM had sold some of its Lenovo holding — a disposal that was long expected. Yet Mr. Amelio views decoupling from IBM as a boost to the PC business, which Big Blue had seen as a low-margin, commoditized industry, and so had neglected. Now, however, there are plenty of dollars to be invested. The American operation's IT system is being updated for the first time in 15 years. "There is a feeling of a team being unleashed," says Mr. Amelio.

Mr. Amelio says that Lenovo is rather like Hewlett-Packard shortly after his former colleague,

Mark Hurd, took over and just before it surged. "As things come together, we are approaching a tipping point in growth," he says. Not everyone is convinced. Some critics think that increased competition in China will hurt Lenovo's margins. And there is the possibility of a revival at Dell, now that its founder, Michael Dell, has taken the reins again. That said, as Mr. Dell surely knows better than most, his former colleague, the master of karate, is ready for a fight.

Words & Expressions

1.	fusion	*n.*	融合，融合物
2.	confess	*v.*	承认，坦白，忏悔，供认
3.	troublesome	*a.*	麻烦的，讨厌的，使人苦恼的
4.	thrive	*v.*	繁荣，兴旺，茁壮成长
5.	ill-fated	*a.*	不幸的，倒霉的
6.	merger	*n.*	（企业等的）合并，并购
7.	equity	*n.*	公平，公正，普通股，抵押资产的净值
8.	stake	*n.*	桩，棍子，赌注，奖金
9.	spurn	*v.*	摒弃，蔑视，唾弃，冷落，一脚踢开
10.	chalice	*n.*	杯，圣餐杯，酒杯
11.	alignment	*n.*	队列，成直线，校准，结盟
12.	meld	*v.*	使……合并，使……混合
13.	beset	*v.*	困扰，镶嵌，围绕
14.	hierarchical	*a.*	分层的，等级体系的
15.	deferential	*a.*	恭敬的，惯于顺从的
16.	confront	*v.*	面对，遭遇，比较
17.	one-off	*a.*	一次性的
18.	retail	*n. & a.*	零售，零售的
19.	tumble	*v.*	摔倒，倒塌，弄乱
20.	unleash	*v.*	发动，解开……的皮带，解除……的束缚
21.	tipping	*a.*	倾翻的，倾斜的
22.	margin	*n.*	边缘，利润，余裕，页边的空白
23.	rein	*n.*	缰绳，驾驭，统治，支配

Notes

1. Lenovo：联想集团有限公司于 1984 年由中国科学院计算技术研究所投资 20 万元创办，由 11 名科技人员组成，是一家在信息产业内多元化发展的大型企业集团和富有创新性的国际化的科技公司。从 1996 年开始，联想电脑的销量一直位居中国国内市场首位；2005 年，联想集团收购 IBM PC（personal computer，个人电脑）事业部；2013 年，联想电脑的销售量升居世界第一，成为全球最大的 PC 生产厂商。2014 年 10 月，联想集团宣布该公司已经完成对摩托罗拉公司的收购。

2. Bill Gates：比尔·盖茨，美国商业巨头、投资家、慈善家、作家、前首席执行官、微软现任董事长，他与保罗·艾伦共同创立了微软公司。在微软任职期间，盖茨担任了首席执行官和首席软件架构师的职务，并且是最大的个人股东，拥有超过 8%的股份。

3. Texas Pacific Group：得克萨斯州太平洋集团，美国最大的私人股权投资公司之一，由大卫·波德曼、吉姆·科尔特等于 1992 年创立。公司业务主要是为公司转型、管理层收购和资本重组提供资金支持，该集团在通过杠杆收购、资本结构调整、分拆、合资及重组而进行的全球股市和私募投资上有着丰富的经验。

4. Best Buy：百思买集团，于 1966 年成立于明尼苏达州，并在 1983 年更名为百思买，是全球最大的家用电器和电子产品的零售商。百思买集团包括 Best Buy 零售、音乐之苑集团、未来商场公司、Magnolia Hi-Fi、热线娱乐公司、Future Shop、五星电器等。

Exercises

I. Match the words on the left with the meanings on the right.

1. fusion   a. to be polite and respectful

2. merger   b. the joining of two or more companies to form one larger one

3. beset   c. a combination of separate qualities or ideas

4. deferential   d. the profit of a company

5. margin   e. to make someone experience serious problems or dangers

II. Fill in the blanks with the following words and change the forms if necessary.

compete   literate   chain   generate   intercultural

1. A better supply _____ should also help the company attain its fourth goal of a credible global brand.

2. In the past decade, there has become an increasing pressure for universities across the world to incorporate _____ and international understanding and knowledge into the education of their students.

3. International _____ and cross-cultural understanding have become critical to a country's cultural, technological, economic, and political health.

4. Students must possess a certain level of global _____ to understand the world they live in and how they fit into this world.

5. This level of global competence starts at ground level — the university and its faculty — with how they _____ and transmit cross-cultural knowledge and information to students.

III. Decide whether the following statements are true (T) or false (F).

(　　) 1. In 2005 Lenovo bought the personal-computer business of IBM, to build China's first successful global brand.

(　　) 2. Mr. Yang runs the board of directors and sets the strategic direction and Mr. Amelio has operational control.

(　　) 3. Mr. Amelio now lives in Japan, partly because it is an easy base from which to travel in the region.

(　　) 4. The Chinese part of Lenovo, beset by deeply hierarchical and deferential behaviour, needs to get people to talk more openly to each other — even if that means confronting a superior.

(　　) 5. Some critics think that increased competition in China will benefit Lenovo's margins.

 Tips：专题介绍

跨文化管理类型

随着世界经济一体化的进行，跨国之间的经济活动和企业活动包括人员之间的流动也必然越来越频繁。跨文化管理会发生在企业到本土之外进行的活动，以及企业之间的合并、兼并等行为中。这包括三种情况，即强势文化和强势文化之间，强势文化和弱势文化之间，弱势文化和弱势文化之间的整合和融合。各种跨文化管理的方法和手段也在不断接受着实践的检验，概括起来，可以分为三种类型，也是跨文化管理的三个层次。

1. 移植

这是最简单的方式，也就是直接将母公司的文化体系全套照搬到子公司所在国家或地区，而无视子公司所在地的本土文化或合作方的原有组织文化。这在具体的文化贯彻和实施过程中，都不可避免地带有强制的色彩。如果母公司文化是强势文化，而子公司的地域文化或原有文化是弱势文化，那么在移植过程中反映出的冲突相对会小些。但如果两种文化势均力敌，都属于强势文化，那么就会产生较为激烈的冲突。第三种情况就是两种文化均为弱势文化，则这种移植就会毫无结果，徒劳无功。而如果子公司所在地域或组织文化为强势文化，则弱势的母公司文化的移植很有可能不仅不能保持母公司文化中的精华，反倒会更为弱势，或者被子公司的文化所同化。这是最低层次的跨文化管理。

2. 嫁接

这种类型的跨文化管理是在母公司认识到子公司所在地域文化的特征并尊重当地文化的前提下采取的方式。嫁接多以子公司的地域或组织文化为主体，然后选择母公司文化中关键和适应的部分与之结合。这种方式的优点在于对当地文化的充分认识和尊重，但容易出现的问题则是母公司文化特征不突出或是没有尽取精华，对当地文化中的不适宜成分也没有充分地剥离，使协同效应无法充分地发挥出来。

3. 文化合金

这是跨文化管理的最高层次，也是经实践证明最有效的方式。文化合金是两种文化的有机结合，选择各自精华的部分紧密融合，成为兼容性强的、多元化的合金。它不是以哪一种文化为主体，而是两种文化直接融合。具有这样性质的文化也可以兼容更多的文化，适应更多不同文化的环境，具有普遍推广的能力，因此是经济全球化下跨国公司最强的核心竞争力。

Corporate Culture

Text A

Getting to Know Corporate Culture

导读： 美国学者托马斯·彼得斯和小罗伯特·沃特曼在其著作《寻求优势》中说道，企业文化是摄取传统文化的精华，结合当代先进的管理策略，为企业职工构建的一套价值观念、行为规范和环境氛围。在现代社会企业中，企业文化非常重要。每个企业的文化都有不同点和共同点，我们可以借鉴，可以学习，可以模仿，但我们不能没有，我们要塑造属于自己的企业文化。企业文化是重中之重，是不可或缺的，是企业的灵魂，是成功的主导线。

In the modern social enterprises, corporate culture[1] is very important. The cultural factors heavily affect the outcome of the company. Each enterprise has its own and unique corporate culture with its own history, its own ways of approaching problems and conducting activities, its own mix of managerial personalities and styles — in other words its own atmosphere, folklore and personality. We can use for reference, we can study but we cannot do without. We must construct corporate culture which belongs to our own. Corporate culture is top priority, is indispensable, is the soul of an enterprise, and is the successful leading line.

What Is Corporate Culture?

Corporate culture refers to the shared values, attitudes, standards, and beliefs that characterize members of an organization and define its nature. Corporate culture is rooted in an organization's goals, strategies, structure, and approaches to labor. As such, it is an essential component in any business's ultimate success or failure.

The impact of corporate and national cultures on decentralization in multinational corporations argues that culture is present everywhere and a factor impossible to overlook in a company's strategic efforts toward success. It may seem problematic to define the concept of culture as the definition varies depending on the context. Hill, the author of *International Business: Competing in the Global Marketplace* (2005) defines culture as a system of values and norms that are shared among a group of people and together give guidelines on how things ought to be. The values reflect the abstract ideas about good, right and desirable, norms reflect the social rules and guidelines on how to behave in certain situations, and values form the basis of a culture. The values and basis of culture provide the context where the norms are created and justified. Furthermore, the author points to the fact that international business is different because the culture differs between countries. There are national differences in the way of doing business, different restrictions and legal systems.

"It is an unwritten value-set that management communicates directly or indirectly and that all employees know and work under," stated John O'Malley in *Birmingham Business Journal*. "It is the underlying soul and guiding force within an organization that creates attitude alliance, or employee loyalty. A winning corporate culture is the environmental keystone for maintaining the highest levels of employee satisfaction, customer loyalty, and profitability." In a healthy culture, employees view themselves as part of a team and gain satisfaction from helping the overall company succeed.

Forms of Corporate Culture

There are many forms of expression of corporate culture, such as company philosophy, corporate ethics, entrepreneurship, business goals, business fashion, corporate democracy, corporate image, enterprise value, enterprise quality, corporate code of conduct, etc. Because of many forms of corporate culture, it involves many things of business. So the corporate culture cannot be ignored.

The Relationship between Corporate Culture and Enterprise Development

First, from the view of business point, corporate culture is a cultural value that the enterprise depends on. From the surface, the enterprise is an economic entity. The enterprise undertakes all activities around the production and management, only with the economic values, not cultural values. But the fact is that in all economic activities of enterprises, the atmosphere is full of culture, and cultural values still dominate all marketing activities of the business and its economic values. From the view of economic value, of course the answer is not. But considered the long-term development, the products must be replaced. Today, we lose many profits. After years, the losses will be compensated, and sometimes the interests of the gains and losses will affect the future development and growth. This involves the issue that the enterprise will support what concept of a culture. Such example can be seen everywhere in the enterprise specific activities, and the key point is how the corporate officers and employees deal with treatment. The handling of specific cases will reflect the cultural values of the enterprise. What kind of culture will produce what kind of economy, what kind of culture will produce what kind of business effect, and what kind of culture will produce what kind of quality of personnel and so on. Corporate culture will integrate into all aspects of enterprise management without shift of people's will. This shows the importance of corporate culture. However, the corporate culture is abstract. In daily life it is often not recognized by the people's attention and attachment. In fact, it is the same as the oxygen in the air around us at all times. Though it is invisible, we cannot be away from it. Therefore, the corporate culture is the "oxygen" that makes the enterprise be survival and developed. Once the "oxygen" is missing, the enterprise could not survive, even the development. Therefore, the corporate culture plays an important role in long-term development.

Second, from the view of individual employees, corporate culture is the guiding ideology of employee behavior. The employees in the modern enterprise are not just the "economic man" who pursues material interests and not just to get corresponding economic return through labor in the enterprise. They also serve as "social man" that requires recognized by society and business, and a personal sense of accomplishment and belonging. In this sense, the enterprise is the environmental sustenance in which the employees could realize their own values, and the enterprise also is the family of employees. Employees do not want to make the enterprise which is dependence and dream of the employees be in ruin. If the "home" is well managed, full of unity, harmony, positive culture in the community, and has a good image in public, then the employees will be proud of her, and work with great enthusiasm to cherish her, create more efficiency, and also sincerely hope that the enterprise has faster and greater development. The staff recognize that the business is their own business, which is a good corporate culture and generates a positive role. On the contrary, employees believe that companies are not their own business. This is the failure and the negative effect of a corporate culture. A good enterprise must have its own successful corporate culture, use a common recognition of cultural values to influence all employees, and promote employees to make progress, love their job and fulfill their duty, work hard, and ensure that business performance continues to increase. Conversely, it is a downturn in enterprise if there is no corporate culture, even no cultural values that all employees recognize. Therefore, from the view of employee's point, corporate culture is the core value recognized and shared by all staff.

Third, corporate culture is the soul of enterprise. From a strategic perspective, corporate culture can clearly distinguish one enterprise from other enterprises. It can convey the company's business philosophy and promote the corporation with imaging visual form. It also can increase the corporate identity which the employees have. From an economic point of view, only achieving the development of material productive forces and economy, then there will be the rise of the culture. This is a general law of economic and social development. From a cultural point of view, with the further development of market economy at the time when culture maintains its ideology, the industry properties are also increasing obviously. With the extensive application of high technology especially in digital technology and network technology, transmission of culture will be more and larger and culture will become increasingly of broad coverage. Cultural expression and inspiration will be an unprecedented play. Culture as a kind of spiritual power is increasingly becoming an important engine of economic and social development. With the standardization of social development, the further improvement of human attainment, cultural competition in comprehensive national strength is about to do more and more prominent, maybe even global significance of the decision. So, faced with another blend of cultural and economic development, we should effectively grasp the enterprise culture and the dialectical relationship between the economies, and better play the role of culture in economic development.

Finally, the relationship between corporate culture and enterprise development can be said that it is the relationship between consciousness and matter. No enterprise development, corporate culture is empty talk. Construction of corporate culture is inseparable from the material basis of enterprise development. Material basis of enterprise development is restricting the construction of corporate culture. Construction of corporate culture cannot be divorced from the corporate status.

Corporate culture has a great power. Some material resources may be exhausted, but only culture will be endless. The development of business is like the development of society. Culture is the factor that cannot be lack of. Corporate culture is a complex subject. We cannot learn everything from it, because it is changing at each time. We should study day by day. We should learn it by heart. Culture is never a substitutive competitive factor.

Words & Expressions

1. underlying	a.	潜在的，隐含的，根本的
2. shift	n.	转换，转变
3. sustenance	n.	维持，供养，支持
4. indispensable	a.	不可或缺的
5. downturn	n.	低迷时期，衰退
6. dialectical	a.	方言的，辩证的
7. substantive	a.	实质的，独立的

Notes

1. corporate culture：企业文化是一个组织由其价值观、信念、仪式、符号、处事方式等组成的特有的文化形象。企业文化是企业的灵魂，是推动企业发展的不竭动力。它包含非常丰富的内容，其核心是企业的精神和价值观。这里的价值观不是泛指企业管理中的各种文化现象，而是企业或企业中的员工在从事商品生产与经营中所持有的价值观念。

I. Match the words on the left with the meanings on the right.

1. priority   a. the most important though not easily noticed

2. underlying   b. famous and important

3. recognition   c. the thing that you think is most important

4. prominent   d. to happen one after another in a repeated pattern

5. alternate   e. the act of realizing and accepting that something is true or important

II. Fill in the blanks with the following words and change the forms if necessary.

keystone	distinguish	application	root	material

1. Corporate culture is _____ in an organization's goals, strategies, structure, and approaches to labor.

2. A winning corporate culture is the environmental _____ for maintaining the highest levels of employee satisfaction, customer loyalty, and profitability.

3. The employees in the modern enterprise are not just the "economic man" who pursues _____ interests and not just to get corresponding economic return through labor in the enterprise.

4. From a strategic perspective, corporate culture can clearly _____ one enterprise from other enterprises.

5. With the extensive _____ of high technology especially in digital technology and network technology, transmission of culture will be more and larger and culture will become increasingly of broad coverage.

III. Decide whether the following statements are true (T) or false (F) .

(　　) 1. Each enterprise has its own and unique corporate culture with its own history, its own ways of approaching problems and conducting activities, its own mix of managerial personalities and styles — in other words its own atmosphere, folklore and personality.

(　　) 2. Corporate culture is something we can study and can do without.

(　　) 3. Corporate culture refers to the shared values, attitudes, standards, and beliefs that characterize members of an organization and define its nature.

(　　) 4. From the view of business point, corporate culture is the guiding ideology of employee behavior.

(　　) 5. The relationship between corporate culture and enterprise development can be said that it is the relationship between consciousness and matter.

Text B

Changing a Corporate Culture Towards a Customer–driven One

导读： 企业为什么会注重自身的文化建设呢？因于它们深知，企业文化是企业成功不可或缺的关键性要素。企业文化兴旺的企业拥有一套卓有成效的办法，与客户建立了亲密的联系。企业文化有两种：一是先锋文化，二是紧跟文化。

"Building the corporate culture" is among the top concerns of China executives, as revealed in various *Chief Executive China* surveys. An equally important concern is "satisfying customers".

When you put the two together, you get what many high-performance companies in the world are doing their best to achieve — developing a corporate culture that is geared toward satisfying customers.

Why do they care so much? Because they know that the concept of corporate culture, formerly associated with small "nice to have" things, is actually a primary indicator of business success. According to research from InMomentum Inc., companies that display specific facets of corporate culture grow 10 times faster than companies that don't. The average net sales growth for so-called high-culture companies is 141 percent, compared with 9 percent growth at "low-culture" companies.

These high-culture companies have specific practices that enable the company to get closer to the customer. A famous example is that of Adobe Systems Inc., where Chairman and CEO John Warnock visits customer chat rooms every day, then drops by Adobe's idea-and product-development centers, where employees raise business ideas and proposals for products they want to develop. "He's translating his direct customer experience back to the development process," says Lynne Waldera, CEO and president of InMomentum, as quoted by *eWEEK*. And that culture of exchange, driven from the top, translates to financial success for the PC software maker, which had sales growth of 25 percent over the past year.

So how does one go about building a culture for customer satisfaction? Or more importantly, how does one change a culture to one whose values support customer satisfaction? To answer these questions, we have compiled the following list of best practices.

Is Your Present Culture Causing Customer Dissatisfaction? Build a New One

Acxiom[1]'s leaders knew their company's culture wouldn't carry it into the 21st century, so they built a new one to replace it.

Without some fundamental changes to the company's culture, growth would not be sustainable. The company was a new player in data mining industry — collecting information such as phone numbers, addresses, and demographic data for client companies and analyzing the data to identify potential new customers and serve existing ones. In order to stay ahead of its competitors, Acxiom had to be quick to capitalize on business opportunities. More important, it had to be flexible enough to meet its clients' highly specialized needs.

But meeting customer needs is difficult when the CEO has to be involved in almost every decision, as it was at Axciom. Decision making was long and laborious, and nobody felt empowered to take initiative. Customer satisfaction, associate satisfaction, and process efficiency were all suffering. Chief Executive Charles Morgan told his managers and executives that the company would never be able to reach its potential if the organization could not find a new way to operate.

The top-driven chain of command was replaced by a decentralized, results-oriented culture in which managers of individual business units were empowered to be responsive to customers.

"We literally slashed the organizational structure, flattened it substantially and created teams," says an Acxiom spokesperson. Old job titles were abolished, and a rating system was developed to differentiate employees by experience level. In the past, says one executive, "when there was a decision to be made, people tended to defer to whoever had the most senior title in the room. Now employees closest to each situation are empowered to make decisions." They're also encouraged to manage themselves and choose the best way to get the work done, and managers are trained to focus on goals and outcomes instead of on the process.

Decide to Have a "Pioneering" Culture and Not Just a "Close-following" Culture

So what's the difference between these two cultures? A close-following culture is focused on competitors. A pioneering culture doesn't watch what its competitors are doing; instead, it pursues its own paths. Pioneering cultures have a higher chance of being customer-focused, precisely because it is obsessed more with innovating products and services for customers, and less with doing battle with competitors.

For example, amazon.com[2] is known to have a pioneering culture. The online retailer does not concern itself as much with competitors. CEO Jeff Bezos believes that pioneering cultures tend to be more focused on customers. To build this kind of culture, he says, the key is to find people that fit, and to know what kind of people do not fit. Those that are looking for a stable environment will not like working in pioneering cultures. "Those kinds of employees leave amazon.com in large numbers," says Bezos.

Train Your People to View Customers as "Customers for Life"

How much could a person spend with you in the course of a lifetime? That's the question you and your people should ask every time you meet with a customer. Says Carl Sewell, author of *Customers for Life*: "You don't want to deal with somebody just once, you want his business forever."

To reinforce this practice, train your people not to look at customers as people who make a one-time purchase. Instead, they should think about all the money that customer will spend with you — or your competitor — in the course of a lifetime.

And keep score: You should know who your lifetime customers are and treat them accordingly. While you are going to be nice to everybody, these customers should get extra attention. They should never have to wait — or want — for anything.

Become a Company That Invents New Ideas

Bernd Pischetsrieder, chairman of Volkswagen[3], likes to host "cigar evenings". At such events, he and his executives just sit around and talk about new ideas, while puffing on fine cigars. The benefits in terms of socializing may be apparent, but the rituals point to something that is strategic. Volkswagen knows that it cannot compete with Toyota[4] or Ford[5] or General Motors on the basis of being lean and efficient. It must produce the kind of creative ideas that lead to premium products.

Creativity on behalf of customers is the foundation of the culture that Pischetsrieder aims to instill. The biggest obstacle to achieving that is — guess what — market research. While it may seem that market research helps a company get closer to its customers, the VW chairman does not see it quite that way.

"The biggest difficulty in our industry is the marketing departments," he said in an interview with *Car* magazine last August. "They are run by people who know what customers have liked in the past but have no idea what the customer wants to drive in five years. You don't learn from customer research what people like — you learn what people don't like. What they don't like today, they will continue to dislike in the future. But what they like — that changes. The customer is never right when you ask him what he wants in five or ten years. But if our engineers know what is on their shelves and what can't be done in the future, and the customer tells us what he doesn't like about today's cars — this combination brings innovation."

Stop and think about it for a moment. Do you have a corporate culture that is committed to using customer research to find out what the customer wants? Or would you rather have one that aims to invent the new ideas that customer research alone cannot uncover?

Build a Culture That Will Help You Succeed in Overseas Markets

If your business is international in scope, hiring people with skills in marketing to people in different countries is a must. But don't stop there — it would help to build a culture that helps your people operate in a global environment.

Mattel, the toy maker, faced a situation where its financial performance was deteriorating. To turn around the company, CEO Robert Eckert disposed of its investments in some businesses and, instead, invested in building the culture and developing people.

Working together with Thunderbird, the American Graduate School of International Management, Mattel developed leadership programs. These programs emphasized the day-to-day management skills that help build a more strategic, more performance-oriented culture that is capable of churning out innovative products for its customers.

Workforce reports that the global leadership programs have increased the knowledge and skills of management worldwide, and now "global management is more closely aligned with the corporate strategies and goals," says Grace MacArthur, vice president of leadership development, who spearheaded the design of the programs. "This, in turn, produces innovative and creative products, reduces costs and improves employee satisfaction." Now employees are becoming "one Mattel company", rather than a number of companies operating separately, she says.

Another success story from workforce of building a culture for operating globally is that of Novo Nordisk, a Denmark-based company that specializes in the treatment of diabetes. The creation of a winning culture is only one part of the company's five-pronged "People Strategy", which also targets customer relations, development of people, equal opportunities, and attracting and retaining the best people.

Novo Nordisk arms each of the business units with a guide for making the "People Strategy" work. It spells out the five focus areas. It explains that year's target for each focus point, such as what percentage of employees expect to meet with a diabetes patient and talk to him about the illness and its impact, which is a cornerstone of the company's customer-relations focus. "Our challenge is to develop a global mind-set and at the same time hold on to our values and culture," says Novo Nordisk CEO Lars Rebien Sørensen.

Choose the Right People for Your New Culture

A mistake many companies make is to turn over the task of culture change to their human resources departments. Culture change is a leadership task, not just an HR task, and unless it's owned by the top leaders, successful culture change won't happen.

There is one area, however, in which HR can have the greatest impact on creating a customer-oriented culture — hiring the right kind of people for such a culture.

Rosenbluth International, one of the most successful travel agencies, has long held to an important set of beliefs: First, that customer service is the most critical factor in an organization's long-term success and even survival; And second, that customer service greatly depends on how you hire and train people.

Rosenbluth is hardly a maverick in its viewpoint. Increasingly, throughout the corporate world, HR departments are focusing their efforts on improving customer satisfaction. They're using HR activities — hiring, training, coaching, and evaluation programs — to give employees the tools and support they need to develop and nurture positive, lasting relationships with clients.

For concrete proof of these practices, they can refer to an analysis of 800 Sears Roebuck stores, which demonstrated that for every 5 percent improvement in employee attitudes, customer satisfaction increased 1.3 percent and corporate revenue rose a half-percentage point.

But it all starts with hiring the right people. Which kinds of people are suitable for a customer-friendly culture? Management author Ron Zemke cites qualities such as optimism, flexibility, the ability to empathize with others, and the ability to handle stressful situations or criticism without feeling emotionally threatened. These are qualities that are not easy to teach and, therefore, need to be found in people the company hires.

And which are the wrong kinds of people to hire for a customer-oriented culture? Starbucks founder Howard Schultz has a clear answer to that: Beware of hiring people from bureaucratic companies. After all, when you hire workers, you're hiring more than their skills. You're also hiring the culture they bring from the companies they used to work for. "I would not rule out someone because they come from a bureaucratic company," Schultz said in the book *Business Leaders and Success*. "But I would be more skeptical and more probing to see if that person can escape that culture."

Change the Systems and Processes

One of the most often-told business success stories in changing a culture towards one that is more customer-driven is that of IBM under Louis Gerstner. By some accounts, the culture was "suffocating" and "counterproductive". IBM had become a company "more concerned with form than substance and a company that was intent above all on self-perpetuation at the expense of all else".

Gerstner brought his perspective as a former customer of IBM. He emphasized the importance of focusing on customers and the marketplace, and spending time learning from competitors and meeting with key customers.

Gerstner himself sums up the experience: "The culture didn't want to change. It didn't buy into the strategy. The culture, which is made up of all kinds of practices and behaviors in the institution, fought the change. So what you have to do is go in and change all the processes that underlie cultural behavior."

Gerstner targeted the compensation process, among others. "We changed the organization system. We said, it doesn't matter any more what your unit does, the whole company has to succeed before you get any payoff."

If you're aiming to change or improve your processes, Richard C. Whiteley, author of *The Customer-Driven Company*, suggests starting with these processes, especially those that cause problems for customers:

(1) Create more consistent input. If you're improving the method for taking orders, can you create a new form to ensure that all order data are taken in the same way? Can you reduce the number of suppliers — one source for a service rather than three or four?

(2) Reduce handoffs. Look at the process and count the number of times one person or group must turn over work to another. Each is an opportunity for misunderstandings, delays, and errors. Can a process be designed with fewer handoffs?

(3) Combine steps. Determine whether two or more steps can become one.

(4) Perform steps in parallel rather than serial order. Save time by having different people do different tasks simultaneously rather than carrying out each step in a sequence.

(5) Add value and eliminate waste. For example, reduce the distance to transport work in process from one workstation to another. Or increase the benefits the process provides.

Words & Expressions

1. laborious	*a.*	艰苦的，费劲的
2. accordingly	*ad.*	相应地，因此
3. on behalf of		代表
4. churn out		大量炮制，艰苦地做出
5. align	*v.*	使结盟，使一致，使成一行，调整，排列

Notes

1. Acxiom：安客诚，成立于 1969 年，总部在美国阿肯色州的小石城，是帮助企业利用信息创造最大价值的全球领导者。该公司致力于用创新的信息管理解决方案为企业提供关键性的客户洞察，帮助企业获得并建立稳固而有利润价值的客户关系。作为全球最大、最复杂的商业智能和数据库营销的发展者，该公司还致力于帮助客户策划和执行营销解决方案。

2. Amazon：亚马逊，是美国最大的一家网络电子商务公司，位于华盛顿州的西雅图，是网络上最早开始经营电子商务的公司之一。亚马逊成立于 1995 年，一开始只经营网络的书籍销售业务，现在已涉及范围相当广的产品，并成为全球商品品种最多的网上零售商和全球第二大互联网企业。

3. Volkswagen：大众汽车公司，成立于 1938 年，总部位于德国沃尔夫斯堡，是欧洲最大的汽车公司，也是世界汽车行业中最具实力的跨国公司之一。在全球建有 68 家全资和参股企业，业务领域包括汽车的研发、生产、销售、物流、服务、汽车零部件、汽车租赁、金融服务、汽车保险、银行、IT 服务等。始终秉承"追求卓越，永争第一"为核心价值观的卓越文化。

4. Toyota：丰田，是一家总部设在日本爱知县丰田市和东京都文京区的日本汽车制造公司，是目前全世界排名第一的汽车生产公司。

5. Ford：福特，1903 年由亨利·福特先生创立于美国底特律市。现在的福特汽车公司是世界上的超级跨国公司，总部设在美国密歇根州迪尔伯恩市。福特汽车的标志是采用福特的英文 Ford 字样，蓝底白字。由于创建人亨利·福特喜欢小动物，所以标志设计者把福特的英文画成一只小白兔样子的图案。

I. Match the words on the left with the meanings on the right.

1. reveal　　　　　　　　a. to become worse

2. fundamental　　　　b. to make sth known to sb

3. reinforce　　　　　c. a sign that shows you what sth is like or how a situation is changing

4. indicator　　　　　d. serious and very important

5. deteriorate　　　　e. to make a feeling stronger

II. Fill in the blanks with the following words and change the forms if necessary.

satisfaction	labor	concern	indicator	capital

1. According to various *Chief Executive China* surveys, "Building the corporate culture" is among the top _____ of China executives.

2. They know that the concept of corporate culture is actually a primary _____ of business success.

3. In order to build a culture for customer _____, we need to do as follows.

4. In order to stay ahead of its competitors, Acxiom had to be quick to _____ on business opportunities.

5. Decision making was long and _____, and nobody felt empowered to take initiative.

III. Decide whether the following statements are true (T) or false (F).

(　　) 1. Creativity on behalf of customers is the foundation of the culture that Amazon aims to instill.

(　　) 2. The average net sales growth for so-called high-culture companies is 41 percent, compared with 9 percent growth at "low-culture" companies.

(　　) 3. The top-driven chain of command was replaced by a decentralized, results-oriented culture in which managers of individual business units were empowered to be responsive to customers.

(　　) 4. In the past, when there was a decision to be made, people tended to defer to whoever had the most senior title in the room.

(　　) 5. The creation of a winning culture is only one part of the company's five-pronged "People Strategy"

Tips：专题介绍

健康的企业文化从这七个方面体现价值

　　企业文化是企业在长期生产经营过程中形成的价值观念、经营理念、团体意识和行为规范的总和。企业文化的建立是与企业发展的不同时期和企业自身的特点相适应的，且与企业的发展目标和发展战略是一致的，也是与企业自身条件相吻合的，是理性化的，绝不能掺杂个人的情感成分。企业文化不是一成不变的，它应该及时得到创新，只有这样才能显现出它的生机，跟上时代的步伐。那么，企业文化最重要的价值体现在哪里呢？

1. 效率第一的原则

效率是什么？简单地说就是业绩。在一个企业的内部，对员工的业绩考核应是第一位的，并且在考核的过程中，必须坚持公正的原则，通过这一原则的建立，企业会很自然地把它在市场上的竞争压力传递到每个员工身上，并且使员工心甘情愿地接受。对企业的贡献度（业绩）越大，企业就会越多地为你考虑和着想，也就是说，身价越高（相对于本企业和其他人），就会得到越高的重视。相反，如果工作业绩平平，企业是不会舍得付出的。或许有人对这一做法感到不理解，甚至会认为企业没有人情味，但如果仔细考虑，就会很容易地找到答案：企业毕竟就是企业，尤其是市场经济下的企业，不是什么慈善机构，它的本质是获取更多、更大的利润，以便扩大再生产。企业更多地为它内部的人力资本（技术创新者和职业经理人）及那些业绩突出的员工着想，是为了让他们从日常生活琐事中抽出身，从而把更多的时间和精力用于工作，以便充分发挥他们的积极作用，为企业创造更高的价值。至于那些确实存在生活或其他方面困难的职工，可以通过社会保障机构或其他途径解决。不是企业对职工无情而是市场对企业太残酷，更何况，市场经济运作的规律本来就是优胜劣汰，市场上没有怜悯、没有同情。通过以上不难看出，在一个企业内部，效率第一应该是绝对的而不是相对的，它没有任何的附加条件，如果有谁不理解或不适应这样一种运行机制，那么他将会被优化到公司的运行机构之外，即公司管理外，因为一个企业要想在激烈的市场竞争中"打赢下一场战争"，就必须把制约企业发展的所有隐性负担变成显性负担，从而最终解除这一没必要的负担。

2. 承认人的能力差别

我们都知道，人的能力是有差别的，有的甚至会有质的差别，例如教育背景相同的人，有的有辉煌的一生，有的却一事无成；在同一个部门里的相同的工作，有的人做得很轻松，有的很吃力，甚至有的做不了。所以不承认人的能力有差别是不对的，最起码人的能力有不同的专长，有的人综合素质好一些，有的就不行。

人的综合素质是有差别的，企业就是由这些综合素质有差别的人组成的一个组织，在这样一个组织中，由于能力的差别决定了每个人权利的差别，也是责任的差别，那么，报酬的具体分配方式和数量也是不同的（人力资本的回报是分红、期权或股份，而人力资源的回报就只是薪水），由此最终决定了各人的收入是有差别的，甚至是巨大的差距。

综合素质高低的体现是以效率为考评的第一要素，能力的大小也是以效率的高低为标准来衡量的。那么，毫无疑问，效率和能力是分不开的，效率证明能力，能力体现效率。企业所有的人力资源经过努力，最终成为人力资本，这是我们所期望的。但我们必须承认，一个人的能力通过努力是完全可以改变和提高的，我们不能用静止的眼光看待一个人的发展，我们应该鼓励和激励员工学习提高，发掘潜力，创造性、创新性地发挥自己的能力。要知道，成功的机遇对每个人都是平等的，只是努力的程度不同。只要努力，所有人都有可能走上"金字塔的顶尖"。

3. 责、权、利相统一的原则

责、权、利三者的有效统一是企业建立科学管理体系的基础。企业应如何用责任来约束人们的权利？又如何用权利和利益来激励其责任付出呢？众所周知，世界上没有不负责任的权利，也不存在只负责任而不享有权利的事情。二者是相辅相成的，享有权利是为了更好地承担责任，有多大责任的付出，就必然有多少利益的回报，任何孤立或偏重责任与权利关系的做法都是错误的。企业之中每一个岗位都是责、权、利的统一体。例如，要使磨子工对磨粉机的正常运转负责，那么就必须授予他操作磨子的权利，同样，他也应相应地获得磨子工岗位的薪酬，这三者有一方出现问题，就会引起整个体系失衡，进而引发管理上的混乱。因此，为保证责、权、利三者的有效统一，使企业管理更具有科学性，各部门在工作过程中需重新核定各岗位的岗位描述，使与这一原则不相符的得到及时修改。只有承担更多的责任，才能获得更大的权利和利益，岗位赋予员工权利是为了使其更好地开展工作，而不是提高身价，更不是损公济私，权利的运用最终是以承担相应责任为代价的。

4. 建立企业利益与员工利益相一致的理念

在市场经济下，企业经营是带有风险的，也就是说，企业的经营业绩并不是理想化直线上升的，而是有波折的。既然这样，职工收益也将随着企业经营业绩的变化而变化。例如，不管工作热情有多高涨，努力有多大，只要企业的业绩下降，那么员工的收入也必将会是降低的。试想，如果没有效率作支撑，企业靠什么来增加员工的薪酬呢？因此，对于平时人们常提的"厂兴我荣，厂衰我耻""我与企业共兴衰"的说法也就不难理解了——"荣"就是为自身劳动得到市场承认而荣；"耻"就是因企业衰败，员工付出的劳动没有被市场承认而耻。所以，最终给工作绩效定性的是市场而不是企业。

市场经济下唯一不变的东西就是"变化"，适应这一规律，员工必须全身心地融入企业的生产经营中，通过学习，不断提高自身的能力，使付出得到市场的肯定，从而使个人与企业共同进步和发展，这才是最需要做的。

5. 管理者能力的提高与被管理者素质的提高相适应

在市场经济条件下，要提升一个企业的综合竞争能力，必须有这个企业各管理层和操作层总体素质的提高来支持，它是影响企业发展的软性因素。素质是什么？简单来说，素质就是除了岗位对必需的知识和技能以外的要求，例如"诚信"就是很多岗位极其重要的素质指标要求。为适应素质考核的要求，人力资源部将分别对各种素质指标进行充分的研究，制定出一套完善的素质能力考核标准，以便在公司内建立起一个适于招聘的操作平台，使具有不同能力的人处于相应的能级（岗位）中，以实现对人才的各尽其用，充分发挥各类人才的能动作用。这一平台的建立，使人力资源的配置更规范、更合理，从而要求管理者与被管理者素质相适应的提高，这样才具有现实的意义。

6. 树立良好的职业道德

企业中的任何一个岗位都存在与社会接触的接口，工作中难免会受到社会不良风气的影响，因此，倡导职业道德就显得非常重要。世上不存在不受约束的权力，行使权力是为了更好地开展工作，而不是用于玩忽职守。强调处事要讲原则、讲公平，这是职业道德最基本的要求。对企业中的管理层来说，各自都不同程度地掌握着一定的权力，需要特别指出的是，这些权力的运用是要对企业、对领导、对同事、对客户负责的，诚实是最基本的道德要求。另外，对企业生产经营及其他方面的信息及时传递，不隐瞒，也是应遵循的一条至为重要的道德行为准则。

良好的职业道德能映射出一个人的能力和这个人的社会价值。没有过硬的技能作支撑，职业道德也会失去它生存的空间。因此，要树立良好的职业道德必须先打好"根基"。

7. 逐步推行合约化管理

在人力资源的管理上，需奉行"人本管理"的原则，发挥人的主体作用。即在人员配置上遵循部门与员工双方平等、相互选择的原则。也就是说，只要有能力，谁都有机会；很显然，如果没能力，将会失去机会。

总之，企业文化的建设是一个循序渐进、逐步升级的过程。只有基础做好了，才能一步步向前推进，不能期望一夜之间就能达到一个让人满意的理想境界，但需坚信，只要选准了方向，加上追求的执着，企业文化理念在人们脑海深处会很快由开始的模糊不清渐渐变得清晰起来。

Corporate Social Responsibility

Text A

A Webless Social Network:
Mobile Phones in India

导读：印度一直以来都是软件大国，然而其互联网信息通信系统还有待国外商家的不断注入与开发。印度人热衷于发信息，Just Dial 公司就成了最大受益者。起初它只提供固定电话语音服务，现在它已不再是过去的语音黄页，而转变成以短信形式为人们提供便捷的信息查询服务，回馈社会。

India may be home to software giants, like Wipro[1] or Infosys[2], which have thrived by harnessing the internet's potential, but few of the country's 1.2 billion people have so far embraced the web. Telecom Regulatory Authority of India reported that at the end of March the country had just 8.8 million broadband connections. By contrast, it boasts some 812 million mobile subscribers. According to Gartner, a market-research outfit, in 2013 Indians sent almost 192 billion text messages.

With 57 million registered users, Just Dial is one of the biggest beneficiaries of Indians' love of texting. Set up in 1996 as a sort of phone-based yellow pages[3], it initially offered a fixed-line voice-based service dispensing information about the nearest coffee shop, electrician, tarot-card reader, hospital, or whatever else the caller happened to be looking for. Many users preferred it to the clunky, state-published phone directories. Cost was limited since all queries were handled in a single call, by a human assistant. "We would read out information which they would then write down on a piece of paper," recalls V.S.S. Mani, the company's founder.

Then, in 2002, India discovered mobile phones. Soon, the cheapest handsets cost as little as 900 rupees[6] ($18), with call rates as low as 1 rupee per minute. The pieces of paper were replaced by a text message. Today, 95% of Just Dial's callers ask for the response to be texted to them; this is done within a minute of their call.

Just Dial has become more than just a talking yellow pages. In many ways it is more akin to Places, a mobile app for Android[5] and Apple's iPhone[4] which tracks the user's location and directs him to whatever it is he needs. Just Dial informs the caller about the nearest desired merchant, as well as several alternatives. The operator also offers to connect the caller directly, at no extra charge, to one of the company's "preferred vendors", a ruse reminiscent of Google's sponsored links. These pay Just Dial from a few thousand to several hundred thousand rupees a month to get talk-time with punters. (No pay per dial just yet, then.)

It is easy to create a user profile based on his search history and, just as in the online world, companies are willing to pay for such information. On occasions, after the caller hangs up, he may be assailed by up to four phone calls from competing vendors. This can be irksome, but many customers find it handy. (When your correspondent was stranded on a Mumbai[7] motorway during a torrential downpour, a call from a nearby towing service came as a relief.) Of course, it means Just Dial needs to share the caller's phone number with participating businesses. Some see this as an invasion of privacy. Unsurprisingly, Mr. Mani assures that Just Dial never misuses information entrusted to it by users. "The numbers we share are only to help the caller make an informed decision."

Just Dial has borrowed other ideas from the social media, too. It has its own recommendation service: before hanging up, each caller is asked to rate the last vendor discovered through Just Dial on a scale of one to five. The database now comprises more than 2.5 million ratings. Another feature, called "tag friends", allows people to tag up to 25 mobile numbers whose owners also use Just Dial. Next time a user is looking for a nearby restaurant, say, the operator may warn him that the closest one has been rated poorly by his pals, whereas one just a few street down got the thumbs-up.

The challenge now is scaling up. Earlier this month Just Dial attracted $10 million from private-equity firms SAP Ventures and Sequoia Capital. Vibhor Mehra, a partner at SAIF Capital, another private-equity outfit which has held a minority stake in Just Dial since 2006, says that the company may file for an initial public offering later this year.

That would be a milestone in Just Dial's chequered history. Mr. Mani first came up with the idea of phone-based search in 1989. It flopped, largely because of inadequate infrastructure: back then, Mumbai had only 600,000 telephone lines. The company took another hit during the dot com craze in the early 2000s. Its nascent web portal, justdial.com, failed to attract traffic and had to be shut down. (Today it is backed up, with 325,000 visits a day.)

Having survived these growing pains, Just Dial now boasts more than 5 million corporate listings accessible in 2000 Indian towns and cities. But Mr. Mani's ambitions extend beyond India. He wants to expand across the English-speaking world. He began last year in America, with a toll free number, 1-800-JUSTDIAL. His dream of becoming the world's leading local-search service while staying largely offline might yet prove less outlandish than it seems.

Words & Expressions

1. thrive	v.	繁荣，兴旺，茁壮成长
2. harness	v.	治理，驾驭
3. embrace	v.	拥抱，信奉，包含
4. telecom	n.	电信，远距通信
5. broadband	n.	宽频，宽波段
6. subscriber	n.	订户，签署者，捐献者
7. dispense	v.	分配，分发，免除，豁免
8. clunky	a.	沉重的，影响不好的
9. query	n.	疑问，质问，疑问号
10. akin	a.	类似的，同类的，同族的
11. alternative	n.	二者择其一，供替代的选择
12. vendor	n.	卖主，小贩
13. ruse	n.	策略，计策，诡计
14. reminiscent	n.	回忆录作者，回忆者
15. sponsor	v.	赞助，发起
16. assail	v.	攻击，质问，着手解决
17. irksome	a.	令人厌烦的，讨厌的，令人厌恶的
18. handy	a.	便利的，手边的，就近的，容易取得的，敏捷的
19. strand	v.	使搁浅，使陷于困境，弄断，使落后
20. torrential	a.	猛烈的，汹涌的，奔流的
21. towing service		拖救服务，拖吊服务
22. tag	n.	标签，名称
23. pal	n.	朋友，伙伴，同志
24. thumbs-up	n.	（表示赞赏的）跷拇指
25. voucher	n.	收据，证人，保证人，证明者
26. equity	n.	公平，公正，抵押资产的净值
27. milestone	n.	里程碑
28. chequered	a.	有方格的，多变的
29. flop	v.	失败，扑拍，扑通落下，笨重地摔
30. nascent	a.	初期的，开始存在的，发生中的

1. Wipro：威普罗科技公司，是一家具有 60 多年历史的综合性企业集团，市值近 230 亿美元，是印度领先的完整服务解决方案供应商，同时也是印度领先的信息科技外包和业务流程外包企业。Wipro 提供信息技术基础设施产品、产品支持、系统整合、信息技术管理、全外包服务、应用开发、组合实施解决方案和咨询服务。其总裁阿兹姆·普雷姆吉（Azim Premji）被誉为印度的"比尔·盖茨"。

2. Infosys：印孚瑟斯信息系统技术公司，印度历史上第一家在美国上市的公司。总部位于印度信息技术中心——班加罗尔市，在全球拥有雇员超过 10 万名，在 56 个主要城市设有办事处或分公司。该公司已在上海张江高科技园区设立分公司，在 1999 年通过了 CMMI5 级（软件工程规范最高级别）认证。

3. Yellow Pages：黄页，国际通用按企业性质和产品类别编排的工商企业电话号码簿，以刊登企业名称、地址、电话号码为主要内容，相当于一个城市或地区的工商企业的户口本，国际惯例用黄色纸张印制，故称黄页。黄页，起源于北美洲，1880 年世界上第一本黄页电话号簿在美国问世，至今已有 100 多年的历史。

4. iPhone：苹果手机，美国苹果公司研发的智能手机系列，搭载苹果公司研发的 iOS 操作系统，第一代苹果手机于 2007 年问世。

5. Android：安卓系统，是一种基于 Linux 的自由及开放源代码的操作系统，主要使用于移动设备，如智能手机和平板电脑，由 Google 公司和开放手机联盟领导及开发。

6. Rupee：卢比，是印度、斯里兰卡、尼泊尔、巴基斯坦、毛里求斯、塞舌尔、印度尼西亚、马尔代夫的货币单位的共同名称。在马尔代夫，货币单位被称为 rufiyah，它是印地语 rupiya 的同源词。印度卢比和巴基斯坦卢比都被细分为 100 个 paise（单数为 paisa）或 pice。毛里求斯和斯里兰卡卢比再细分为 100 分。尼泊尔卢比分为 100 个 paisas（单数和复数）或 4 个苏卡或 2 个摩尔。

7. Mumbai：孟买，印度最大的海港，是印度马哈拉施特拉邦的首府。孟买港是一个天然深水良港，承担印度超过一半的客运量，货物吞吐量相当大。孟买是印度的商业和娱乐业之都，拥有重要的金融机构——印度储备银行、孟买证券交易所、印度国家证券交易所，也是许多印度公司的总部。该市是印度印地语影视业（常称为"宝莱坞"）的大本营。

I. Match the words on the left with the meanings on the right.

1. milestone   a. easy for anyone to obtain and use

2. accessible   b. an amount of money that you pay to use a bridge or a road

3. subscriber   c. extremely strange and unusual

4. outlandish   d. an event or achievement that marks an important stage in a process

5. toll   e. someone who pays money in order to receive something regularly

II. Fill in the blanks with the following words and change the forms if necessary.

dispense	access	register	nascent	query

1. With 57 million _____ users, Just Dial is one of the biggest beneficiaries of Indians' love of texting.

2. Cost was limited since all _____ were handled in a single call, by a human assistant.

3. Its _____ web portal, justdial.com, failed to attract traffic and had to be shut down.

4. Having survived these growing pains, Just Dial now boasts more than 5 million corporate listings _____ in 2000 Indian towns and cities.

5. It initially offered a fixed-line voice-based service _____ information about the nearest coffee shop, electrician, tarot-card reader, hospital, or whatever else the caller happened to be looking for.

III. Decide whether the following statements are true (T) or false (F).

(　　) 1. Set up in 1996 as a sort of phone-based yellow pages, Just Dial initially offered a fixed-line voice-based service dispensing information about the nearest places or whatever else the caller happened to be looking for.

(　　) 2. Today, 85% of Just Dial's callers ask for the response to be texted to them; this is done within a minute of their call.

(　　) 3. On occasions, after the caller hangs up, he may be assailed by up to four phone calls from competing vendors.

(　　) 4. In 1989, Just Dial flopped, largely because of poor service.

(　　) 5. Having survived these growing pains, Just Dial now boasts more than 5 million corporate listings accessible in 2000 Indian towns and cities.

Text B

The Corporate Responsibility Commitment

　　导读： 企业的社会责任是指企业在创造利润、对股东承担法律责任的同时，还要承担对员工、消费者、社区和环境的责任。这要求企业必须超越把利润作为唯一目标的传统理念，强调要在生产过程中对人的价值的关注，强调对消费者、对环境、对社会的贡献，更好地用行动回馈社会。企业社会责任作为一种新的企业经营策略已被越来越多的公司和机构采用，因为良好的企业社会责任会给公司带来长远而巨大的效益，这是一个毋庸置疑的事实。

CR and CSR[1] sit among those sets of initials — like B2B[2], CRM[3], SME — that have simply become assimilated into everyday business speak. CR is a broader term for CSR. To understand what these initials literally stand for is the easy part but, as a casual trawl of the web will reveal, to define what corporate responsibility or the older term corporate social responsibility means has not proved so simple.

There are myriad definitions of corporate social responsibility, with analysts seemingly divided on whether it is the "Corporate", the "Social" or the "Responsibility" that demands the most focus. Along with this confusion of meaning comes a host of bold claims that seemingly position corporate social responsibility as the Holy Grail. Little wonder that businesses of every size are both irresistibly attracted to corporate social responsibility but also somewhat daunted by the prospect of meeting such grand expectations.

It is up to companies then to define for themselves what those expectations should be. As a company, Pitney Bowes has decided to use the term corporate responsibility, extending the concept to caring for the environment and seeing to the proper disposal and recycling of equipment and consumables. It means taking on responsibilities beyond the "social" and committing to having a positive impact on the physical state of the community as well.

It is important to remember that there are no hard and fast rules for corporate responsibility programs although there are general guidelines emerging such as those from the Global Reporting Initiative, an independent institution that provides a framework for tracking social and environmental activities. Still, there is no precise definition of what a corporate responsibility program should encompass, but there are definite pitfalls to avoid.

Commitment and Budget

Certainly, there is little point in a corporate responsibility program for the sake of it. Arguably, businesses that take up a corporate responsibility initiative in a bid to appear forward-thinking and progressive, only to then withdraw once the spotlight moves to the next business trend, will do themselves more harm than good. Any corporate responsibility policy must represent a long-term commitment which takes planning, staff commitment and budget.

Equally, businesses should avoid over-committing and making promises that simply aren't realistic or affordable. Businesses are not charities and there should be no shame in being overt about the commercial advantages that a strong corporate responsibility program can deliver.

When looking at our own program, a major consideration was that much of the activity should relate back to our core business. We run an annual auction event called "Pushing the Envelope" to raise funds for the National Literacy Trust (NLT)[4]. We got involved with the NLT five years ago because, as a company, Pitney Bowes is all about improving communications for our customers. The National Literacy Trust (NLT) is driving to improve standards of literacy across all age groups — and improved literacy obviously means improved communication.

The "Pushing the Envelope" event relates back to our core business activity because we ask celebrities and artists to design envelopes. The fact that these designs are on envelopes makes the event stand out, but also references our core strength of mail and messaging technology.

On the environmental side, Pitney Bowes takes back equipment and either disposes of it responsibly — recycling parts and recovering precious metals — or refurbishes it to sell in other markets. The company is committed to protecting the environment and is an accredited ISO 14001[5] company.

A Differentiator?

There is clear evidence that customers are beginning to expect the businesses they deal with to be corporate responsibility advocates — taking on social responsibilities and meeting green standards. In the consumer market, businesses are dedicating significant budget to declaring their corporate responsibility colors.

In the business to business arena, corporate responsibility is by no means yet a critical influencer. But, in a competitive market, corporate responsibility can represent a differentiator from competitors and an area of common ground with clients in initial new business discussions.

Equally, corporate responsibility can be important for improving a company's standing in its own community — which in turn can aid the recruitment process. Similarly, existing employees like to feel part of a company that is seen to be responsible and "giving back" to the wider community.

Of course, as with any new business strategy, corporate responsibility has its detractors. Critics argue that corporate responsibility distracts from the fundamental economic role of businesses while others argue that it is nothing more than superficial window-dressing.

Certainly, our own involvement with the National Literacy Trust has been well received by both staff and customers. But more than this — and a point that's often overlooked — it's been enormous fun! Pitney Bowes has been able to align its brand to such stellar names as Damien Hirst, Sir Ian McKellan, Kate Winslet and hundreds of others, whilst raising much valued funds for an extremely deserving cause.

The message is — don't simply adopt corporate responsibility for the sake of it. Think long-term, find relationships that make sense for your brand and be creative. Big businesses can often be accused of a myopic, navel-gazing approach but sensible corporate responsibility partnerships suggest a company that is more aware of its wider role.

Corporate responsibility champions argue that there is a strong business case in that corporations benefit in multiple ways by operating with a perspective broader and longer than their own immediate, short-term profits. Whatever one's personal opinion there is little doubt that corporate responsibility is no flash-in-the-pan and that, increasingly, consumers and organizations are looking to do business with companies that display this broader perspective.

Words & Expressions

1. assimilate	v.	吸收，使同化
2. consumable	n.	消费品，消耗品
3. refurbish	v.	刷新，再磨光
4. encompass	v.	包含，包围，环绕，完成
5. recruitment	n.	补充，招聘，聘任，人员招募
6. myopic	a.	近视的，目光短浅的
7. stellar	a.	和电影明星有关的，主要的，一流的，极好的
8. navel-gazing		钻牛角尖，纸上谈兵
9. flash-in-the-pan		昙花一现的人或物
10. window-dressing	n.	装饰门面，弄虚作假
11. detractor	n.	贬低者，诽谤者
12. overt	a.	明显的，公然的，蓄意的
13. trawl	n.	拖网，排钩
14. confusion	n.	混淆，混乱，困惑
15. daunt	v.	使气馁，使畏缩
16. disposal	n.	处理，支配，清理，安排
17. emerge	v.	浮现，摆脱，暴露
18. pitfall	n.	陷阱，圈套，缺陷，诱惑
19. accredit	v.	授权，信任，委派，归因于
20. standing	n.	站立，持续，身份
21. align	v.	使结盟，使成一行，匹配

Notes

1. CSR：企业社会责任（corporate social responsibility），指企业在创造利润、对股东和员工承担法律责任的同时，还要承担对消费者、社区和环境的责任，企业的社会责任要求企业必须超越把利润作为唯一目标的传统理念，强调要在生产过程中对人的价值的关注，强调对环境、消费者和社会的贡献。

2. B2B：商业到商业（business to business），指企业与企业之间通过专用网络或 Internet，进行数据信息的交换、传递，开展交易活动的商业模式。它将企业内部网和企业的产品及服务，通过 B2B 网站或移动客户端与客户紧密结合起来，通过网络的快速反应，为客户提供更好的服务，从而促进企业的业务发展。

3. CRM：客户关系管理（customer relationship management），企业为提高核心竞争力，利用相应的信息技术及互联网技术协调企业与顾客之间在销售、营销和服务上的交互，从而提升其管理方式，向客户提供个性化的客户交互和服务。其最终目标是吸引新客户、保留老客户，以及将已有客户转化为忠实客户，增加市场份额。

4. National Literacy Trust (NLT)：全国扫盲基金，它是一家独立的慈善机构，总部位于英国伦敦，旨在通过扫盲改变人们的生活。自 1993 年成立以来，它创新性地与学校和社区合作，努力打造一个人人都具备阅读、写作、口语和听力技能的社会，以充分发挥各自的潜力。

5. ISO 14001：环境管理体系认证的代号，是由国际标准化组织制订的环境管理体系标准。为使用者（企业、事业、政府）提供了综合管理包括质量管理等体系兼容并蓄的环境管理依据，规定了环境管理的共同语言和准则要求。

I. Match the words on the left with the meanings on the right.

1. detractor   a. to publicly support a political group

2. daunt   b. to be officially declared

3. pitfall   c. to make someone feel afraid or less confident about something

4. accredit   d. someone saying sth bad about others in order to make them see less good

5. align   e. a problem or difficulty that is likely to happen in a particular job

II. Fill in the blanks with the following words and change the forms if necessary.

detractor	accredite	myopic	consumable	assimilate

1. CR and CSR have simply become _____ into everyday business speak.

2. The company has decided to use the term corporate responsibility, extending the concept to caring for the environment and seeing to the proper disposal and recycling of equipment and _____.

3. The company is committed to protecting the environment and is a(n) _____ ISO 14001 company.

4. Of course, as with any new business strategy, corporate responsibility has its _____. Critics argue that corporate responsibility distracts from the fundamental economic role of businesses while others argue that it is nothing more than superficial window-dressing.

5. Big businesses can often be accused of a _____, navel-gazing approach but sensible corporate responsibility partnerships suggest a company that is more aware of its wider role.

III. Decide whether the following statements are true (T) or false (F).

(   ) 1. It is up to the society then to define for themselves what those expectations should be.

(   ) 2. Any corporate responsibility policy must represent a long-term commitment which takes planning, staff commitment and facilities.

( ) 3. The National Literacy Trust (NLT) is driving to improve standards of literacy across all age groups — and improved literacy obviously means improved communication.

( ) 4. Corporate responsibility can be important for improving a company's standing in its own community — which in turn can aid the recruitment process.

( ) 5. Big businesses can often be accused of a myopic, navel-gazing approach but sensible corporate responsibility partnerships suggest a company that is more aware of its wider role.

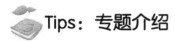 **Tips：专题介绍**

企业社会责任

"企业社会责任"概念最早由西方发达国家提出，近些年来这一思想广为流行，连《财富》和《福布斯》这样的商业杂志在企业排名评比时都加上了"社会责任"这一标准，可见西方社会对企业社会责任的重视。

1999 年 1 月，在瑞士达沃斯世界经济论坛上，联合国秘书长安南提出了"全球协议"，并于 2000 年 7 月在联合国总部正式启动。该协议号召公司遵守在人权、劳工标准和环境方面的九项基本原则，其内容如下。

（1）企业应支持并尊重国际公认的各项人权。

（2）绝不参与任何漠视和践踏人权的行为。

（3）企业应支持结社自由，承认劳资双方就工资等问题谈判的权利。

（4）消除各种形式的强制性劳动。

（5）有效禁止童工。

（6）杜绝任何在用工和行业方面的歧视行为。

（7）企业应对环境挑战未雨绸缪。

（8）主动增加对环保所承担的责任。

（9）鼓励无害环境科技的发展与推广。

分析这九项原则，从企业内部看，就是要保障员工的尊严和福利待遇；从外部看，就是要发挥企业在社会环境中的良好作用。总得来说，企业的社会责任可分为经济责任、文化责任、教育责任、环境责任等方面。就经济责任来说，企业主要为社会创造财富，提供物质产品，改善人民的生活水平；就文化责任和教育责任来说，企业要为员工提供符合人权的劳动环境，教育职工在行为上符合社会公德，在生产方式上符合环保要求。

有学者将企业的社会责任的内容做了如下概括和归纳：

（1）对股东：证券价格的上升；股息的分配（数量和时间）。

（2）对职工或工会：相当的收入水平；工作的稳定性；良好的工作环境；提升的机会。

（3）对政府：对政府号召和政策的支持；遵守法律和规定。

（4）对供应者：保证付款的时间。

（5）对债权人：对合同条款的遵守；保持值得信赖的程度。

（6）对消费者/代理商：保证商品的价值（产品价格与质量、性能和服务的关系）；产品或服务的方便程度。

（7）对所处的社区：对环境保护的贡献；对社会发展的贡献（税收、捐献、直接参加）；对解决社会问题的贡献。

（8）对贸易和行业协会：参加活动的次数；对各种活动的支持。

（9）对竞争者：公平的竞争；增长速度；在产品、技术和服务上的创新。

（10）对特殊利益集团：提供平等的就业机会；对城市建设的支持；对残疾人、儿童和妇女组织的贡献。

但是，在战略决策的过程中，各个与企业利害相关的团体的利益总是相互矛盾的，很难有一个能使各方都满意的战略。因此，一个高层管理者应该知道哪些团体的利益是要特别重视的。美国管理协会（AMA）曾经对 6 000 位经理进行调查，最后得出了表 15-1。

表 15-1 各种利益相关团体对企业的重要性

利益相关团体	得分排序（最高为 7 分）
顾客	6.40
职工	6.01
主要股东	5.30
一般大众	4.52
一般股东	4.51
政府	3.79

Keys

Unit 1

Text A

I

1. e 2. d 3. b 4. c 5. a

II

1. recruitment 2. evaluation 3. priority 4. internal 5. seniority

III

1. F 2. T 3. T 4. F 5. T

Text B

I

1. e 2. c 3. d 4. b 5. a

II

1. utility 2. businesses 3. interconnected 4. expanded 5. collaborate

III

1. F 2. T 3. F 4. F 5. T

Unit 2

Text A

I

1. c 2. d 3. a 4. e 5. b

II

1. adulthood 2. measurements 3. veiled 4. portion 5. deliver

III

1. F 2. T 3. F 4. F 5. T

Text B

I

1. b 2. c 3. d 4. e 5. a

II

1. engaged   2. involving   3. across   4. position   5. recite

III

1. F   2. T   3. F   4. T   5. T

Unit 3

Text A

I

1. c   2. e   3. b   4. a   5. d

II

1. compact   2. offerings   3. expansion   4. coached   5. prospect

III

1. T   2. F   3. T   4. F   5. T

Text B

I

1. d   2. c   3. b   4. e   5. a

II

1. standby   2. match   3. tailored   4. wealth   5. loyalty

III

1. F   2. T   3. T   4. T   5. F

Unit 4

Text A

I

1. c   2. e   3. d   4. a   5. b

II

1. zero   2. appropriate   3. committed   4. outset   5. practice

III

1. F   2. T   3. F   4. T   5. F

Text B

I

1. c   2. e   3. d   4. b   5. a

II

1. ensure   2. temperament   3. link   4. disappointed   5. thoughtful

III

1. F   2. F   3. T   4. F   5. T

Unit 5

Text A

I

1. e   2. c   3. d   4. a   5. b

II

1. intern   2. premises   3. outshine   4. underlings   5. ferreting

III

1. T   2. F   3. T   4. F   5. T

Text B

I

1. a   2. c   3. d   4. e   5. b

II

1. future   2. concerned   3. essential   4. isolated   5. emanates

III

1. T   2. F   3. F   4. T   5. F

Unit 6

Text A

I

1. d   2. a   3. e   4. b   5. c

II

1. qualified   2. quality   3. transparent   4. value   5. matched

III

1. F   2. T   3. F   4. T   5. F

Text B

I

1. d   2. c   3. b   4. a   5. e

II

1. relationship 2. particular 3. demonstrated 4. impressions 5. reliability

III

1. F 2. F 3. T 4. F 5. F

Unit 7

Text A

I

1. b 2. c 3. e 4. a 5. d

II

1. efficiency 2. feedback 3. satisfaction 4. emphasis 5. appraised

III

1. F 2. F 3. F 4. T 5. T

Text B

I

1. c 2. e 3. d 4. b 5. a

II

1. foresight 2. supervisor 3. noncompliance 4. loyalty 5. appraisal

III

1. F 2. T 3. F 4. F 5. T

Unit 8

Text A

I

1. a 2. e 3. b 4. c 5. d

II

1. genuine 2. eligible 3. rehabilitation 4. premium 5. incorporate

III

1. F 2. T 3. F 4. F 5. T

Text B

I

1. d 2. e 3. c 4. a 5. b

II

1. lifestyles   2. obligations   3. valid   4. propositions   5. partnership

III

1. T   2. F   3. T   4. F   5. T

Unit 9

Text A

I

1. d   2. b   3. a   4. e   5. c

II

1. primarily   2. budget   3. privatize   4. significance   5. employment

III

1. T   2. F   3. T   4. T   5. F

Text B

I

1. b   2. c   3. d   4. e   5. a

II

1. base   2. strengthen   3. annually   4. incremental   5. solve

III

1. T   2. T   3. F   4. T   5. T

Unit 10

Text A

I

1. c   2. d   3. a   4. e   5. b

II

1. significantly   2. fixes   3. abundant   4. taxation   5. privileges

III

1. T   2. F   3. F   4. T   5. T

Text B

I

1. e   2. a   3. b   4. c   5. d

II

1. support 2. austerity 3. unemployment 4. recessions 5. suffered

III

1. F 2. F 3. T 4. T 5. F

Unit 11

Text A

I

1. a 2. e 3. b 4. c 5. d

II

1. reward 2. motivators 3. capital 4. hierarchy 5. preserved

III

1. F 2. F 3. F 4. F 5. T

Text B

I

1. b 2. e 3. a 4. c 5. d

II

1. aspects 2. examine 3. void 4. common 5. heterogeneous

III

1. T 2. T 3. F 4. F 5. T

Unit 12

Text A

I

1. c 2. e 3. a 4. b 5. d

II

1. accounts 2. broad 3. ethical 4. assumes 5. exploitation

III

1. T 2. T 3. T 4. F 5. T

Text B

I

1. d 2. e 3. b 4. a 5. c

II

1. equation 2. subject 3. negotiate 4. concerned 5. interests

III

1. F　2. F　3. F　4. T　5. T

Unit 13

Text A

I

1. a　2. c　3. d　4. e　5. b

II

1. stagnation　2. coordination　3. emphasizes　4. absorb　5. cohesive

III

1. T　2. F　3. F　4. T　5. F

Text B

I

1. c　2. b　3. e　4. a　5. d

II

1. chain　2. intercultural　3. literacy　4. competence　5. generate

III

1. F　2. T　3. F　4. T　5. F

Unit 14

Text A

I

1. c　2. a　3. e　4. b　5. d

II

1. rooted　2. keystone　3. material　4. distinguish　5. application

III

1. T　2. F　3. T　4. F　5. T

Text B

I

1. b　2. d　3. e　4. c　5. a

II

1. concerns　2. indicator　3. satisfaction　4. capitalize　5. laborious

III

1. F   2. F   3. T   4. T   5. T

Unit 15

Text A

I

1. d   2. a   3. e   4. c   5. b

II

1. registered   2. queries   3. nascent   4. accessible   5. dispensing

III

1. T   2. F   3. T   4. F   5. T

Text B

I

1. d   2. c   3. e   4. b   5. a

II

1. assimilated   2. consumables   3. accredited   4. detractors   5. myopic

III

1. F   2. F   3. T   4. T   5. T

References

[1] STEVEN P, ZHIANG L. Promotion systems and organizational performance: a contingency model[J]. Computational & mathematical organization. 2001, 7(3): 207-232.

[2] WILLIAMS C, VAN TRIEST S. The impact of corporate and national cultures on decentralization in multinational corporations[J]. International business review. 2009, 18(2): 156-167.

[3] FELDSTEIN M. Rethinking social insurance[J]. American economic review. 2005, 95(1): 1-24.

[4] ATLESON J B. Values and assumptions in American labor law[M]. Amherst, Massachusetts: University of Massachusetts Press, 1983.

[5] DANNIN E. Taking back the workers' law: how to fight the assault on labor rights[M]. Ithaca, N Y: Cornell University Press, 2006.

[6] GREGORY C O. Labor and the law[J]. Journal of political economy. 1947, 55(4): 395-396.

[7] KEYSERLING L H. Wagner Act: its origin and current significance[M]. George Washington law review. 1960, 29(5): 199-233.

[8] MIKVA A J. The changing role of the Wagner Act in the American labor movement[J]. Stanford law review, 1986, 38(4): 1123-1140.

[9] MORRIS, CHARLES. The blue eagle at work: reclaiming democratic rights in the American workplace[M]. Ithaca, NY: Cornell University Press, 2004.